WALLACE STEVENS

Wallace Stevens

LUCY BECKETT

CAMBRIDGE UNIVERSITY PRESS

Published by the Syndics of the Cambridge University Press
Bentley House, 200 Euston Road, London NW1 2DB
American Branch: 32 East 57th Street, New York, N.Y.10022

© Cambridge University Press 1974

Library of Congress Catalogue Card Number: 73-80485

ISBN: 0 521 20278 7

First published in 1974

Printed in Great Britain
by W & J Mackay Limited, Chatham

ACKNOWLEDGMENTS:

Quotations from *Opus Posthumous*, by Wallace Stevens, edited with Introduction by Samuel French Morse. Copyright © 1957 by Elsie Stevens and Holly Stevens. Reprinted by permission of Alfred A. Knopf, Inc. and Faber and Faber Ltd.

Quotations from *The Necessary Angel*, by Wallace Stevens. Copyright 1951 by Wallace Stevens. Reprinted by permission of Alfred A. Knopf, Inc. and Faber and Faber Ltd.

Quotations from *Letters of Wallace Stevens*, edited by Holly Stevens. Copyright © 1966 by Holly Stevens. Reprinted by permission of Alfred A. Knopf, Inc. and Faber and Faber Ltd.

Quotations from *The Collected Poems of Wallace Stevens*. Copyright 1923, 1931, 1935, 1936, 1937, 1942–52, 1954 by Wallace Stevens. Reprinted by permission of Alfred A. Knopf, Inc. and Faber and Faber Ltd.

Quotations from *To Criticize the Critic* by T. S. Eliot. Copyright 1965 by T. S. Eliot. Reprinted by permission of Farrar, Straus and Giroux, Inc. and Faber and Faber Ltd.

Quotations from *The Use of Poetry and the Use of Criticism* by T. S. Eliot. Reprinted by permission of Harper and Row, Inc. and Faber and Faber Ltd.

Quotations from *Personae* by Ezra Pound. Copyright 1926 by Ezra Pound. Reprinted by permission of New Directions Publishing Corporation and Faber and Faber Ltd.

Quotations from *The Cantos* by Ezra Pound. Copyright 1948 by Ezra Pound. Reprinted by permission of New Directions Publishing Corporation and Faber and Faber Ltd.

Quotations from *Literary Essays* by Ezra Pound. Copyright 1918, 1920, 1935 by Ezra Pound. Reprinted by permission of New Directions Publishing Corporation and Faber and Faber Ltd.

Frontispiece: Faber and Faber Ltd, photograph Sylvia Salmi.

To J.

Truth, therefore, in the anger of disappointment, called upon her father, Jupiter, to re-establish her in the skies, and leave mankind to the disorder and misery which they deserved, by submitting willingly to the usurpation of Falsehood.

Jupiter compassionated the world too much to grant her request, yet was willing to ease her labours, and mitigate her vexation. He commanded her to consult the Muses by what methods she might obtain an easier reception, and reign without the toil of incessant war. It was then discovered, that she obstructed her own progress by the severity of her aspect, and the solemnity of her dictates; and that men would never willingly admit her, till they ceased to fear her, since, by giving themselves up to Falsehood, they seldom made any sacrifice of their ease or pleasure, because she took the shape that was most engaging, and always suffered herself to be dressed and painted by Desire. The Muses wove, in the loom of Pallas, a loose and changeable robe, like that in which Falsehood captivated her admirers; with this they invested Truth, and named her Fiction. She now went out again to conquer with more success...

Dr Johnson   *The Rambler*
16 February 1751

CONTENTS

1

Introductory

In 1954, the year before his death, Wallace Stevens was asked by a periodical reprinting some of his poems to provide a biographical note and a statement of what he considered to be the major ideas in his work. After giving the briefest possible details of his life and publications, he wrote:

The author's work suggests the possibility of a supreme fiction, recognised as a fiction, in which men could propose to themselves a fulfilment. In the creation of any such fiction, poetry would have a vital significance. There are many poems relating to the interactions between reality and the imagination, which are to be regarded as marginal to this central theme.

The scope of the ambition behind these words and the tentativeness with which it is presented give some indication of the demands Stevens made both on himself and on his readers. He is a difficult poet because in the whole extent of his work, covering a period of some forty years, he was attempting to find or to make – the two processes cannot be separated – some kind of answer to the most profound and central of all human problems, the problem of belief.

Such an undertaking has by no means always been required of the poet or even among his concerns. As Stevens wrote at the beginning of his poem 'Of Modern Poetry', published in 1942:

> The poem of the mind in the act of finding
> What will suffice. It has not always had
> To find: the scene was set; it repeated what
> Was in the script.
>   Then the theatre was changed
> To something else. Its past was a souvenir.

From the beginning of historical time till the closing years of the eighteenth century there prevailed in European civilisation in all areas of intellectual and spiritual enquiry an atmosphere, if not of actual certainty, at least of potential certainty. However various the fortunes and factious the upholders of faith and reason, the feeling that truth evident to all not only should be but could be established never failed. Poetry written in such an atmosphere, except perhaps by Shakespeare, could never escape confinement to a subordinate position within a larger edifice of intellectual or spiritual truth. When Dryden and Johnson spoke of 'instruction' as the chief end of poetry, there was no need for them to elaborate their meaning. The context was always that of moral truth external to poetry, which poetry should serve and adorn but could not in any way change or influence.

Johnson died in 1784. Twenty years later the familiar limits set to the moral and intellectual autonomy of poetry by inclusive structures of conviction had vanished for good. Poems 'of the mind in the act of finding' what would suffice had already been written by Blake, Wordsworth and Coleridge. The imagination was being discovered or invented as a fresh, vital source of meaning and justification in human life, its appeal cutting right across the ancient polarity of faith and reason. The individual poet found himself liberated from the constraints of systems of thought and networks of assumptions woven by the past and other people. At the same time he was confronted by the terrifying responsibility of this freedom, by the need to make through his work some sense of this new world which the old patterns of sense seemed no longer to fit. The best poets of the period since Johnson's death have been those who have most persistently devoted all their resources of talent and character to the meeting of this challenge. It is here and not in the technical reform engendered by 'the group denominated imagists in London about 1910' and 'usually and conveniently taken as the starting-point of modern poetry'[1] that the real difference between modern and pre-modern poetry lies.

Eliot, whose own best poetry amounts to one of the fullest and subtlest responses there has been to the demands that the modern world makes of its poets, was much to blame for the confusion that has obscured this issue. In 1927 in a famous passage which has often

[1] T. S. Eliot 'American Literature and the American Language' 1953.

been quoted by Dr Leavis, he described the situation of the modern poet as he then saw it:

I cannot see that poetry can ever be separated from something which I should call belief, and to which I cannot see any reason for refusing the name of belief, unless we are to shuffle names together. It should hardly be needful to say that it will not inevitably be orthodox Christian belief, although that possibility can be entertained, since Christianity will probably continue to modify itself into *something* that can be believed in (I do not mean *conscious* modifications like modernism, etc., which always have the opposite effect). The majority of people live below the level of belief or doubt. It takes application and a kind of genius to believe anything, and to believe anything (I do *not* mean merely to believe in some 'religion') will probably become more and more difficult as time goes on.

These sentences cast light not only on Eliot's own work, on the preoccupations which produced *The Waste Land*, *Ash-Wednesday* and *Four Quartets*, but also on the efforts of all the poets and critics who, since the beginning of the nineteenth century, have seen and tried to strengthen a connexion between poetry and something that might satisfy the need for belief. In the main body of his critical writing, however, Eliot disowns this representative point of view and attacks these same poets and critics for finding a connexion between two areas of life that must, he insists, be kept rigidly distinct.

In *The Use of Poetry and the Use of Criticism*, for instance, which was first published in 1933 but which Eliot in 1963 'was still prepared to accept' as 'a statement of [his] critical position', Wordsworth, Shelley and Goethe are said to 'belong with the numbers of the great heretics of all times'. The argument by which this astonishing judgment is reached shows how harshly the now Anglo-Catholic Eliot wished to limit the degree of significance which poetry should be allowed.

I believe that for a poet to be also a philosopher he would have to be virtually two men; I cannot think of any example of this thorough schizophrenia, nor can I see anything to be gained by it: the work is better performed inside two skulls than one. Coleridge is the apparent example, but I believe that he was only able to exercise the one activity at the expense of the other. A poet may borrow a philosophy or he may do without one. It is when he philosophises upon his own *poetic* insight that he is apt to go wrong.

The reference to Coleridge derives from the conventional view that Coleridge allowed his poetic genius to lose itself in a marsh of philosophical speculation, a view which fails to take into account both Coleridge's perception of and desire to explain the possible power of poetry, and his own correct opinion of himself as, however unfortunately, a temporary and less than great poet. In spite of his psychological troubles, the range of his interests, and the diversity of his theories at various periods of his life, there is nothing schizophrenic about Coleridge. But there is a damaging lack of connexion, a lack of integrity in its root sense, in the mind of a man who is capable of writing *Ash-Wednesday* and two years later capable of saying that 'a poet may borrow a philosophy or he may do without one'. This amounts to the condemnation of what we may assume to be a serious man to the darkness of defeatism over the central issue of intelligent existence, a condemnation that is rammed home in the next sentence. 'It is when he philosophises upon his own *poetic* insight that the poet is apt to go wrong.' What if his poetic insight seems to a poet to be the one means left to him of constructing 'what will suffice'? He is in 'error' says Eliot, detaching himself with distaste from the conscientious struggles of a century and a half.

More fiercely objected to than the poets are the critics, particularly Matthew Arnold and I. A. Richards, who have dared to suggest that poetry might have some relevance to the fulfilment of spiritual need. Forgetting his own inability to 'see that poetry can ever be separated from something which I should call belief', Eliot, both in *The Use of Poetry* and elsewhere, dismisses much of Arnold's work from serious consideration with patronising condescension. 'In philosophy and theology he was an undergraduate; in religion a Philistine.'[1] '*Literature and Dogma, God and the Bible*, and *Last Essays on Church and Religion*, have served their turn and can hardly be read through.'[2] If Arnold's contribution to the history of ideas is limited to his purely literary criticism he does indeed become, as Eliot would have him, a rather weak and only sporadically interesting figure. But in his religious books and in *Culture and Anarchy*, which Eliot also despises, he made a very powerful appeal for the value of idealism and for new flexibility and courage in the approach to problems of belief. This appeal arises from Arnold's

[1] *The Use of Poetry.*   [2] 'Arnold and Pater' 1930.

sense of the basic connexion between literature and religion. The great achievement of the religious books is his finding that the language of religion is poetic, literary and approximate, while those who use it tend to think of it as dogmatic, literal and exact. In *Literature and Dogma* he recommends to his readers' attention the 'reservedness of affirmation about God' to be found in the Old Testament, against 'the astounding particularity and licence of affirmation of our dogmatists'. In the Preface to *God and the Bible* he summarises his view. Religious language, he says,

is approximative merely, while men imagine it to be adequate; it is *thrown out* at certain realities which they very imperfectly comprehend. It is materialised poetry, which they give as science; and there can be no worse science than materialised poetry. But poetry is essentially concrete; and the moment one perceives that the religious language of the human race is in truth poetry, which it mistakes for science, one cannot make it an objection to this language that it is concrete...Everything turns on it being at realities that this...language is aimed.

This conception of religious language, this confidence in the symbolic as opposed to the literal use of words, should be felt as the weight behind all Arnold's hopes for the ability of poetry 'to interpret life for us, to console us, to sustain us'. Eliot saw it as irresponsible dabbling in matters that should be left to experts. 'For Arnold the best poetry supersedes both religion and philosophy', he says, with gross distortion, in *The Use of Poetry*, and continues 'Nothing in this world or the next is a substitute for anything else; and if you find that you must do without something, such as religious faith or philosophic belief, then you must just do without it.' With neat and careless pronouncements such as this Eliot sought to disguise the fact that Arnold was prepared to probe more deeply than he was himself, except in his poetry, into the real nature of both poetry and belief. But for those who do not share the dogmatic confidence of Eliot's prose, Arnold's world of dissolution and tentative suggestion, which is also the world of *Four Quartets*, seems the more recognisable.

While Eliot's personal convictions closed his mind and his sympathies to Arnold's speculations, he adopted Dryden as his critical hero, presumably in the hope that the certainties that supported

Dryden's terminology – 'edification', 'refinement', 'moral truth' – might somehow be restored. In the same spirit of nostalgia for days when the poet's task was limited to the job of writing well he exempts Keats from his general disapproval of nineteenth century poets and absolves him from the 'error' of crossing the barrier that should separate poetry from belief.

Wordsworth and Shelley both theorise. Keats has no theory, and to have formed one was irrelevant to his interests, and alien to his mind. If we take either Wordsworth or Shelley as representative of his age, as being a voice of the age, we cannot so take Keats. But we cannot accuse Keats of any withdrawal or refusal; he was merely about his business.

Here Eliot is looking to Keats to support his own reluctance to consider enquiry into the possible nature and purpose of poetry as anything but a distracting and probably pernicious waste of time. But the truth is that Keats, even though very young and intellectually not at all precocious, did not confine his attention to the craft for which he had such a great natural gift. On the contrary, he showed every sign of finding himself confronted with the issues which concerned Wordsworth, Coleridge, the very precocious Shelley and, later, Arnold, those issues to which Eliot would deny existence. The path that Keats travelled between the first draft of *Endymion* and the composition of the second *Hyperion* is revealed in his letters as a journey from naive delight in the power of his own sensibility towards a passionate desire to learn and think enough to settle the confusions of his own mind and to establish his existence as a poet as one of significance and use. 'Keats has no theory' not because 'to have formed one was irrelevant to his interests and alien to his mind' but because his illness did not give him enough time to form one. Had he lived he would almost certainly have arrived at a view of poetry and its relation to belief of which Eliot would have disapproved as much as he disapproved of the views of Wordsworth and Shelley.

The young Stevens was perhaps closer in spirit to Keats than to any other poet of the past. Whether or not he was conscious of the affinity, it had nothing to do with influence. These two young men were simply alike, in their high spirits and seriousness, in their independence and impatience of eyewash, and in their delight in the particular, the real, the sensuous detail of the actual world. As a poet Stevens was, compared with Keats, a very late starter; but, in their bracing immediacy and absence of received opinion, his early reflections on poetry and the poet have a distinctly Keatsian tang. Here are a few remarks from the nineteen-year-old Stevens's journal, written in 1899 when the high tide of nonsense about poetry was only too likely to sweep an impressionable boy along with it. 'Art for art's sake is both indiscreet and worthless' (there is a great deal of the later Stevens in that 'indiscreet'). 'Many of us deceive ourselves... that we are glorious but mute. I doubt it.' 'Poetry and Manhood: Those who say poetry is now the peculiar province of women say so because ideas about poetry are effeminate...Silly verse is always the work of silly men. Poetry itself is unchanged.' In 1910, now newly married and at the beginning of his career in the insurance business, Stevens quotes a few lines of Keats in a letter to his wife. They are the last lines of the following passage from the verse letter to J. H. Reynolds:

> O that our dreamings all, of sleep or wake,
> Would all their colours from the sunset take:
> From something of material sublime,
> Rather than shadow our own soul's day-time
> In the dark void of night. For in the world
> We jostle, – but my flag is not unfurl'd
> On the Admiral-staff, – and so philosophize
> I dare not yet! Oh, never will the prize,
> High reason, and the lore of good and ill,
> Be my award! Things cannot to the will
> Be settled, but they tease us out of thought;
> Or is it that imagination brought
> Beyond its proper bound, yet still confin'd,
> Lost in a sort of Purgatory blind,
> Cannot refer to any standard law
> Of either earth or heaven? It is a flaw
> In happiness, to see beyond our bourn, –
> It forces us in summer skies to mourn,
> It spoils the singing of the Nightingale.

There is in these lines a sense of loneliness and weakness in a world
without absolutes, a sense that mere reality must somehow by some
effort of the solitary mind be made to suffice, its separate existence
from the transient self conquered but not changed, however impossible such a task might appear. This whole complex of feeling is
behind almost every poem that Stevens ever wrote. And in 'Sunday
Morning', the first of his major poems, it finds expression in verse
whose Shakespearean weight and whose tone, style and flavour
(almost literally – Keats and Stevens shared a highly articulate sense
of taste and their grapes, plums and sick-tasting brass have a particular pungency) show a remarkable similarity to Keats's May Odes.
Here is one stanza of the poem's eight:

> She says, 'But in contentment I still feel
> The need of some imperishable bliss.'
> Death is the mother of beauty; hence from her,
> Alone, shall come fulfilment to our dreams
> And our desires. Although she strews the leaves
> Of sure obliteration on our paths,
> The path sick sorrow took, the many paths
> Where triumph rang its brassy phrase, or love
> Whispered a little out of tenderness,
> She makes the willow shiver in the sun
> For maidens who were wont to sit and gaze
> Upon the grass, relinquished to their feet.
> She causes boys to pile new plums and pears
> On disregarded plate. The maidens taste
> And stray impassioned in the littering leaves.

If Keats had lived he might well have reached just such assurance
as this in the expression of ideas in poetry, and the ideas might not
have been dissimilar. Keats like Stevens set his mind to the problem
of accommodating the idea of death without the help of a structure
of belief, and each of them considered the evils and sufferings of the
real world to be an essential element in his personal theory. Towards
the end of a long letter much occupied with the question of death
and containing the 'Death is Life's high meed' sonnet, Keats produced his famous parable explaining how the soul acquires its identity,
how the world takes on meaning for the individual:

I will call the *world* a School instituted for the purpose of teaching little children to read – I will call the *human heart* the *horn Book* used in that School – and I will call the *Child able to read*, the *Soul* made from that *School* and its *hornbook*. Do you not see how necessary a World of Pains and troubles is to school an Intelligence and make it a Soul? A Place where the heart must feel and suffer in a thousand diverse ways. Not merely is the Heart a Hornbook, it is the Minds Bible, it is the Minds experience, it is the teat from which the Mind or intelligence sucks its identity.... This appears to me a faint sketch of a system of Salvation which does not affront our reason and humanity.

The elaborate theory of reality and the imagination, their balance and interaction, that Stevens over many years evolved, adjusted and came to depend on is fundamentally exactly this. The soul must be made by the heart with no help except that given it by the manifold reality of the actual world. What Keats here calls the heart is for Stevens the imagination – 'the Minds Bible, the Minds experience' – and the 'necessary World of Pains and troubles' Stevens calls the necessary angel of reality.

Keat's theory of the world as the vale of soul-making is one of the signs of his increasing sense, in the last months of his working life, of the high possibilities that might be latent in poetry. If the heart was to make the soul by means of the real world, poetry as a medium of reconciliation between the heart and the infinite detail of the real world might have a vital role to play. Two days after the composition of the ode 'To Autumn' Keats wrote to his brother: 'Some think I have lost that poetic ardour and fire 'tis said I once had – the fact is perhaps I have: but instead of that I hope I shall substitute a more thoughtful and quiet power.' As it turned out, 'To Autumn' was his last serious poem; but the 'thoughtful and quiet power' which had produced it amounted to the achievement of the high place for poetry in Keats's mind towards which he had been intermittently struggling throughout his thinking life. This raising of poetry to the level, in significance and in the potentiality for good, of what he had always called 'philosophy' had taken place earlier in the same month (September 1819) in and through the composition of the 'induction' to the revised version of *Hyperion* which Keats attempted and then abandoned. This induction, the vision of Moneta in Saturn's temple, shows Keats battling with the ideas of death, evil and pain, and

9

simultaneously with the problem of what the poet must set himself
to do in a world which contains all these things and no solid structure
of consolation.

The poet arrives, after a nightmare struggle, at the feet of the
enigmatic figure of Moneta. She tells him:

> 'None can usurp this height...
> Save those to whom the miseries of the world
> Are misery, and will not let them rest'

and when he expresses his surprise at finding himself there alone,
without the 'thousands who labour for mortal good', she describes to
him the peculiar nature of the poet's sensibility:

> 'Those whom thou spak'st of are no vision'ries',
> Rejoin'd that voice – 'They are no dreamers weak,
> They seek no wonder but the human face;
> No music but a happy-noted voice –
> They come not here, they have no thought to come –
> And thou art here, for thou art less than they –
> What benefit canst thou, or all thy tribe,
> To the great world? Thou art a dreaming thing,
> A fever of thyself – think of the Earth;
> What bliss even in hope is there for thee?
> What haven? every creature hath its home;
> Every sole man hath days of joy and pain,
> Whether his labours be sublime or low –
> The pain alone; the joy alone; distinct:
> Only the dreamer venoms all his days,
> Bearing more woe than all his sins deserve.'

The poet then objects, with the following question:

> 'Majestic shadow, tell me: sure not all
> These melodies sung into the World's ear
> Are useless: sure a poet is a sage;
> A humanist, physician to all men.
> That I am none I feel, as vultures feel
> They are no birds when eagles are abroad.
> What am I then: Thou speakest of my tribe:
> What tribe?'

To which Moneta answers:

> 'Art thou not of the dreamer tribe?
> The poet and the dreamer are distinct,
> Diverse, sheer opposite, antipodes.
> The one pours out a balm upon the World,
> The other vexes it'.

This draws from the poet a great curse on unworthy poets. Then the atmosphere changes and there follows a terrifying vision of Moneta as an image so deathly as to be beyond death and yet with a compelling benignancy shining from her eyes:

> I ask'd to see what things the hollow brain
> Behind enwombed: what high tragedy
> In the dark secret chambers of her skull
> Was acting, that could give so dread a stress
> To her cold lips, and fill with such a light
> Her planetary eyes; and touch her voice
> With such a sorrow.

And she reveals to the poet the heavy silence of the fallen Saturn, the picture, now much expanded, that had possessed Keats in the first version of *Hyperion*.

Keats in this poem achieves an imaginative strength that defies translation into other terms. If one bears in mind that it is concerned both with the poet's responsibility to the suffering world and with the decline of a divine rule, however remote the chosen image of Saturn may seem, it becomes a representative document of modern poetry. A possible commentary on it is a look at two Stevens poems written when the poet was in his sixties and had travelled far from the exquisite victories of 'Sunday Morning'.

'Esthétique du Mal' is a long poem, or rather, as was Stevens's habit with long poems, a series of short poems moving about a central theme. The problem that is the poem's subject is one of Keats's subjects, the problem of how the poet is to justify his existence and his art in a world in which he perceives pain and misery and knows that these things are not to be ignored. For 'Pain is human', as Stevens says in the first section:

> This is a part of the sublime
> From which we shrink. And yet, except for us,
> The total past felt nothing when destroyed.

When Stevens says 'the sublime' here, he means human reality with all its manifold and shifting richness of significance. Both Stevens and Keats were facing the existence of human pain and misery in a world without divine sanctions or heavenly reparation; and Dante, the supreme poet of such sanctions and reparation, lurks as a figure of contrast behind both these poems. The atmosphere of *Hyperion* and the role of Moneta as guide are derived from parallels in the *Inferno*: in Stevens's poem Dante is referred to in terms that catch the mixed emotions with which the modern poet must regard him:

> His firm stanzas hang like hives in hell
> Or what hell was, since now both heaven and hell
> Are one, and here, O terra infidel.

These lines begin a section which reveals very clearly Stevens's ambivalent attitude to the specific beliefs of Christianity. As such we will return to it later; my present purpose is to show how close to *Hyperion* the conclusions of this poem come.

Stevens makes, though less explicitly, Keats's distinction between the poet, who can 'pour out a balm upon the world', and the dreamer, who 'vexes it'. The last section begins:

> The greatest poverty is not to live
> In a physical world, to feel that one's desire
> Is too difficult to tell from despair.

One remembers Moneta's words:

> 'Thou art a dreaming thing,
> A fever of thyself – think of the Earth;
> What bliss even in hope is there for thee...
> Only the dreamer venoms all his days,
> Bearing more woe than all his sins deserve.'

In the previous section Stevens has described one kind of dreamer, the revolutionary, the

> lunatic of one idea
> In a world of ideas, who would have all the people

Live, work, suffer and die in that idea
In a world of ideas. He would not be aware of the clouds,
Lighting the martyrs of logic with white fire.

One remembers Keats's opening for the revised *Hyperion*:

Fanatics have their dreams, wherewith they weave
A paradise for a sect;

and his hopeful thought:

Whether the dream now purpos'd to rehearse
Be poet's or fanatic's will be known
When this poor scribe my hand is in the grave.

Throughout Keats's poem there is an uncertainty, not only as to
whether he himself is poet or dreamer, but as to what it is that the
poet must do to become 'a sage, a humanist, physician to all men'.
The sixty-five-year-old Stevens, though no surer than Keats that he
himself is able to achieve it, has a clearer vision of the poet's object.
A large part of the poet's struggle, he says, is not to exclude, as the
fanatic does; not to limit but to extend significance; not to deny but
to explore the endless conjunctions of the imagination and reality,
however sad and however disparate. All this the unworthy poets
whom Keats had cursed as 'careless Hectorers in proud bad verse'
cannot achieve.

To lose sensibility, to see what one sees,
As if sight had not its own miraculous thrift,
To hear only what one hears, one meaning alone,
As if the paradise of meaning ceased
To be paradise, it is this to be destitute.
This is the sky divested of its fountains.
Here in the west indifferent crickets chant
Through our indifferent crises. Yet we require
Another chant, an incantation, as in
Another and later genesis, music
That buffets the shapes of its possible halcyon
Against the haggardie...A loud, large water
Bubbles up in the night and drowns the crickets' sound.
It is a declaration, a primitive ecstasy,
Truth's favours sonorously exhibited.

(The point of the coinage 'haggardie' is the contrast with 'halcyon': peace against wildness, and, in the etymological background, the miraculous bird of calm seas against the 'haggard', the correct word for an untamed falcon.) The last lines of the passage well describe the peculiar beneficence of such poems as 'To Autumn' and Stevens's 'Credences of Summer', written two years after 'Esthétique du Mal'. But both Keats and Stevens were aware that truth's favours include the mysterious, the sad and the painful; that the world to which people may be helped by the poet to acclimatise themselves is not a world from which it is possible to extract only the good and the beautiful for 'sonorous exhibiton'. As Stevens said in a poem written at about the same time as 'Esthétique du Mal':

> It is here, in this bad, that we reach
> The last purity of the knowledge of good.

The poet's music means nothing in relation to the 'haggardie' if the poet excludes from his vision the miseries and haphazard disasters that are part of reality. The most moving section of 'Esthétique du Mal' begins like this, its playful language and neat French borrowings sharpening the irony of its initial pronouncement:

> Life is a bitter aspic. We are not
> At the centre of a diamond. At dawn,
> The paratroopers fall and as they fall
> They mow the lawn. A vessel sinks in waves
> Of people, as big bell-billows from its bell
> Bell-bellow in the village steeple. Violets,
> Great tufts, spring up from buried houses
> Of poor, dishonest people, for whom the steeple,
> Long since, rang out farewell, farewell, farewell.
>
> Natives of poverty, children of malheur,
> The gaiety of language is our seigneur.

The figure of Moneta, terrifying, sorrowful and kind, knowledge revealing itself to the poet, is above all a figure of death. The mixture of cold fear and inexplicable comfort that pervades the poet's encounter with her perhaps represents Keats's feelings towards the imminent death that he must have thought of as an ever-present possibility. In 1947 Stevens's closest friend, Henry Church, died.

In the poem Stevens wrote after his death, 'The Owl in the Sarco-phagus', there is a figure who casts some light into the darkness surrounding Moneta. There are actually three figures in Stevens's poem, 'two brothers', sleep and peace, and a shadowy female third:

> she that says
> Good-by in the darkness, speaking quietly there,
> To those that cannot say good-by themselves.

The poem continues:

> These forms are visible to the eye that needs,
> Needs out of the whole necessity of sight.

These figures are no more 'real' than Moneta; no mystical claim for their 'existence' is made. They are no more than the embodiment of things impossible to define in terms other than those the poem gives them, things that a man may hope to find confronting him at his death. They are figures of pure significance, and the significance they have is no more than human. Here, for instance is the figure of peace:

> An immaculate personage in nothingness,
> With the whole spirit sparkling in its cloth,...

> This is that figure stationed at our end,
> Always, in brilliance, fatal, final, formed
> Out of our lives to keep us in our death.

The third figure is not named; she is perhaps the figure of significance itself. She is not terrifying, as Moneta was, but she has the same remoteness, the same sense of consolation in knowledge, of withheld explanation that somehow will justify death, and the same power to rescue the transient fragments of events into a memory that will save them from loss:

> She spoke with backward gestures of her hand,
> She held men closely with discovery...

> It was not her look but a knowledge that she had,
> She was a self that knew, an inner thing,
> Subtler than look's declaiming, although she moved

> With a sad splendor, beyond artifice,
> Impassioned by the knowledge that she had,
> There on the edges of oblivion.

This passage is not obscure any more than the description of the encounter with Moneta is obscure; but each is impossible to paraphrase. The last lines of 'The Owl in the Sarcophagus' make the nature of both Stevens's poem and Keats's somewhat clearer:

> It is a child that sings itself to sleep,
> The mind, among the creatures that it makes,
> The people, those by which it lives and dies.

In the last few weeks of his writing life Keats was surely approaching something like the conviction that Stevens was to put in these words: 'My own way out toward the future involves a confidence in the spiritual role of the poet.' There was of course no time for this promise of a new and more considered phase in his work to be fulfilled, nor for him to organise into a firm attitude what half-consciously and in flashes of intuition he had glimpsed of the modern poet's possible role. The parallel between Keats and Stevens must for this reason be incomplete, and sensed rather than proved. That they were the same kind of poet is perhaps the most one can say; but one should add that this shows not that Stevens was a late throwback to 'romanticism' – a term which when contrasted with 'the modern' generates nothing but darkness – but that Keats, like Blake, Wordsworth and Coleridge before him, found himself confronted by the same challenge as Stevens.

In 1946, in reply to *Yale Literary Magazine*'s question as to what he considered the greatest problem facing the young writer, Stevens made the following bald statement:

Today, in America, all roles yield to that of the politician.

The role of the poet may be fixed by contrasting it to that of the politician. The poet absorbs the general life: the public life. The politician is absorbed by it. The poet is individual. The politician is general. It is the personal in the poet that is the origin of his poetry. If this is true respecting the relation of the poet to the public life and respecting the origin of his poetry, it follows that the first phase of his problem is himself.

This does not mean that he is a private figure. On the other hand, it does mean that he must not allow himself to be absorbed as the politician is absorbed. He must remain individual. As individual he must remain free. The politician expects everyone to be absorbed as he himself is absorbed. This expectation is part of the sabotage of the individual. The second phase of the poet's problem, then, is to maintain his freedom, the only condition in which he can hope to produce significant poetry.

If people are to become dependent on poetry for any of the fundamental satisfactions, poetry must have an increasingly intellectual scope and power. This is a time for the highest poetry. We never understood the world less than we do now nor, as we understand it, liked it less. We never wanted to understand it more or needed to like it more. These are the intense compulsions that challenge the poet as the appreciatory creator of values and beliefs. That, finally, states the problem.

I have not touched on form which, although significant, is not vital today, as substance is. When one is an inherent part of the other, form, too, is vital.

Or, as Stevens said in a letter of his old age: 'To me, poetry is not a literary activity: it is a vital activity.' This is an integrative view. The poet's personality cannot be separated from his work; its worth cannot be separated from his independence and intellectual strength; form cannot be separated from substance and made an issue in its own right. On all these questions, disregarding both his pioneering work on the seventeenth century and his own best poetry, Eliot, because of his personal doctrinal priorities, often took the opposite, the divisive, view. It was, in other words, in spite of his own limiting ideas that he was a modern poet of precisely the kind aimed at in Stevens's statement. Hence the contradictions and paradoxes of Eliot's criticism which, on account of his very high reputation, have led to widespread confusion and the mistaken assumption that he and the school of poetry founded by him and Pound are somehow set apart from the 'heretical' concerns of Wordsworth, Shelley and Goethe by a devotion to pure craftsmanship in the spirit of Dryden. In fact Eliot, whether he liked it or not, was a man of his own period and there was, therefore, in essential respects more in common between him and Coleridge or Blake than between him and Dryden or, for that matter, Donne. It is only if the early nineteenth century poets are thought to be an aberration, an extraneous episode as Eliot would have them, that modern poetry can be said to have begun in 1910 or 1914. If Blake, Wordsworth, Coleridge, Shelley and Keats were, on the other hand, an evolutionary stage, part of the main story, then it must be accepted that the crisis which produced modern poetry was not the crumbling of Victorian complacencies in the catastrophe of the Great War – how complacent in any case were the anxious intellectuals of the nineteenth century? – but the period of profound revolution when, for the sensitive and intelligent man, the truth stopped being something you were told by the experts, philosophical or theological, and started to be something you had to make for yourself.

The first and plainest account of this crisis and its formation of a modern poet was given by Wordsworth in the 1805 *Prelude*. Here is recorded the collapse of authority, both Christian and rationalist, and the realisation of the excitement and the terrors of individual freedom

> in the very world which is the world
> Of all of us, the place in which, in the end,
> We find our happiness, or not at all.

Something never felt before in Christian times, the sense of nature as a source of moral strength, was produced from the struggle to find significance in a world where nothing could be relied upon apart from the mind in conjunction with reality. If the earth were the only realm of goodness and beauty rather than a place of necessary travail on the road to absolute goodness and beauty, then it was newly deserving of love for itself alone. As Stevens was to write in 'Sunday Morning':

> And shall the earth
> Seem all of paradise that we shall know?
> The sky will be much friendlier then than now,
> A part of labor and a part of pain,
> And next in glory to enduring love,
> Not this dividing and indifferent blue.

The Prelude tells us how Wordsworth arrived at this feeling by instinct before it became his conscious attitude. It also tells us, in Book x, how the idea of rapid human perfectibility on the grand scale of nations and institutions, an idea born in the first glamour of the French Revolution, faded into disillusion and a long confusion of thought, and how the poetic spirit was forced back upon itself and its relationship with the natural world. In this process Wordsworth had Coleridge's intellectual companionship and his sister Dorothy's moral support:

She, in the midst of all, preserv'd me still
A Poet, made me seek beneath that name
My office upon earth, and nowhere else,
And lastly, Nature's Self, by human love
Assisted, through the weary labyrinth
Conducted me again to open day.

Most modern poets who have faced such a task have had to do so alone. The kind of courage that this requires can be seen in Stevens's 'Extracts from Addresses to the Academy of Fine Ideas'. This poem was written in 1940; the panache of Stevens's early poems has faded like Wordsworth's bliss of the revolutionary dawn, and the 'fine ideas' of the title are very like the succession of philosophical 'contrarieties' that perplexed and muddled Wordsworth in his 'weary labyrinth'. Stevens glossed this poem in a letter:[1] 'One of the characteristics of the world today is the Lightness with which ideas are asserted, held, abandoned, etc. That is what this poem grows out of.' In the midst of such 'Lightness', and at the same time watching with horror the early stages of the new World War, it is himself that Stevens makes 'seek beneath the name' of Poet his 'office upon earth and nowhere else'. Here is the end of the poem:

The chants of final peace
Lie in the heart's residuum.

How can
We chant if we live in evil and afterward
Lie harshly buried there?

If earth dissolves
Its evil after death, it dissolves it while
We live. Thence come the final chants, the chants
Of the brooder seeking the acutest end
Of speech: to pierce the heart's residuum
And there to find music for a single line,
Equal to memory, one line in which
The vital music formulates the words.

Behold the men in helmets borne on steel,
Discolored, how they are going to defeat.

1 To Oscar Williams, 18 November 1940.

In this passage Stevens defines a tenable role for the poet in a world whose growing tendency to enormous public disaster might appear to make his occupation seem at best unnecessary and at worst mere blinkered frivolity. Against such appearances Stevens often, as here, insists that even, or perhaps particularly, in such a world the poet has a serious part to play. The area of his concern is the individual mind, the privacy of the spirit in which both freedom to think and the possibility of peace are to be found. There is optimism as well as a truth in the words: 'The chants of final peace/Lie in the heart's residuum', and later in the passage this optimism is extended to the poet and to what he can do to create an orientation in the distracted mind.

> to pierce the heart's residuum
> And there to find music for a single line,
> Equal to memory,

Behind these words lies a perception of all that is involved in the mimetic aspect of poetry, in that accuracy with respect to reality which produces in the reader a sense of recognition not only of his world but of himself in that world, a sense of the significance of the conjunction of himself and the world, a sense of home. The powerful effect of the poem's concluding couplet is made largely by how we have been prepared for it. It is itself 'at the acutest end of speech', 'equal to memory'. More than something said about war and its futility, it is something achieved by the poet for those who despair at what they see in the world and also for the soldiers on their tanks. It is a tribute, remote and tactful, to that human quality which dissolves the earth's evil 'while we live', a quality which Stevens, with extreme caution in his use of the word, elsewhere refers to as 'nobility'.

In the preceding section of 'Extracts from Addresses to the Academy of Fine Ideas', Stevens has been more explicit about the relationship between man and his world. He describes more directly than Wordsworth with his varying philosophical apparatus ever does that sense of the earth as home which lies near the centre of Wordsworth's best poetry. The quotation has to be a long one:

> Ecstatic identities
> Between one's self and the weather and the things

Of the weather are the belief in one's element,
The casual reunions, the long-pondered
Surrenders, the repeated sayings that
There is nothing more and that it is enough
To believe in the weather and in the things and men
Of the weather and in one's self, as part of that
And nothing more. So that if one went to the moon,
Or anywhere beyond, to a different element,
One would be drowned in the air of difference,
Incapable of belief, in the difference.
And then returning from the moon, if one breathed
The cold evening, without any scent or the shade
Of any woman, watched the thinnest light
And the most distant, single color, about to change,
And naked of any illusion, in poverty,
In the exactest poverty, if then
One breathed the cold evening, the deepest inhalation
Would come from that return to the subtle centre.

The word 'poverty' was a favourite of Stevens's. He used it like this, and often with a denser load of connotation, to evoke the condition of modern man, without certainty, without truths acceptable as authoritative, without anything but himself and his planet to make something of that will satisfy his need for belief and for significance. All Stevens's work should be seen against the background of this 'poverty' because it was towards the making of something out of and for it that his whole effort was directed.

Wordsworth in 1800[1] contemplated with gloom the decline of literary sensibility into the craving for news and sensation, but at the same time hoped that 'the time is approaching when the evil will be systematically opposed by men of greater powers and with far more distinguished success' than his own. As it turned out, few poets since his time have approached Wordsworth's goal for literary endeavour in comprehension let alone in actual achievement. It was not the poets but the novelists of the nineteenth and early twentieth centuries who were to come closest to fulfilling his hope. There have nevertheless been poets, the poets who for this very reason matter

[1] In the Preface to *Lyrical Ballads*.

most, who have understood and accepted the challenge involved, and of them none has done both with more clarity and more resolution than Stevens.

The nature of the challenge, of the momentous change in the place and purpose of poetry to which Wordsworth and Keats, Eliot and Stevens each in his own way responded, is beautifully put by Stevens, with the oblique lightness characteristic of his prose, in a passage from his late (1951) essay 'A Collect of Philosophy'. It is appropriate that his example should be drawn from the pre-Christian world. Jean Paulhan, a friend of Stevens's, was a distinguished critic and the editor for many years of the *Nouvelle Revue Française*. He was also a decorated survivor of four years in the trenches and a hero of the Resistance. He died in 1968. 'When we read the *Phaedo*', writes Stevens,

we stand in the presence of Socrates, in the chamber in which he is shortly to die and we listen to him as he expounds his ideas concerning immortality. We observe that the confidence in the immortality of what was really Socrates was no less a confidence in the world, in which he reclined and spoke, a hostile and a fatal world. When we look over the shoulder of Jean Paulhan, in Paris, while he writes of 'la confiance que le poète fait naturellement – et nous invite à faire – au monde' and stop to consider what a happy phrase that is, we wonder whether we shall have the courage to repeat it, until we understand that there is no alternative. So many words other than confidence might have been used – words of understanding, words of reconciliation, of enchantment, even of forgetfulness. But none of them would have penetrated to our needs more surely than the word confidence.

2

Imagination as Value

Arnold's true successor was not Pater or any other English writer of
the generation immediately following his own but George Santayana,
the Spanish philosopher and critic who lived in America from his ninth
to his forty-ninth year, and was for the last twenty-three of those
years on the Faculty of Harvard University. After his resignation in
1912 he never returned to America. He lived in England during the
war and later in Paris; in 1924 he settled in Rome and died there in
1952. All his writings were in English. As a critic, or, rather, a
philosopher who frequently turned his attention to literary questions,
he was certainly not Arnold's successor in any conscious or deliberate
sense. Like Eliot (whom perhaps Santayana influenced in this as in
other, more fortunate directions) he attributed to Arnold the high-
flown vagueness that should have been laid at Pater's door. He
launched, against Arnold's famous verdict, a defence of Shelley as a
poet[1] which not only reveals a distorted and unjust view of Arnold,
but also defies the critical principles that he himself had earlier laid
down in substantial agreement with Arnold. And in a note on
'Liberalism and Culture' published in 1915, he attacked Arnold without mercy and with very little understanding:

Liberalism does not go very deep; it is an adventitious principle, a mere
loosening of an older structure. For that reason it brings to all who felt
cramped and ill-suited much comfort and relief. . .It opens to them that
sweet, scholarly, tenderly moral, critically superior attitude of mind which
Matthew Arnold called culture. . .Piety and learning had their intrinsic
charms, but, after all, they had been cultivated for the sake of ulterior duties
and benefits, and in order to appropriate and hand down the revealed wisdom
which opened the way to heaven. Culture, on the contrary, had no ulterior

---

[1] 'Shelley: or the Poetic Value of Revolutionary Principles', *Winds of Doctrine*, 1913.

purpose, no forced unity. It was an aroma inhaled by those who walked in the evening in the garden of life.

Santayana is here as unfair to Arnold as Eliot was later to be: Arnold's view of culture, for instance, was always informed by precisely the 'ulterior purpose' which Santayana denies. But Santayana's unfairness is more unexpected than Eliot's, since his own best writing on literature, and particularly on its relation to religion, shows such striking and complete concordance with Arnold that, but for such passages as this, one might guess him to have read all Arnold's works with care and enthusiasm.

For Santayana's critical idealism is as strong as Arnold's, if more rigorous; it is formulated and substantiated by his study of literature in very much the same way; and it is seen as subject to very much the same threats and dangers, though these looked even direr to the younger man. Arnold, visiting America at the end of his life could see that its faith in 'the *average man*' was a menace to the standards that he had passionately preached. Santayana, who could have heard Arnold's lecture 'Literature and Science' as an undergraduate, was revolted by the prevailing values of the university in which he lived and worked. In *Character and Opinion in the United States*, he tells this story:

The president of Harvard College, seeing me once by chance soon after the beginning of a term, inquired how my classes were getting on; and when I said I thought they were getting on well, that my men seemed to be keen and intelligent, he stopped me as if I were about to waste his time. 'I meant' said he, '*what is the number* of students in your classes?'

Santayana's refusal to knuckle under to this atmosphere was un-qualified: 'I object to and absolutely abhor', he wrote to William James, who had accused him of 'impertinence and superior airs', 'the assertion that all the eggs indiscriminately are good because the hen has laid them.' And, in another letter:

While I wish to be just and to understand people's feelings, wherever they are at all significant, I am deliberately minded to be contemptuous towards what seems to me contemptible, and not to have any share in the conspiracy of mock respect by which intellectual ignominy and moral stagnation are kept up in our society.

It is not surprising to find that when Santayana applied his unpopular principles of moral and intellectual excellence to contemporary literature, he found nothing to satisfy him. For one who felt as he did, and as Arnold had, that: 'The sole advantage in possessing great works of literature lies in what they can help us to become', the literary scene in America and England in the 'nineties was not encouraging. Surveying it in 1896 he wrote: 'The crudity we are too distracted to refine, we accept as originality, and the vagueness we are too pretentious to make accurate, we pass off as sublimity.' And in his critical essays collected and published in 1900 under the title *Interpretations of Poetry and Religion* he presents as it were the firm conclusions about the poet's task in the modern world towards which all Arnold's work had tended but which Arnold himself had never definitely stated.

In his Preface Santayana summarises the idea which connects the essays in terms which show how closely his view approached Arnold's:

Religion and poetry are identical in essence, and differ merely in the way in which they are attached to practical affairs. Poetry is called religion when it intervenes in life, and religion, when it merely supervenes upon life, is seen to be nothing but poetry. It would naturally follow from this conception that religious doctrines would do well to withdraw their pretension to be dealing with matters of fact...For the dignity of religion, like that of poetry and of every moral ideal, lies precisely in its ideal adequacy, in its fit rendering of the meanings and values of life, in its anticipation of perfection.

Santayana may have thought that he was attacking Arnold in this passage later in the Preface: 'The liberal school that attempts to fortify religion by minimizing its expression, both theoretic and devotional, seems...to be merely impoverishing religious symbols and vulgarizing religious aims.' But Arnold's constant insistence on the fundamental value of the Bible itself, and his leaning towards the liturgy (though not the theology) of the Catholic Church absolve him from such a charge; and he would have agreed with every word of Santayana's conclusion to the Preface:

Not to see in...rational activity the purpose and standard of all life is to have left human nature half unread...In comparison with such apathetic naturalism, all the errors and follies of religion are worthy of indulgent sympathy, since they represent an effort, however misguided, to interpret and to use the materials of experience for moral ends, and to measure the value of reality by its relation to the ideal.

Just as Santayana shared, though apparently without realising it, Arnold's view of the relation between poetry and religion and of the nature of religious language and symbolism, so he shared with Arnold a vision of the enormous imaginative and intellectual responsibility confronting the modern poet, and a despairing perception of the failure to meet it. In the well-known essay 'The Poetry of Barbarism', of which Whitman and Browning are the particular targets, he diagnoses this failure in these words:

We find our contemporary poets incapable of any high wisdom, incapable of any imaginative rendering of human life and its meaning. Our poets are things of shreds and patches; they give us episodes and studies, a sketch of this curiosity, a glimpse of that romance; they have no total vision, no grasp of the whole reality and consequently no capacity for a sane and steady idealization. The comparatively barbarous ages had a poetry of the ideal; they had visions of beauty, order and perfection. This age of material elaboration has no sense for those things. Its fancy is retrospective, whimsical, and flickering; its ideals, when it has any, are negative and partial; its moral strength is a blind and miscellaneous vehemence...This poetry should be viewed in relation to the general moral crisis and imaginative disintegration of which it gives a verbal echo; then we shall avoid the injustice of passing it over as insignificant, no less than the imbecility of hailing it as essentially glorious and successful.

This passage, like the whole essay from which it comes is most remarkable for its date (1900). It not only crystallises, in terms stronger and clearer than Arnold's own, the situation as Arnold had seen it; it also looks forward across the chasm of 1914–18 to the Yeats of 'The Second Coming' – 'The best lack all conviction' – to *The Waste Land* and the 'imaginative disintegration' of the *Cantos*, and also to *Four Quartets* and Stevens's later poetry which are the only fully-achieved victories in this century and in English of poetry against barbarism.

Santayana had a closer and more accurate appreciation than Arnold of the way in which the poetic imagination actually works. In 'The

Elements and Function of Poetry', the essay which concludes *Interpretations of Poetry and Religion,* he says:

The great function of poetry...is...to repair to the material of experience, seizing hold of the reality of sensation and fancy beneath the surface of conventional ideas, and then out of that living but indefinite material to build new structures, richer, finer, fitter to the primary tendencies of our nature, to the ultimate possibilities of the soul.

And a little further on he coins a concept, a celebrated shorthand description of the poetic process, for which Eliot has taken the credit. The poet's imagination, he says, operates like the day-dreaming child's: 'The glorious emotions with which he bubbles over must at all hazards find or feign their correlative objects.' This is, as far as I know, the first appearance in criticism of the objective correlative. But whereas Eliot leaves the causal relationship between object and emotion undefined, so that one suspects him of suggesting that the poet, like the child, sets out to find or feign a correlative in the real world. Santayana makes it clear that it is 'the seed of sensation' which comes first.

The passions are naturally blind, and the poverty of the imagination, when left alone, is absolute. The passions may ferment as they will, they can never breed an idea out of their own energy. This idea must be furnished by the senses, by outward experience, else the hunger of the soul will gnaw its own emptiness for ever.

Both Eliot and Stevens were undergraduates at Harvard while Santayana was teaching there. Eliot took two of Santayana's courses of lectures, in 1908 and (as a graduate student) in 1909. Stevens, who was at Harvard from 1897 to 1900, took no courses in philosophy and was therefore never officially one of Santayana's pupils. But he knew him, was often invited by Santayana to come and see him, and read him his early poems. Both poets were influenced by him to a very considerable degree. To anyone who has read *Interpretations of Poetry and Religion* and *Three Philosophical Poets* (1910), ideas first organised by Santayana are plainly visible in Eliot's early criticism, though their derivation, as with the objective correlative, is usually not acknowledged. It is above all a toughness, an intellectual rigour in thought about poetry and an unwillingness to tolerate emotional self-indulgence that Santayana strengthened in the young Eliot. But Santayana's fundamental view of poetry, his vision of its relation to religion, and the consequent vast reach of his hope for it – all so like Arnold's – were ultimately to prove, of course, far from sympathetic to Eliot. One can hardly imagine him, at least after the late 1920s, agreeing with this pronouncement in 'The Elements and Function of Poetry':

Where poetry rises from its elementary and detached expressions in rhythms, euphemism, characterization and story-telling, and comes to the consciousness of its highest function, that of portraying the ideals of experience and destiny, then the poet becomes aware that he is essentially a prophet, and either devotes himself to the loving expression of the religion that exists, or like Lucretius or Wordsworth, to the heralding of one that he believes to be possible. Such poets are aware of their highest mission; others, whatever the energy of their genius, have not conceived their ultimate function as poets. They have been willing to leave their world ugly as a whole, after stuffing it with a sufficient profusion of beauties. Their contemporaries, their fellow-countrymen for many generations, may not perceive this defect, because they are naturally even less able than the poet himself to understand the necessity of so large a harmony...Such insensibility to the highest poetry is no more extraordinary than the corresponding indifference to the highest religion; nobility and excellence, however, are not dependent on the suffrage of half-baked men, but on the original disposition of the clay and the potter; I mean on the conditions of the art and the ideal capacities of human nature.

The irony and the paradox of Eliot is that, although in *Four Quartets* he fulfilled the 'ultimate function' of the poet as Santayana here defines it, as a critic he consistently evaded the admission that such a function exists even for the Christian poet, let alone for the non-Christian.

The challenge that Santayana formulated for the modern poet, more cogently and carefully than Arnold had done, though less optimistically, was essentially post-Christian. It was connected, that is to say, to a view of religion incompatible with orthodox Christianity, in so far as orthodox Christianity imposes upon its poets the service of specific and unquestionable truths. When Santayana uses phrases like 'the loving expression of the religion that exists', he is speaking of the past. He sees the present, his own period, as a time of 'general

moral crisis and imaginative disintegration', and nowhere does he
envisage a return to the orthodoxy of the past as the modern poet's
proper response to this crisis. It was thus inevitable that Eliot, the
convert to Anglo-Catholicism, should move altogether away from
the influence of a man whose theology he would presumably have
considered as juvenile as that of Arnold which it so closely resembles.
'That fallacy', wrote Santayana in a characteristic passage,

from which the pagan religion alone has been free, that πρῶτον ψεῦδος of all
fanaticism, the natural but hopeless misunderstanding of imagining that
poetry in order to be religion, in order to be the inspiration of life, must first
deny that it is poetry and deceive us about the facts with which we have to
deal – this misunderstanding has marred the work of the Christian imagination
and condemned it, if we may trust appearances, to be transitory.

It is hardly likely that Eliot would have regarded such an observation
with enthusiasm, still less all in Santayana's critical thought which
depends directly upon such a conception of religion.

Santayana's influence on Stevens was altogether different, in kind,
in duration, and in intensity. It was not only that Santayana's
critical ideas, some of them much elaborated, remained permanently
at the centre of Stevens's thought, so that the vision of the poet's
task sketched by Santayana comes to seem a bright unbroken
thread reappearing again and again throughout Stevens's work. It
was also that the figure of Santayana himself, whom after 1900 he
never saw again, assumed for Stevens over the years a strangely
symbolic, almost a numinous quality. In a passage from the very
difficult and important essay 'Imagination as Value', which Stevens
delivered as a lecture in 1948, Santayana appears as the single illustration illuminating a whole complex of ideas essential to the understanding of Stevens himself. I quote at length because the force of
Stevens's peculiar prose, at once tentative and dense with integrity,
is lost in the short extract. The neat and quotable conclusion is not
the object of his method of thought; as he wrote elsewhere,[1] of
Santayana: 'His pages are part of the *douceur de vivre* and do not
offer themselves for sensational summary.' The following passage
from 'Imagination as Value' is part of a meditation exploring and

[1] In 'A Collect of Philosophy', *Opus Posthumous*, p. 187.

defining the suggestion contained in these two sentences: 'To regard the imagination as metaphysics is to think of it as part of life, and to think of it as part of life is to realize the extent of artifice. We live in the mind.'

The discussion of the imagination as metaphysics has led us off a little to one side. This is justified, however, by the considerations, first, that the operation of the imagination in life is more significant than its operation in or in relation to...arts and letters; second, that the imagination penetrates life; and finally that its value as metaphysics is not the same as its value in arts and letters. In spite of the prevalence of the imagination in life, it is probably true that the discussion of it in that relation is incomparably less frequent and less intelligent than the discussion of it in relation to arts and letters. I suppose that the reason for this is that few people would turn to the imagination, knowingly, in life, while few people would turn to anything else, knowingly, in arts and letters. In life what is important is the truth as it is, while in arts and letters what is important is the truth as we see it. There is a real difference here even though people turn to the imagination without knowing it in arts and letters. There are other possible variations of that theme but the theme itself is there. Again in life the function of the imagination is so varied that it is not well-defined as it is in arts and letters. In life one hesitates when one speaks of the value of the imagination. Its value in arts and letters is aesthetic. Most men's lives are thrust upon them. The existence of aesthetic value in lives that are forced on those that live them is an improbable sort of thing. There can be lives, nevertheless, which exist by the deliberate choice of those that live them. To use a single illustration: it may be assumed that the life of Professor Santayana is a life in which the function of the imagination has had a function similar to its function in any deliberate work of art or letters. We have only to think of this present phase of it,[1] in which, in his old age, he dwells in the head of the world, in the company of devoted women, in their convent, and in the company of familiar saints, whose presence does so much to make any convent an appropriate refuge for a generous and human philosopher. To repeat, there can be lives in which the value of the imagination is the same as its value in arts and letters and I exclude from consideration as part of that statement any thought of poverty or wealth, being a *bauer* or being a king, and so on, as irrelevant.

What is being aimed at in this remarkable paragraph, as in the whole of the essay, is nothing less than a definition of the human

---

[1] In 1948 the octogenarian Santayana was living in the convent in Rome where, in 1952, he died.

qualities and human powers by which man is able to confer value on his life and on his relation to the world. The definition is not arrived at by the ordinary process of consequential statement but evoked, as it were, by an accumulation of suggestions lit by Stevens's incandescent caution. The large words 'by which men long lived well' but which in the modern world have lost the firmness and credit that vanished structures gave them, words like 'goodness', 'freedom', 'nobility', even 'meaning', are consistently avoided. Yet it is precisely towards the conviction such words used to carry that Stevens moves with due and elaborate care both in his poetry and in his prose. Within the convolutions of the passage above lurks the proposition that the freedom to create significance, a commonplace of perception and discussion in the aesthetic sphere, can be related to the freedom from which a man may choose to create the significance of his own life. And within even this proposition there is the suggestion, made with the subtlest circumspection, that Santayana is a good man, and that his goodness has to do with just such created significance as is usually thought of in connexion with the arts. These large words belong, of course, to 'sensational summary'. Stevens knew what he was about when he denied himself the use of them: he was seeking to outwit the easy neglect that follows upon the easy classification. 'Your use of the word nobility causes some difficulty', he told a critic[1] who had thus labelled a recurrent theme of his poetry. 'Not long ago I wrote to John Crowe Ransom and told him that I thought that while the word was essentially the right word it was a most impolitic word to use.' But by evading the dangers referred to in the phrase 'a most impolitic word', Stevens took on the simpler danger of not being understood. If what he was saying is to be heard, it must in the end be said in the old, large words, sharpened and strengthened a little, perhaps, by his own refusal to rely on them.

On the basis of this passage alone it would seem extravagant to claim that the figure of Santayana came, towards the end of both their lives, to represent for Stevens the saving goodness, the emblematic victory over life, that in another age would have been represented by the figure of a saint. The claim is substantiated, however, by the poem 'To an Old Philosopher in Rome' which Stevens wrote

[1] Letter to Robert Pack, 14 April 1955.

four years later (it was published, by coincidence, in the month that Santayana died, September 1952). The subject of the poem is not only Santayana himself, the old philosopher dying 'in the head of the world'; it is also 'the imagination as value'. Stevens sees Santayana's life as a representative and sufficient answer to the question posed elsewhere in the essay of that name: 'What, then, is it to live in the mind with the imagination, yet not too near to the fountains of its rhetoric, so that one does not have a consciousness only of grandeurs, of incessant departures from the idiom and of inherent altitudes?' The question implies an insistence on the normal, on the tethering of the imagination to reality, which is highly characteristic of Stevens. The imagination, in his view, is not to transcend, to leave behind as worthless and despised, what he called the poverty of human life. On the contrary, it is this inescapable poverty which the imagination, as only the imagination can, must inform with significance. The point is clearly made in these sentences from the closing passage of 'Imagination as Value':

My final point, then, is that the imagination is the power that enables us to perceive the normal in the abnormal, the opposite of chaos in chaos. It does this every day in arts and letters. This may seem to be a merely capricious statement; for ordinarily we regard the imagination as abnormal per se...It is natural for us to identify the imagination with those that extend its abnormality. It is like identifying liberty with those that abuse it. A literature overfull of abnormality and, certainly, present-day European literature, as one knows it, seems to be a literature full of abnormality, gives the reason an appearance of normality to which it is not, solely, entitled...Those that insist on the solitude and misery and terror of the world...will ask of what value is the imagination to them; and if their experience is to be considered, how is it possible to deny that they live in an imagination of evil? Is evil normal or abnormal? And how do the exquisite divinations of the poets and for that matter even the 'aureoles of the saints' help them? But when we speak of perceiving the normal, we have in mind the instinctive integrations which are the reason for living. Of what value is anything to the solitary and those that live in misery and terror, except the imagination?...

The chief problems of any artist, as of any man, are the problems of the normal and...he needs, in order to solve them, everything that the imagination has to give.

The possible triumph suggested here, the triumph of human value

achieved by the imagination, is the triumph described and saluted in
'To an Old Philosopher in Rome'. An essential constituent of any
such triumph, as Stevens sees it, is the ordinariness, the poverty and
the sadness inseparable from human existence, and here it is exemplified
by the ordinary objects surrounding Santayana's, as any man's,
deathbed. It is hard to quote from this poem: the long sentences move
through the sixteen stanzas with such mastery of measure that
quotation seems more than usually like mutilation. The two worlds,
reality and the imagination, are established at the beginning:

> On the threshold of heaven, the figures in the street
> Become the figures of heaven, the majestic movement
> Of men growing small in the distances of space,
> Singing, with smaller and still smaller sound,
> Unintelligible absolution and an end –
>
> The threshold, Rome, and that more merciful Rome
> Beyond, the two alike in the make of the mind.
> It is as if in a human dignity
> Two parallels become one, a perspective, of which
> Men are part both in the inch and in the mile.

The mind, in its 'making', unites the two worlds by endowing the
bare particulars of reality with the imagination's value, inventing
nothing and exaggerating nothing, always acknowledging the nakedness and poverty of the human condition.

> Be orator but with an accurate tongue
> And without eloquence, O, half-asleep,
> Of the pity that is the memorial of this room,
>
> So that we feel, in this illumined large,
> The veritable small, so that each of us
> Beholds himself in you, and hears his voice
> In yours, master and commiserable man,
> Intent on your particles of nether-do,
>
> Your dozing in the depths of wakefulness,
> In the warmth of your bed, at the edge of your
>   chair, alive
> Yet living in two worlds, impenitent
> As to one, and, as to one, most penitent,

> Impatient for the grandeur that you need
> In so much misery; and yet finding it
> Only in misery, the afflatus of ruin,
> Profound poetry of the poor and of the dead. . .

After the long sentence comes the simple statement:

'It is poverty's speech that seeks us out the most', and then the stanza which forms the summit, as it were, of the whole poem:

> And you – it is you that speak it, without speech,
> The loftiest syllables among loftiest things,
> The one invulnerable man among
> Crude captains, the naked majesty, if you like,
> Of bird-nest arches and of rain-stained vaults.

After this stanza the emotional intensity of the poem dies away towards the serenity of its close:

> It is a kind of total grandeur at the end,
> With every visible thing enlarged and yet
> No more than a bed, a chair and moving nuns,
> The immensest theatre, the pillared porch,
> The book and candle in your ambered room,
>
> Total grandeur of a total edifice,
> Chosen by an inquisitor of structures
> For himself. He stops upon this threshold,
> As if the design of all his words takes form
> And frame from thinking and is realized.

This was the last long poem that Stevens published (though not the last he wrote). In the year of its composition he was 73, and had not seen Santayana for more than half a century. It is obvious that mixed with his veneration for a figure who had become for him a symbol of a certain kind of victory, is reflection, meditation, perhaps even hope almost amounting to prayer, about his own approaching death. The religious connotations of the poem, which certainly exist, we shall examine later. For the moment the point is only to demonstrate how deeply Santayana, alone among all the people he had known and all the writers he had read, became involved in the innermost texture of Stevens's intellectual and emotional life, in this poem to the point of complete imaginative identity. The root of this relationship of the mind was clearly a strong sympathy between the two men as individuals when both were at Harvard, together with a close similarity of aim. They shared an aloof and lonely determination of spirit which each may have detected in the other; and they also shared an ambition for poetry which Santayana was formulating at the time and which Stevens spent the rest of his life attempting to put into practical effect. Beneath the extreme reticence of a passage in one of Stevens's letters it is possible to detect a sense of his having assumed a role that Santayana abandoned when he gave up writing poetry.

I doubt if Santayana was any more isolated at Cambridge than he wished to be...He invited me to come to see him a number of times and, in that way, I came to know him a little. I read several poems to him and he expressed his own view of the subject of them in a sonnet which he sent me...This was forty years ago,[1] when I was a boy and when he was not yet in mid-life. Obviously, his mind was full of the great projects of his future and, while some of these have been realized, it is possible to think that many have not. It would be easy to speak of his interest and sympathy; it might amuse you more to know that Sparklets were then something new and that Santayana liked to toy with them...I always came away from my visits to him feeling that he made up in the most genuine way for many things that I needed. He was then still definitely a poet.

With the hints of this passage in mind, one wonders whether it is Santayana the old philosopher or Stevens the old poet who is the more strongly referred to in the lines:

> He stops upon this threshold,
> As if the design of all his words takes form
> And frame from thinking and is realized.

The ideas expressed with odd elliptical precision in 'Imagination as Value' are very close to much that Santayana had expounded in a more orderly, but nevertheless a less definite, manner many years before. This is by no means to suggest 'influence' in any crude or careless sense. 'Imagination as Value', like all his prose, is most clearly the fruit of Stevens's own experience and thought. Its ideas are related to Santayana's ideas in the same way that the two men are

---

[1] This letter was written in 1945 (to José Rodríguez Feo, 4 January 1945).

related in the one's poem about the other: by an identity of feeling and of aim. 'It is as if...two parallels become one, a perspective.' We have observed Stevens's insistence on the normal, on the tethering of the imagination to reality. Here, in another passage from the essay, is this insistence pitched at its highest:

The world may, certainly, be lost to the poet but it is not lost to the imagination. And I say that the world is lost to him, certainly, because, for one thing, the great poems of heaven and hell have been written and the great poem of the earth remains to be written. I suppose it is that poem that will constitute the true prize of the spirit and that until it is written many lesser things will be so regarded, including conquests that are not unimaginable.

Santayana several times expressed the same hope, with the same lack of confidence. In *Three Philosophical Poets*, published in 1910, he wrote:

It is time some genius should appear to reconstitute the shattered picture of the world. He should live in the continual presence of all experience, and respect it; he should at the same time understand nature, the ground of that experience; and he should also have a delicate sense for the ideal echoes of his own passions, and for all the colours of his possible happiness. All that can inspire a poet is contained in this task, and nothing less than this task would exhaust a poet's inspiration...But this supreme poet is in limbo still.

And in *Reason in Art* (1905) there is a passage describing the relation between reality and the imagination which might serve as an epigraph, not only for 'To an Old Philosopher in Rome', but for the whole of Stevens's work:

Literary art in the end rejects all unmeaning flourishes, all complications that have no counterpart in the things of this world or no use in expressing their relations; at the same time it aspires to digest that reality to which it confines itself, making it over into ideal substance and material for the mind... [The writer's] art is relative to something other than its own formal impulse; it comes to clarify the real world, not to encumber it; and it needs to render its native agility pertinent to the facts and to attach its volume of feeling to what is momentous in human life. Literature has its piety, its conscience; it cannot long forget, without forfeiting all dignity, that it serves a burdened and perplexed creature, a human animal struggling to persuade the universal Sphinx to propose a more intelligible riddle. Irresponsible and trivial in its abstract impulse, man's simian chatter becomes noble as it becomes symbolic;

its representative function lends it a serious beauty, its utility endows it with moral worth.

There is much in Santayana's hope for poetry, and in Stevens's, that seems reminiscent of Emerson. Among the hazy rhetorical paragraphs of, for instance, Emerson's essay 'Poetry and Imagination', one finds remarks that seem to anticipate the two later writers:

Poetry must be affirmative. It is the piety of the intellect...The poet who shall use Nature as his hieroglyphic must have an adequate message to convey thereby.

The poet is rare because he must be exquisitely vital and sympathetic, and, at the same time, immoveably centred...The poet is representative, – whole man, diamond merchant, symboliser, emancipator; in him the world projects a scribe's hand and writes the adequate genesis.

We must not conclude against poetry from the defects of poets.

But Emerson's ideas about poetry, as about other things, are vitiated by a vagueness, a lack of respect not only for the discipline of organised thought but also for the hard facts of reality and for plain common-sense, that Santayana himself exposed in a devastating essay in *Interpretations of Poetry and Religion*. The object of his attack is Emerson's tendency towards the elevation of the imagination, as some sort of faculty of the absolute, above the real world and ordinary human understanding of it. This tendency Santayana calls 'mystical'. Of Emerson's 'alternately ingenuous and rhapsodical' reliance upon the imagination alone Santayana writes:

By attacking the authority of the understanding as the organon of knowledge, by substituting itself for it as the herald of a deeper truth, the imagination... prepares its own destruction. For if the understanding is rejected because it cannot grasp the absolute, the imagination and all its works – art, dogma, worship – must presently be rejected for the same reason.

On this issue, which is really the issue of a satisfactory definition of the imagination, Stevens, though some critics have linked him with Emerson in an escapist realm of pure wishful thinking, is unequivocally on the same side as Santayana.

Again and again Stevens insists, in full accord with Santayana, that the imagination divorced from reality is nothing. His view of it, unlike Emerson's, is never transcendental or absolutist. Emerson, defining the imagination, says:

Whilst common sense looks at things or visible nature as real and final facts, poetry, or the imagination which dictates it, is a second sight, looking through these, and using them as types or words for thoughts which they signify... The very design of imagination is to domesticate us in another, in a celestial nature. This power is in the image because this power is in Nature. It so affects, because it so is...Or, shall we say that the imagination exists by sharing the ethereal currents

He believes, in other words, with whatever degree of optimistic imprecision, that there exists a rival reality, beyond or above mundane reality, to which the imagination alone has access. Stevens's view of the imagination could not be more firmly opposed to such a belief. 'To be at the end of fact is not to be at the beginning of imagination but it is to be at the end of both', he wrote in his notebook. And here is a typical pronouncement:

Poetry is a passion, not a habit. This passion nourishes itself on reality. Imagination has no source except in reality, and ceases to have any value when it departs from reality. Here is a fundamental principle about the imagination. It does not create except as it transforms...Imagination gives, but gives in relation.

These crisp sentences, from a letter of 1940,[1] are part of a gloss on section XXII of 'The Man with the Blue Guitar', the long and difficult poem about his theory of poetry that he had written three years before. Nothing could better illustrate the distance that separates Stevens from Emerson's soft woolliness of thought than these dry lines, pared to the very bone of accuracy:

> Poetry is the subject of the poem,
> From this the poem issues and
>
> To this returns. Between the two,
> Between issue and return, there is
>
> An absence in reality,
> Things as they are. Or so we say.

[1] To Hi Simons, 10 August 1940.

But are these separate? Is it
An absence for the poem, which acquires

Its true appearances there, sun's green,
Cloud's red, earth feeling, sky that thinks?

From these it takes. Perhaps it gives,
In the universal intercourse.

The unexpectedness both of the colours and of the sudden pathetic fallacies in the penultimate couplet, particularly in their close proximity to the word 'true', are a swift and subtle indication of the part played by the poet himself in the process described. As Stevens was to put it, concluding 'Effects of Analogy', a lecture delivered in the same year as 'Imagination as Value': 'Poetry... is a transcendent analogue composed of the particulars of reality, created by the poet's sense of the world, that is to say, his attitude, as he intervenes and interposes the appearances of that sense.' The 'transcendent analogue' is quite unrelated to Emerson's 'celestial nature': Stevens insists always that 'The imagination is the faculty by which we import the unreal into what is real.' And Stevens's parallel insistence on the essential role of the creative individual in any act of the imagination is equally remote from Emerson's neoplatonist visions of the world-soul common to all men. Whenever Stevens in his prose writings moves towards a tentative definition of poetry, his stress is, as above, on 'the poet's sense of the world'. In 'The Noble Rider and the Sound of Words' (written in 1941), the first of the lectures in *The Necessary Angel*, the emphasis takes this form:

The pressure of reality is, I think, the determining factor in the artistic character of an individual. The resistance to this pressure or its evasion in the case of individuals of extraordinary imagination cancels the pressure so far as those individuals are concerned...The role of the poet...is paramount. In this area of my subject I might be expected to speak of the social, that is to say sociological or political, obligation of the poet. He has none...What is his function? Certainly it is not to lead people out of the confusion in which they find themselves. Nor is it, I think, to comfort them while they follow their leaders[1] to and fro. I think that his function is to make his imagination theirs and that he fulfils himself only as he sees his imagination become the light in the minds of others. His role, in short, is to help people to live their

[1] Misprinted as 'readers', *The Necessary Angel*, p. 29.

lives...He has had immensely to do with giving life whatever savour it possesses. He has had to do with whatever the imagination and the senses have made of the world. He has, in fact, had to do with life except as the intellect has had to do with it and, as to that, no one is needed to tell us that poetry and philosophy are akin.

It is worth remarking that in the middle of this passage Stevens makes an observation whose realism sharply limits the apparent extravagance of his argument: 'Time and time again it has been said that [the poet] may not address himself to an élite. I think he may. There is not a poet whom we prize living today that does not address himself to an élite.'

In 'The Figure of the Youth as Virile Poet' (1943) – his bizarre titles reflects the luxuriance of his care for accurate speech – he approaches the same theme with the same emphasis, but from a humbler direction. He suggests 'that we define poetry as an un-official view of being', and continues:

This is a much larger definition of poetry than it is usual to make. But just as the nature of the truth changes, perhaps for no more significant reason than that philosophers live and die, so the nature of poetry changes, perhaps for no more significant reason than that poets come and go.

In the light of this use of the word 'truth' the puzzling firmness of a sentence in the long passage quoted above from 'Imagination as Value' begins to quiver. 'In life what is important is the truth as it is, while in arts and letters what is important is the truth as we see it.' It becomes clear that 'reality' rather than 'the truth' is what is meant here, as, indeed, the rest of the passage suggests. Meanwhile 'The Figure of the Youth as Virile Poet' circles for a little round the question of defining poetry and then settles on a conclusion of resilient exactness.

Since we have no difficulty in recognizing poetry and since, at the same time, we say that it is not an attainable acme, not some breath from an altitude, not something that awaits discovery, after which it will not be subject to chance, we may be accounting for it if we say that is a process of the personality of the poet...There can be no poetry without the personality of the poet, and that, quite simply, is why the definition of poetry has not been found and why, in short, there is none.

On this conclusion Stevens comments: 'One does not have to be a cardinal to make the point.' Possibly one had to be a poet: at any rate, those who write about poetry as if it had some mysterious life of its own, and, worse, those who write it as if it had, should be healthily embarrassed by the sanity of these remarks. Stevens adds:

We are talking about something a good deal more comprehensive than the temperament of the artist as that is usually spoken of. We are concerned with the whole personality and, in effect, we are saying that the poet who writes the heroic poem that will satisfy all there is of us and all of us in time to come, will accomplish it by the power of his reason, the force of his imagination and, in addition, the effortless and inescapable process of his own individuality.

It might seem unnecessary to say things about poetry and the poet which are so obviously true were it not for the vast quantities of pretentious absurdity that are perpetrated in the name of criticism. Stevens knew that there was not only room, but a great need, for some central sense to be spoken about poetry. He wrote, in 1951, in the short Introduction to *The Necessary Angel*:

The theory of poetry, as a subject of study, was something with respect to which I had nothing but the most ardent ambitions. It seemed to me to be one of the great subjects of study. I do not mean one more *Ars Poetica* having to do, say, with the techniques of poetry and perhaps with its history. I mean poetry itself, the naked poem, the imagination manifesting itself in its domination of words. The few pages that follow are, now, alas! the only realization posssible to me of those excited ambitions.

The pages of the essays that follow, with all their fine and elaborate affirmation, imply several targets for attack. One is what Leavis has called, with scorn, the upholding of 'purely literary values' – 'Nor are [these] merely literary pages', says Stevens in his Introduction, 'They are pages that have to do with one of the enlargements of life.' Another target as we have seen, is the wishing of a 'social obligation' upon the poet. Between these two, the idea that imaginative literature is useless and the idea that it should be deliberately and specifically useful, lies a path which Stevens (like Leavis) devoted much time and thought to charting. A third target of Stevens's essays, and perhaps the one that was to him the most important, is the idea to which Emerson among many others was prone, that the imagination is some sort of involuntary absolute power involving the existence of some sort of alternative reality. It is above all to counter this idea, or any variant of it, that he repeatedly dwells upon both the interdependence of reality and the imagination and the creative responsibility of the poet in the whole of his personality. A passage towards the end of 'The Figure of the Youth as Virile Poet' shows how inextricably the two themes are related:

It is important to believe that the visible is the equivalent of the invisible; and once we believe it, we have destroyed the imagination; that is to say, we have destroyed the false imagination, the false conception of the imagination as some incalculable *vates* within us, unhappy Rhodomontade. One is often tempted to say that the best definition of poetry is the sum of its attributes. So, here, we may say that the best definition of true imagination is that it is the sum of our faculties. Poetry is the scholar's art. The acute intelligence of the imagination, the illimitable resources of its memory, its power to possess the moment it perceives – if we were speaking of light itself, and thinking of the relationship between objects and light, no further demonstration would be necessary. Like light, it adds nothing, except itself.

The imagination 'adds nothing, except itself'. Behind such a statement is Stevens's constant devotion to reality, his belief that the phrase 'the truth of the imagination' has a meaning only with respect to the imagination's relation with reality, his descriptions of metaphor, of poetry itself, in terms of 'accuracy', 'appositeness', 'rightness'. All these ideas involve to the highest degree the responsibility of the poet himself. When Stevens, as he does in this same essay, makes a gnomic pronouncement like: 'The morality of the poet's radiant and productive atmosphere is the morality of the right sensation', one should not dismiss it as a piece of wilful and question-begging obscurantism. Stevens's essays have frequently, particularly in England, provoked such reactions. But, to take only this instance, the thought is fully achieved, the support for the use of the word 'morality' is there. What Stevens is proposing to the poet is a discipline from which the moral element cannot be abstracted. 'The poet', he says, two sentences later, 'must get rid of the hieratic in everything that concerns him and must move constantly in the direction of the credible'. When he comes to explain what he means by 'the credible', we begin to see also what he means by 'the morality of the right sensation'.

Desiring with all the power of our desire not to write falsely, do we not begin to think of the possibility that poetry is only reality, after all, and that poetic truth is a factual truth, seen, it may be, by those whose range in the perception of fact – that is, whose sensibility – is greater than our own?... What we have called elevation and elation on the part of the poet, which he communicates to the reader, may be not so much elevation as an incandescence of the intelligence and so more than ever a triumph over the incredible.

These ideas are put forward in the form of suggestions. But the suggestions derive from the mature experience of a poet of unassailable integrity whose own work displays unassailable quality. They should be tested not against some vague and misleading notion of 'poetry-in-general' but against the best poetry that we have. From Johnson on, the critical theories that have crashed on the rock of Shakespeare have been legion. It is an indication of the value of what Stevens has to say about poetry that Shakespeare is the name that most frequently occurs to one as vindicating proof when one is reading Stevens's prose. This is true for instance of a passage from 'Effects of Analogy' where Stevens, who is discussing the poetic image and 'the discipline that comes from appositeness in the highest degree', makes finally clear his case against 'the false imagination', above all against what he saw to be the widespread and dangerous tendency 'to identify the imagination with those that extend its abnormality'. Again it is necessary to quote at length:

It [the discipline of the imagination] is primarily a discipline of rightness. The poet is constantly concerned with two theories. One relates to the imagination as a power within him not so much to destroy reality at will as to put it to his own uses. He comes to feel that his imagination is not wholly his own but that it may be part of a much larger, much more potent imagination, which it is his affair to try to get at. For this reason, he pushes on and lives, or tries to live, as Paul Valéry did, on the verge of consciousness. This often results in poetry that is marginal, subliminal. The same theory exists in relation to prose, to painting and other arts. The second theory relates to the imagination as a power within him to have such insights into reality as will make it possible for him to be sufficient as a poet in the very centre of consciousness. This results, or should result, in a central poetry...The proponents of the first theory believe that it will be a part of their achievement to have created the poetry of the future. It may be that the poetry of the future will be to the poetry of the present what the poetry of the present is to the ballad. The proponents of the second theory believe that to create the poetry of the present is an incalculable difficulty, which rarely is achieved, fully and robustly, by anyone... The adherents of the imagination are mystics to begin with and pass from one mysticism to another. The adherents of the central are also mystics to begin with. But all their desire and all their ambition is to press away from mysticism toward that ultimate good sense which we term civilization.

This passage – which sums up much of what is said throughout *The Necessary Angel* – should be borne in mind by those who believe that Stevens was, in more than incidental ways, either Emerson's heir or a French Symbolist in everything but language. 'To an Old Philosopher in Rome' was written by an 'adherent of the central', as were the very few English poems of this century that can be compared with it, 'The Dry Salvages' perhaps, and 'Among School Children'. And of these three, each in its way a masterpiece, Stevens's poem has moved the furthest away from 'mysticism' in Stevens's and Santayana's sense and 'toward that ultimate good sense which we term civilization'. To put this in another way, the quality which Stevens's poem has more of than either Eliot's or Yeats's is the kind of wholeness or complete integration of creative personality indicated by Santayana in a pessimistic passage in *Winds of Doctrine*:

How, then, should there be any great heroes, saints, artists, philosophers, or legislators in an age when nobody trusts himself, or feels any confidence in reason, in an age when the word dogmatic is a term of reproach? Greatness has character and severity, it is deep and sane, it is distinct and perfect. For this reason there is none of it today...The master's eye itself must be single, his style unmistakable, his visionary interest in what he depicts frank and supreme. Hence this comprehensive sort of greatness too is impossible in an age when moral confusion is pervasive, when characters are complex, undecided, troubled by the mere existence of what is not congenial to them, eager to be not themselves; when, in a word, thought is weak and the flux of things overwhelms it.

There are phrases here which catch briefly but exactly some of the fallings from a 'comprehensive sort of greatness' that mark the work of the three 'modern' poets who have been awarded the status of English classics: Eliot, 'troubled by the mere existence of what is not congenial', Yeats, 'eager to be not himself', Pound, 'thought is weak and the flux of things overwhelms it'. There are other phrases here that have their relevance to Stevens, to the best essays in *The Necessary Angel* as well as to the best of his poems: 'greatness has character and severity, it is deep and sane...The master's eye must be single, his style unmistakable, his visionary interest in what he depicts frank and supreme'.

3

The First Phase

'The first phase of the poet's problem is himself.' When we look at the few pages we have (printed in *Letters of Wallace Stevens*) from the journal of the very young Stevens, the undergraduate who found that Santayana 'made up in the most genuine way for many things that I needed', we see that there are already signs of the courage and resolve which the mature poet felt to be of the utmost importance. He was clearly fond of and influenced by his father, who emerges from a handful of his letters to Stevens at Harvard as an affectionate, intelligent man, his admiration for the most talented of his five children tempered with humour and hard-headed commonsense. There are one or two light injunctions in these letters which Stevens fulfilled with remarkable exactness. 'Paint truth but not always in drab clothes.' 'You are not out on a pic-nic – but really preparing for the campaign of life – where self sustenance is essential and where everything depends upon yourself.' 'It will not do to put off the thought of *subsistence* as drone matter, ignoble and unworthy – The "Crack a Jack" is the fellow who is always ready in any emergency, and meanwhile fills his pockets with more stones and his head with more wisdom.' This last piece of advice Stevens followed to the tune of becoming a rich and powerful businessman who did not retire from his job as vice-president of the Hartford Accident and Indemnity Company even at the statutory age of seventy, and was in his office until within a few weeks of his death. His double life, so unlike the careers of most modern literary figures, has seemed puzzling to some, offensively worldly and commercial to others. There is no mystery. As a young man, ambitious, competent, a little priggish, extremely sensible, he was confronted with the necessity of earning his living, and when, after an unsuccessful year as a reporter, he agreed to enter Law School rather than try freelance writing, it was not from weakness but because he felt his father was right. Over the years the career of which he made such a conspicuous success not only bought him the privacy, peace and moderate luxury in which he liked to write, but also, one guesses, provided a discipline, a skeleton of routine for each week and each day, on which his work as a poet came to depend. This, surely, is the explanation of his refusal of the Charles Eliot Norton Chair at Harvard for 1955–6 on the apparently odd grounds that: 'To take the greater part of a year...for something else would be only too likely to precipitate the retirement that I want so much to put off.'[1] (In the event he died before the beginning of the academic year in question.)

Paradoxically perhaps, his job, so much in and of the world, gave him as it were the camouflage that guaranteed his isolation as a poet. 'One of these days', he wrote to a friend in 1942, 'I should like to do something for the Ivory Tower. There are a lot of exceedingly stupid people saying things about the Ivory Tower who ought to be made to regret it.'[2] Six years later, in 'Effects of Analogy', he said in public:

There was a time when the ivory tower was merely a place of seclusion, like a cottage on a hill-top or a cabin by the sea. Today, it is a kind of lock-up of which our intellectual constables are the appointed wardens. Is it not time that someone questioned this degradation, not for the purpose of restoring the isolation of the tower but in order to establish the integrity of its builder? Our rowdy gun-men may not appreciate what comes from that tower. Others do.

Behind these sentences one can detect the detachment from the pressures and demands of the literary world that Stevens guarded for himself, and that his career, begun almost accidentally at the age of twenty-two, helped him to preserve. 'The second phase of the poet's problem...is to maintain his freedom.'

The Journal he kept at Harvard shows how little his almost monastically self-disciplined character changed in the whole course of his life. His devotion to the highest ends of private intellectual and emotional effort was balanced always by an extremely practical awareness of how such devotion could best be fostered and shielded. A paragraph

---

[1] To Archibald MacLeish, 29 November 1954.   [2] To Simons, 18 February 1942.

he wrote in 1899, when he was not yet twenty, contains several clues to the decisive consciousness that governed his life and made it so unlike most poets' lives in its uneventful calm, prosperity, reticence, and marvellously productive old age:

The feeling of piety is very dear to me. I would sacrifice a great deal to be a Saint Augustine but modernity is so Chicagoan, so plain, so unmeditative. I thoroughly believe that at this very moment I get none of my chief pleasures except from what is unsullied. The love of beauty excludes evil. A moral life is simply a pure conscience: a physical, mental and ethical source of pleasure. At the same time it is an inhuman life to lead. . . The only practical life of the world, as a man of the world, not as a University Professor, a Retired Farmer or Citizen, a Philanthropist, a Preacher, a Poet or the like, but as a bustling merchant, a money-making lawyer, a soldier, a politician is to be if unavoidable a pseudo-villain in the drama, a decent person in private life. . . I believe, as unhesitatingly as I believe anything, in the efficacy and necessity of fact meeting fact – with a background of the ideal.

The day before he had written of one of his friends:

[He] ought to have one definite and simple ethical rule which like a weathercock could point every direction and yet be always uppermost. Moods ought not to wreck principles. He needs stability of desire. Personally I mean to work my best and with my might and accept whatever condition that brings me to. Such a principle strikes me as the only true sort of one, the real rockbottom.

This young man, serious but not silly, his idealism firmly rooted in sanity (and controlled by the irony that makes him give those wry capitals to his list of unworldly, impossibly remote occupations), might, in another age, have seen his own feelings in terms of a religious vocation. As it was, in the booming 'Chicagoan' America of the early 1900s, he found both discipline and protection, the complementary practical aspects of monasticism, in the life of 'a money-making lawyer. . .a pseudo-villain in the drama'. The analogy is not far-fetched. To take only a single sign of its appropriateness, 'To an Old Philosopher in Rome' is, among other things, a poem about the death of one solitary contemplative written by another approaching his own. It is also, as we have suggested, a poem that illustrates admirably what Stevens meant when he talked about a certain kind of poet as an 'adherent of the central'. This 'adherence', which he was to describe half a century later ('all their desire and all their ambition is to press away from mysticism...'), is already visible in his Harvard Journal. It takes the form of a very Santayana-like resistance to the current theories of the 'aesthetes'.

When the young Stevens writes: 'The love of beauty excludes evil', the thought, however rashly expressed, has nothing of Pater about it. The feeling behind it is much more that of Arnold, as the context makes clear. Stevens at nineteen, as we have seen, was capable of observing: 'Art for art's sake is both indiscreet and worthless.' And he follows the remark with a fine gloss on 'beauty'.

To say that stars were made to guide navigators etc. seems like stretching a point; but the real use of their beauty...is that it is a service, a food. Beauty is strength. But art – art all alone, detached, sensuous for the sake of sensuousness, not to perpetuate inspiration or thought, art that is mere art – seems to me to be the most arrant as it is the most inexcusable rubbish...What does not have a kinship, a sympathy, a relation, an inspiration and an indissolubility with our lives ought not, and under healthy conditions could not have a place in them.

This, of course, is in exact accord with Santayana, though on this sort of occasion it is probably misleading to use the word 'influence' of two minds in such obvious sympathy. Santayana put the same thought more grandly in *Reason in Art* a few years later:

Any absolute work of art which serves no further purpose than to stimulate an emotion has about it a certain luxurious and visionary taint. We leave it with a blank mind, and a pang bubbles up from the very foundation of pleasures. Art, so long as it needs to be a dream, will never cease to prove a disappointment. Its facile cruelty, its narcotic abstraction, can never sweeten the evils we return to at home; it can liberate half the mind only by leaving the other half in abeyance.

These ideas are central in more than Stevens's sense. They reflect the consensus of English critical thought since it began. Neither Dryden nor Johnson, Coleridge, Wordsworth, Keats in his brief maturity, or Arnold would have disagreed with them. And perhaps the obloquy heaped on Leavis for repeating them only shows how slow we have been to recover from the aestheticism in which some writers of the later nineteenth century took refuge from responsibility.

The young Stevens's sense of responsibility significantly manifests itself more in general reflection and resolution about his own mind and character than in theories about poetry itself. It is as if he were already subconsciously aware that 'the first phase of the poet's problem is himself'. In his Journal after he left Harvard and in the letters, replacing it, to Elsie Moll, the girl from his home town[1] whom he eventually married in 1909, his poet's sensibility is constantly evident. But, unlike most young poets, he is in no hurry. He is content to get on with earning his living and at the same time simply to absorb the particulars of reality that please and move him and to think, in fits and starts, about the enormous issues that underneath it all concern him most. Something of his particular kind of determination can be gathered from these remarks in his Journal a few weeks after he arrived in New York from Harvard. He has just read an article by one Harvard graduate about another:

Harvard feeds subjectivity, encourages an all consuming flame and that, in my mind, is an evil in so impersonal a world. Between lovers and the like personality is well-enough; so with poets and old men etc. and conquerors and lambs etc.; but, for young men etc. it is most decidedly a well-enough to be left alone. Savage was an admirable fellow. Mason calls his attempt at self-support 'praiseworthy though quixotic!' This is absurd...Self-dependence is the greatest thing in the world for a young man and Savage knew it...Savage went into the shoe business and still kept an eye on sunsets and red-winged blackbirds – the summum bonum.

This last sentence well describes Stevens himself at this time. For the next thirteen years he worked very hard to get himself established in his career and wrote no poetry that he later cared to preserve; but many snatches from his journal and letters, full of high spirits, moments of melancholy, the play of a puritan but richly emotional intelligence, show how steadily he kept his eye on 'the summum bonum'. A few examples will give an idea both of what he was like in his twenties and also of how early the preoccupations that underlie all the poetry he was afterwards to write were formed.

I thought, on the train, how utterly we have forsaken the Earth, in the sense of excluding it from our thoughts.

[1] Reading, Pennsylvania. Stevens later traced his paternal ancestry back to Dutch immigrants of the seventeenth century. His mother was Pennsylvania German.

I should like to make a music of my own, a literature of my own, and I should like to live my own life.

I grow infinitely weary of accepting things, of taking things for granted and so on. I sicken of patterns, and trite symbols, and conventions and the lack of thought.

The young man with his star, or the young woman with her dreams are not as happy as the man with his cow – and the woman with her knitting.

Life seems glorious for a while, then it seems poisonous. But you must never lose faith in it, it *is* glorious after all. Only you must find the glory for yourself. Do not look for it either, except in yourself; in the secret places of your spirit and in all your hidden senses.

Been reading poetry. What strikes me is the capable, the marvellous, poetic language; and the absence of poetic thought...We get plenty of moods (and like them, wherever we got them, whether in novels, or poems, or talk, or paintings); and so we get figures of speech, and impressions, and superb lines, and fantastic music. But it's the mind we want to fill – with life. We admit now that Truth is the warrior and Beauty only his tender hide.

The lack that Stevens complains of here, 'the absence of poetic thought', is exactly the lack that both Arnold and Santayana had observed and described. Stevens himself had not yet devoted any-thing like systematic thought to the problems confronting the modern poet. But often in these early diaries and letters there are signs that his ideas and his priorities were very much the same as those of the two older writers. He had not yet, as least as far as the evidence we have indicates, made an organised connexion between what he thought about poetry and what he thought about religion. But the elements of a connexion are there, and his feelings on both subjects are in close sympathy with *Literature and Dogma*, which he had almost certainly not read, as well as with *Interpretations of Poetry and Religion* which he almost certainly had. When Elsie Moll was considering joining a church (of what denomination is not clear) and had been upset by the derogatory remarks of a friend, Stevens wrote her a letter on 10 March 1907 which reveals a great deal about his own attitude to religion:

I don't *care* whether the churches are all alike or whether they're right or wrong. It is not important. The very fact that they take care of [the friend's] 'stupid' people is an exquisite device. It is undoubtedly true that they do not '*influence*' any but the 'stupid'. But they are beautiful and full of comfort and moral help. One can get a thousand benefits from churches that one cannot get outside of them. They purify a man, they soften Life. *Please* don't listen to [the friend], or, at least, don't argue with her. Don't *care* about the Truth. There are other things in Life besides the Truth upon which everybody of any experience agrees, while no two people agree about the Truth. I'd rather see you going to church than know that you were as wise as Plato and Haeckel rolled in one; and I'd rather sing some old chestnut out of the hymn-book with you, surrounded by 'stupid' people, than listen to all the wise men in the world...I am not in the least religious. The sun clears my spirit, if I may say that, and an occasional sight of the sea, and thinking of blue valleys, and the odour of the earth, and many things. Such things make a god of a man; but a chapel makes a man of him. Churches are human. – I say my prayers every night – not that I need them now, or that they are anything more than a habit, half-unconscious. But in Spain, in Salamanca, there is a pillar in a church (Santayana told me) worn by the kisses of generations of the devout. One of their kisses are worth all my prayers. Yet the church is a mother for them – and for us.

One sees how this young man, writing in 1907, a bit patronisingly, to a girl brought up in the respectable bourgeoisie of a provincial town in Pennsylvania, comes to say that he is 'not in the least religious'. After all, 'I sicken of patterns, and trite symbols, and conventions and the lack of thought.' On the other hand, what emerges from the above letter, as from others written in Stevens's youth, is undoubtedly a religious sensibility. Not only do his seriousness, his sense of responsibility, and his reliance on 'the secret places of the spirit' indicate this, but also his poet's need to find the life of the image within the image and not somewhere beyond it. It is such life, the life of meaning and value which 'trite symbols and conventions' do not have, that is acknowledged in the three words 'Churches are human.' The idea that the vitality of religion lies not in its 'truth' – 'Don't care about the Truth...no two people agree about the Truth' – but in the vitality of its imagery, was an important one for Stevens. It was also the fundamental idea without which the poet so earnestly required by Arnold and Santayana could not embark upon the work they hoped for from him. It is many times referred to by Santayana, perhaps most clearly in this passage from Vol. 1 of

The Life of Reason (he is writing, in 1905, of the 'radical school' and 'The after-effects of supernaturalism'):

Like children escaped from school, they find their whole happiness in freedom. They are proud of how much they have rejected, as if a great wit were required to do so; but they do not know what they want...They have discarded the machinery in which their ancestors embodied the ideal; they have not perceived that those symbols stood for the life of reason and gave fantastic and embarrassed expression to what, in itself, is pure humanity; and they have thus remained entangled in the colossal error that ideals are something adventitious and unmeaning, not having a soil in mortal life nor a possible fulfilment there.

Perhaps the most important key to the whole of Stevens's work as a poet is that he could not find his happiness in the 'freedom' Santayana refers to here. It was because he did perceive that the ancient symbolic structure of Christianity, now generally abandoned and deserted, had given 'fantastic and embarrassed expression to what, in itself, is pure humanity', that he devoted himself to trying to find or make 'what will suffice' in the new symbolic structures of his poems. And his faithfulness to 'the necessary angel', to reality in all its manifestations, was, precisely, the result of his belief that 'ideals' do have 'a soil in mortal life and a possible fulfilment there'. This, of course, is a summary (even a 'sensational summary') of a lifetime of effort and thought. But the foundations of the final achievement are plainly visible in these early letters. In one typical letter, written in 1909[1] to Elsie Moll a few months before their marriage, the jumbled outpouring of observations and ideas derived from a summer Sunday walk in New York gives several indications of how free from Santayana's 'colossal error' Stevens was. As the walk had done, the letter rambles from subject to subject without plan, connexion or paragraphing. Its length forbids the complete quotation it deserves; here are some passages from it:

Today I have been roaming about town. In the morning I walked down-town – stopping once to watch three flocks of pigeons circling in the sky. I dropped into St. John's chapel an hour before the service and sat in the last pew and looked around. It happens that last night at the Library I read a life

---

[1] The date is given as Sunday Evening [3 May], but it must have been 2 May, *Letters*, p. 139.

of Jesus and I was interested to see what symbols of that life appeared in the chapel. I think there were none at all excepting the gold cross on the altar. When you compare that poverty with the wealth of symbols, of remembrances, that were created and revered in times past, you appreciate the change that has come over the church. The church should be more than a moral institution, if it is to have the influence that it should have. The space, the gloom, the quiet mystify and entrance the spirit. But that is not enough. – And one turns from this chapel to those built by men who felt the wonder of the life and death of Jesus – temples full of sacred images, full of the air of love and holiness – tabernacles hallowed by worship that sprang from the noble depths of men familiar with Gethsemane, familiar with Jerusalem. – I do not wonder that the church is so largely a relic. Its vitality depended on its association with Palestine, so to speak...

Before today I do not think I have ever realized that God was distinct from Jesus. It enlarges the matter almost beyond comprehension. People doubt the existence of Jesus – at least, they doubt incidents of his life, such as, say, the Ascension into Heaven after his death. But I do not understand that they deny God...

I dropped into a church for five minutes, merely to see it, you understand. I am not pious. But churches are beautiful to see. – And then I came home, observing great masses of white clouds, with an autumnal shape to them, floating through the windy sky...

My chief objection to town-life is the commonness of the life. Such numbers of men degrade Man. The *teeming* streets make Man a nuisance – a vulgarity, and it is impossible to see his dignity. I feel, nevertheless, the overwhelming necessity of thinking well, speaking well. – 'I am a stranger in the earth'. – You see I have been digging into the Psalms – anything at all, so long as it is full of praise – and rejoicing. I am sick of dreariness.

One hesitates to draw too definite connecting lines between poems written years later and episodes in the poet's life that happen to come to light. 'Sunday Morning', the first of Stevens's great poems, did not appear until 1915.[1] Nevertheless, even if many layers of experience and thought settled over this Sunday walk in the intervening years, as no doubt they did, the whole atmosphere and the feeling of the letter describing it are present in the poem. Beneath the return to the richness of reality that is proclaimed in the poem, the necessity of making value and significance out of this mortal

[1] He had published two sequences of short poems, 'Carnet de Voyage' and 'Phases', the year before: the inference is that 'Sunday Morning' was written 1914–15.

life – 'Death is the mother of beauty' – lies both the lack felt in the chapel, the lack of 'sacred images, full of the air of love and holiness', and the terrifying yet exhilarating self-dependence expressed later in the letter. The concentrated power of 'Sunday Morning', written by a man of thirty-five at the very beginning of his poetic career, is perhaps partly explained by the long period of accretion that preceded it. Here are the first two and the last of its eight stanzas:

> Complacencies of the peignoir, and late
> Coffee and oranges in a sunny chair,
> And the green freedom of a cockatoo
> Upon a rug mingle to dissipate
> The holy hush of ancient sacrifice.
> She dreams a little, and she feels the dark
> Encroachment of that old catastrophe,
> As a calm darkens among water-lights.
> The pungent oranges and bright, green wings
> Seem things in some procession of the dead,
> Winding across wide water, without sound.
> The day is like wide water without sound,
> Still for the passing of her dreaming feet
> Over the seas, to silent Palestine,
> Dominion of the blood and sepulchre.
>
> Why should she give her bounty to the dead?
> What is divinity if it can come
> Only in silent shadows and in dreams?
> Shall she not find in comforts of the sun,
> In pungent fruit and bright, green wings, or else
> In any balm or beauty of the earth,
> Things to be cherished like the thought of heaven?
> Divinity must live within herself:
> Passions of rain, or moods in falling snow;
> Grievings in loneliness, or unsubdued
> Elations when the forest blooms; gusty
> Emotions on wet roads on autumn nights;
> All pleasures and all pains, remembering
> The bough of summer and the winter branch.
> These are the measures destined for her soul...
>
> She hears, upon that water without sound,

A voice that cries, 'The tomb in Palestine
Is not the porch of spirits lingering.
It is the grave of Jesus, where he lay.'
We live in an old chaos of the sun,
Or old dependency of day and night,
Or island solitude, unsponsored, free,
Of that wide water, inescapable.
Deer walk upon our mountains, and the quail
Whistle about us their spontaneous cries;
Sweet berries ripen in the wilderness;
And, in the isolation of the sky,
At evening, casual flocks of pigeons make
Ambiguous undulations as they sink,
Downward to darkness, on extended wings.

In 1928 Stevens wrote[1] to someone who had sent him some elaborately explanatory notes on 'Sunday Morning': 'This is not essentially a woman's meditation on religion and the meaning of life. It is anybody's meditation.' To make his point more clearly: the part in the poem played by the woman, in all her rich particularity of circumstance, can perhaps be defined by reference to the letter quoted above. 'The teeming streets make Man a nuisance – a vulgarity, and it is impossible to see his dignity...I am sick of dreariness.' Other passages in the early letters also help, finding in this poem, about which so much that only obscures it has been written, their apotheosis. 'I thought...how utterly we have forsaken the Earth, in the sense of excluding it from our thoughts.' 'What strikes me is the capable, the marvellous poetic language; and the absence of poetic thought.' Despite 'the marvellous poetic language', it is of Wordsworth rather than Keats that 'Sunday Morning' most reminds us. Whereas Keats, except in the revised *Hyperion*, was still writing about the earth itself, Stevens here, like Wordsworth in the greatest passages of *The Prelude*, is writing about the earth in our thoughts. 'Sunday Morning' is, in Coleridge's phrase, a philosophical poem. It has the quality that Coleridge had detected in *The Prelude* and that, to his bitter disappointment, he failed to find in *The Excursion*. 'Whatever in Lucretius is Poetry is not philosophical,

---

[1] To L. W. Payne, 31 March 1928.

whatever is philosophical is not Poetry: and in the very Pride of confident Hope I looked forward to the Recluse as the *first* and *only* true Phil. Poem in existence.'[1]

What Coleridge hoped for from Wordsworth was the poetry that Arnold and Santayana later hoped for from anyone who might be capable of writing it. In the end the best commentary on 'Sunday Morning' as on the other Stevens poems of this highest order, comes from his friend Santayana and was written before Stevens's work as a poet had really begun:

There is a kind of sensualism or aestheticism that has decreed in our day that theory is not poetical; as if all the images and emotions that enter a cultivated mind were not saturated with theory... The life of theory is not less human or less emotional than the life of sense; it is more typically human and more keenly emotional. (*Three Philosophical Poets*)

And, from *Interpretations of Poetry and Religion*:

With a world so full of stuff before him, I can hardly conceive what morbid instinct can tempt a man to look elsewhere for wider vistas, unless it be unwillingness to endure the sadness and the discipline of the truth.

'Sunday Morning', so far from being the celebration of thoughtless hedonism that it has been called, is a poem about the sadness and the discipline of the truth.

---

[1] Letter to Wordsworth, 30 May 1815.

4

The Pressure of Reality

Harmonium, Stevens's first book, was published in 1923. He had wanted to call it *The Grand Poem: Preliminary Minutiae.* As late as 1938, after *Harmonium*'s second edition (1931) and the appearance of three more books, *Ideas of Order* (1935), *Owl's Clover* (1936) and *The Man with the Blue Guitar* (1937), he said: 'The few things that I have already done have merely been preliminary. I cannot believe that I have done anything of real importance...I very much like the idea of something ahead; I don't care to make exhaustive effort to reach it, to see what it is.'[1] This patient confidence turned out to be justified. Stevens died (in 1955) when he was almost seventy-six, having produced the main body of his work, including most of his finest poems and almost all his prose, in the last fifteen years of his life. His extraordinarily fruitful old age was the result of a strenuous effort of thought and reorientation that he made in the middle years of his poetic career, an effort occasionally reflected in his letters, as in this passage of 1935:

When *Harmonium* was in the making there was a time when I liked the idea of images and images alone, or images and the music of verse together. I then believed in *pure poetry,* as it was called. I still have a distinct liking for that sort of thing. But we live in a different time, and life means a good deal more to us now-a-days than literature does. In the period of which I have just spoken, I thought literature meant most. Moreover, I am not so sure that I don't think exactly the same thing now, but, unquestionably, I think at the same time that life is the essential part of literature.[2]

He had been dissatisfied with *Harmonium* even before it came out. 'Gathering together the things for my book has been so depressing that I wonder at *Poetry*'s friendliness', he wrote to Harriet Monroe, *Poetry*'s editor, on 28 October 1922:

[1] Letter to Ronald Lane Latimer, 28 June 1938.
[2] Letter to Latimer, 31 October 1935.

All my earlier things seem like horrid cocoons from which later abortive insects have sprung. The book will amount to nothing, except that it may teach me something...The reading of these outmoded and debilitated poems does make me wish rather desperately to keep on dabbling and to be as obscure as possible until I have perfected an authentic and fluent speech for myself.

Those, led by Yvor Winters in his celebrated essay 'Wallace Stevens or The Hedonist's Progress', who judge *Harmonium* to contain Stevens's best work have, one hopes, been effectively answered by Professor Kermode.[1] Nevertheless Stevens himself in the above passages is misleadingly hard on it. 'Sunday Morning' is scarcely a poem 'of images and images alone'; still less is it a 'horrid cocoon', 'outmoded and debilitated'. There is, admittedly, nothing else in *Harmonium* that has quite 'Sunday Morning''s degree of commanding excellence. But even without 'Sunday Morning' there is enough poetry of very high quality in the volume to put it at least in the same class as the other great books of English verse that appeared in the decade 1915–25, *Homage to Sextus Propertius* and *Hugh Selwyn Mauberley*; *Prufrock*, *Poems 1920* and *The Waste Land*.

When one compares Stevens's poetry of this period with the much more famous contemporary works of Pound and Eliot one finds some striking similarities. The major poetic efforts of all three show an intensely self-conscious, intensely sophisticated preoccupation with the finding of a role for the poet in a world that appears to be inimical to poetry. A text which illuminates the poems of them all at this time is the two sentences Stevens wrote much later in 'The Noble Rider and the Sound of Words': 'The pressure of reality is...the determining factor in the artistic character of an era, and, as well, the determining factor in the artistic character of an individual. The resistance to this pressure or its evasion in the case of individuals of extraordinary imagination cancels the pressure so far as those individuals are concerned.' Pound is perhaps the clearest case. Both the *Homage* and *Mauberley* are, in their different ways, poems about the poet's resistance to the pressure of reality. 'By the pressure of

[1] In his short survey *Wallace Stevens* (Oliver and Boyd, 1960). This is the best book on Stevens, and the only one that is consistently a help rather than a hindrance. To those who know it my debt to it will be obvious.

reality', Stevens explained in 'The Noble Rider', 'I mean the pressure of an external event or events on the consciousness to the exclusion of any power of contemplation.' This is how Pound described his *Homage* to Propertius which he had written during the war and published in 1918:

It presents certain emotions as vital to men faced with the infinite and ineffable imbecility of the British Empire as they were to Propertius some centuries earlier, when faced with the infinite and ineffable imbecility of the Roman Empire...If the reader does not find relation to life defined in the poem, he may conclude that I have been unsuccessful in my endeavour.

Inseparable from the recommendation of 'certain emotions as vital' is, of course, the recommendation of one kind of poetry as opposed to another:

> Out–weariers of Apollo will, as we know, continue
> their Martian generalities,
>> We have kept our erasers in order.
> A new-fangled chariot follows the flower-hung horses;
> A young Muse with young loves clustered about her
> ascends with me into the aether,...[1]
> And there is no high-road to the Muses.
> Annalists will continue to record Roman reputations,
> Celebrities from the Trans-Caucasus will belaud Roman
> celebrities
> And expound the distentions of Empire,
> But for something to read in normal circumstances?
> For a few pages brought down from the forked hill
> unsullied?
> I ask a wreath which will not crush my head.

Throughout the *Homage*, as in this brief example, private love and the high private standards of the poet as craftsman – 'We have kept our erasers in order' – are held up for celebration together. Pound's choice of Propertius as his vehicle, a love-poet in an age of belligerent imperialism, epitomized but also over-simplified the problems confronting Pound himself and his contemporaries. *Hugh Selwyn Mauberley*, begun in the early years of the war and completed, after the *Homage*,

[1] Pound's ellipsis.

in 1920, detaches from the conflict of private and public emotion the central ultimately separate question of whether the poet can resist or evade the pressure of reality without becoming a mere aesthete, writing only in order to write well and in the end abandoning everything real, everything human. *Mauberley* is one of the great poems of this century and it is of the highest significance that its answer to this question is in the negative. The despairing ironies of the short poems that make it up catch aspect after aspect of the complex army of forces that the modern world fields to defeat its poets. Against the collapse of standards, the demand for cheap realism, the defection of artists themselves toward fashionable raptures or quick financial returns or phoney drawing-room reputations, the poet's efforts seem as futile as the deaths of the soldiers dying 'For a botched civilization' in a futile war. In the concluding section of the poem, 'Mauberley 1920', we are shown the final failure of the poet whose devotion to his art – 'His true Penelope was Flaubert' – has led only to complete withdrawal from reality:

> Mildness, amid the neo-Nietzschean clatter,
> His sense of graduations,
> Quite out of place amid
> Resistance to current exacerbations,
>
> Invitation, mere invitation to perceptivity
> Gradually led him to the isolation
> Which these presents place
> Under a more tolerant, perhaps, examination.
>
> By constant elimination
> The manifest universe
> Yielded an armour
> Against utter consternation,
>
> A Minoan undulation,
> Seen, we admit, amid ambrosial circumstances
> Strengthened him against
> The discouraging doctrine of chances,
>
> And his desire for survival,
> Faint in the most strenuous moods,
> Became an Olympian *apathein*
> In the presence of selected perceptions.

So 'the artist's urge' is destroyed, and Mauberley vanishes into the blissful isolation of absolute silence.

This is not, of course, what happened to Pound himself. Mauberley records the perception of one path open to the modern poet, the path of aestheticism, of 'purely literary values'; it also records the realisation that such a path leads to a dead-end where neither the poet himself nor his art retain any significant existence. With *Mauberley* Pound turned his back on the option that had seemed possible to Stevens at the 'time when [he] liked the idea of images and images alone, or images and the music of verse together'. With the *Cantos* Pound, who had been for all his proclamations of revolution, the last notable apostle of 'art for art's sake', wheeled to confront reality with a poem whose enormous sprawling heterogeneity should be as limitless as the pressure of reality itself and has come to a term only with Pound's life. The attempt, held together only by an extraordinary wild consistency of technique, is a failure. In even the best stretches of this vast poem, the early cantos, written before 1930, and the Pisan cantos, written while Pound was imprisoned in a cage awaiting trial for treason in 1945, it is reality rather than the poet who is the victor. The political and economic obsessions that led him to that cage, the vituperative hatreds that erupt again and again, the furious ambition somehow to rescue by himself the relics of world civilisation from a universal conspiracy of fools and murderers – all this combines to swamp both the poet himself and his art almost as completely as the denial of reality had extinguished the fictional Mauberley. The poet of exquisite craftsmanship, whose solitary campaign for discipline in the writing of poetry so deeply influenced Eliot, Yeats and many others, is in the *Cantos* crushed by the violence of reality and the violence of his own responses to it. Again 'the first phase of the poet's problem is himself', and the best passages in the *Cantos* show an increasingly desperate realisation of this truth. It is in the end not the fulfilment but the defeat of the hope expressed in the recurrent line:

In the gloom, the gold gathers the light against it

that the poem illustrates. The gold of the organising imagination does occasionally shine through the gloom, but not nearly often enough. Pound's mind is like a clouded kaleidoscope: the fragments of his own experience and of the civilisations, literatures and histories that have caught his attention remain a shifting heap of splinters until, now and again, the mirrors of the instrument suddenly clear and for a moment a pattern is revealed. In the tragic *Pisan Cantos* his own consciousness of weakness in the face of reality and the poet's necessary struggle with it is at its most apparent. Here the recurrent line, equally wistful, equally defeated, is 'Le Paradis n'est pas artificiel', once followed by its bleak corollary' 'L'enfer non plus'. One is reminded of Stevens's lines from 'Esthétique du Mal' written at almost the same time (1944) as these *Cantos*:

> His firm stanzas hang like hives in hell
> Or what hell was, since now both heaven and hell
> Are one, and here, O terra infidel.

But Pound could not summon the steadiness or concentration to move forwards from such a thought.

His most fundamental weakness, the lopsidedness of his view of poetry and hence of his whole poetic ambition, is clearly visible in the *Cantos*. His emphasis in the many passages that refer to his own situation as a poet is always upon technique. Supremely aware of the poet's responsibility in respect of the disciplined use of language, he is hardly aware at all of the poet's responsibility in respect of thought. The problems of belief and value in a world without established systems of truth, the search for 'what will suffice', the poet's task envisaged by such as Arnold and Santayana, concern him very little. In this sense he is a most un-modern poet. His most powerful response to the modern world is disgust; his most powerful emotion is nostalgia. *Mauberley* shows that he was able to realise that the poet in the modern world must be more than a fine craftsman, but nothing in his work shows that he himself was able to achieve the more that Mauberley could not manage. He loathed first the America he abandoned and then the Europe he adopted for failing to provide him with a sufficient publicly-accepted role as a poet, and, failing to construct a sufficient role for himself, he turned longingly to civilisations of the past which seemed to him to justify his own poetic efforts. 'Out of key with his time', as he wrote in *Mauberley*, he could neither

resign himself, like, say, Robert Graves, to the minor lyric per-
fectionism, careless of fame and influence, that is celebrated in *Homage
to Sextus Propertius,* nor find the intellectual and moral strength to
brave the issues that in the end must confront the more than minor
poet. He took refuge in bitterness, in Fascism, in hopeless yearning
for the moral support of more congenial times, and in a poetic technique that should somehow protect him from responsibilities he could
not cope with. He remains 'il miglior fabbro', and the *Cantos,* that
colossal attempt to master reality with persistence of method rather
than with persistence of thought, remains the saddest of modern
poetic defeats.

Eliot's early poetry (the two small collections that preceded *The
Waste Land, The Waste Land* itself and *The Hollow Men*) is the result
of a more oblique and defensive approach than Pound's to the modern
poet's problems. Whereas Pound in the *Homage* and *Mauberley* faced
the pressure of reality head-on with two varieties of protest, Eliot's
first poetic response to it was a strange mixture of acceptance and
revolted disdain. Pound's nostalgia for worlds that seemed to him
more heroic, more sympathetic, more 'poetic' than his own is simple
and open. His 'make it new' is governed always by the traditional
aesthetic standard that he could call 'beauty' without equivocation.
'Beauty in art reminds one what is worthwhile', he wrote in 'The
Serious Artist' (1913); 'I am not now speaking of shams. I mean
beauty, not slither, not sentimentalising about beauty, not telling
people that beauty is the proper and respectable thing. I mean
beauty. You don't argue about an April wind.' And many of Pound's
early poems, particularly 'Near Perigord', as well as long stretches of
the *Homage,* are beautiful in exactly this direct sense. Eliot, on the
other hand, buries an equally strong feeling for what he would never
have called 'beauty' beneath a portrayal of modern reality that
deliberately emphasises its sordid, grimy, anonymous and ridiculous
aspects. The deflationary devices of the early poems, the absurd
proper names, bathetic rhymes, and ironies either weary, comic or
caustic, seem designed, whether consciously or not, to suppress all
positive emotion in the poet. 'Feeling, love in particular, is the great
moving power and spring of verse', wrote Hopkins. The spring of
Eliot's early poems is a curious obverse of 'feeling, love in particular'.

It is not only that sexual emotion is belittled by a cynical and partial realism. It is that the poet's desire to find in reality that which will reconcile him to his world is treated with a similar puncturing disbelief. There is nothing in these poems of 'la confidence que le poète fait naturellement – et nous invite à faire – au monde'. There is, rather, the creation of an anxiety, a fear, a distrust that is the very opposite of confidence. Prufrock and both the characters in 'Portrait of a Lady', Sweeney and Burbank, Gerontion and the figures in *The Waste Land*: all of them move in an atmosphere of futility and menace. 'And in short, I was afraid.' 'We are really in the dark.' 'I will show you fear in a handful of dust.'

Pound wrote in Canto LXXVI, pathetically among the hatreds of his poem:

> nothing matters but the quality
> of the affection –
> in the end – that has carved the trace in the mind.

But what matters in Eliot's early poems is the quality of the revulsion. The sexual disillusion, the frightening alienation of this world of exiles and refugees, the pervasive dread and unease are held in poems which are themselves victories over the reality they present. The panic, nausea and despair which constantly spill out of Pound's mental and spiritual reach in the *Cantos* are here contained, particularly in *The Waste Land* and *The Hollow Men*, by Eliot's phenomenal creative control. For all his prose protestations in favour of impersonality, 'classicism' and the conformist virtues of the age of Dryden, *The Waste Land* is a modern poet's triumph over reality, and, as such, it is essentially individual, original, and above all personal. Stevens in one of his notebooks praised a comment on Cézanne 'because it adds to subject and manner the thing that is incessantly overlooked: the artist, the presence of the determining personality'. It was the determining personality that Pound had the critical acumen to draw attention to when he reviewed *Prufrock* in 1917:

...the supreme test of a book is that we should feel some unusual intelligence working behind the words. By this test various other new books, that I have, or might have, beside me, go to pieces. The barrels of sham poetry that every decade and school and fashion produce, go to pieces. It is sometimes extremely difficult to find any other particular reason for their being so unsatisfactory. I have expressly written here not 'intellect' but 'intelligence'. There is no intelligence without emotion.

And it was the decisive presence of Eliot's personality and the intelligence and emotion peculiar to it that made *The Waste Land* out of the waste land in which he felt himself to be.

The Waste Land is a very difficult poem whose greatness will never yield to any single commentary. Nevertheless it is safe to say that it consummates the first phase of Eliot's work as a poet, and that the desolation it disturbs us with is the desolation out of which Eliot was to build the affirmations of his later poetry. In *The Hollow Men*, written three years later (1925), the desolation of the poet in the waste land of modern reality is more plainly stated, but the beginnings of affirmation are also present. The question that *The Hollow Men* leaves, agonisingly, unanswered is whether the affirmation, which is of course an affirmation of belief, can have anything to do with poetry. The question is answered in *Ash-Wednesday* (1930) and still more in *Four Quartets* (1935–42) where 'between the conception and the creation' no shadow falls, where the poetry and the affirmation are one. It is as if, in the frightening negations of the poems up to and including *The Waste Land*, Eliot destroyed for himself all the available consolations and assumptions which might be supposed to support the poet in the modern world, and then, in the later poems, constructed with the most scrupulous caution his own statement of 'what will suffice'. The whole of his poetic achievement constitutes an exercise in creative responsibility which, as we shall see, is matched by Stevens's. It has not been even approached by any other poet in English.

One of the sections of Stevens's late (1946) poem, 'Credences of Summer', clarifies better than any prose could the nature both of what is dissolved in Eliot's early poetry and of what is made in his later poetry:

> Fly low, cock bright, and stop on a bean pole. Let
> Your brown breast redden, while you wait for warmth.
> With one eye watch the willow, motionless.
> The gardener's cat is dead, the gardener gone
> And last year's garden grows salacious weeds.

A complex of emotions falls apart,
In an abandoned spot. Soft, civil bird,
The decay that you regard: of the arranged
And of the spirit of the arranged, *douceurs*,
Tristesses, the fund of life and death, suave bush

And polished beast, this complex falls apart.
And on your bean pole, it may be, you detect
Another complex of other emotions, not
So soft, so civil, and you make a sound,
Which is not part of the listener's own sense.

The modern poet's task has perhaps never been so well described as in these lines. The 'sound which is not part of the listener's own sense', the new affirmation that has to be made amid desolation and decay and the collapse of ancient structures, is the affirmation of 'what will suffice'. The poet who can achieve it will conclude his efforts with the serenity of Stevens's late poems and of the last sections of 'East Coker' and 'Little Gidding'. But first he must have fully known the waste land, 'the abandoned spot', 'the gardener gone'.

Harmonium is usually thought of as a volume of gaudy and confident exuberance after which Stevens retreated or advanced, according to the point of view,[1] into the more abstract metaphysical world of his later poetry. It is certainly true that the marvellous luxuriance of language which distinguishes *Harmonium* and runs to fantastic riot in its longest poem 'The Comedian as the Letter C', is later much restrained. It is also true that as Stevens's thought gradually progressed his poems collected an increasing weight of meditative subtlety. What is misleading is the idea that the *Harmonium* poems represent the assumption of a positive relation between the poet and reality which Stevens later relinquished in favour of philosophical enquiry. In fact, the desolation of existence without reconciling structures of belief, the waste land for which Stevens's word was 'poverty', is recognised and accepted in *Harmonium* as definitely as it is in Eliot's early poetry. The real difference between the two poets at this period[2] is that whereas Eliot, in disgust and despair, was making

---

[1] Winters, the best of the adverse critics, said, for instance, that Stevens's 'hedonism' led him, after *Harmonium,* only into an obsessive and destructive ennui and 'experience increasingly elusive and incomprehensible' (*In Defense of Reason,* p. 439).

[2] *Harmonium* appeared within months of *The Waste Land*'s publication.

his poetry out of the waste land itself in its most dispiriting aspects, Stevens was already more concerned with the possibility of affirmations that the poet might be able to construct in defiance of it. The affirmations of *Harmonium* are no more than provisional – hence Stevens's wish to call the book 'The Grand Poem: Preliminary Minutiae', and the dissatisfaction it caused him. These poems are skirmishes at the beginning of the battle that Stevens was to wage for the rest of his life, his fundamental object being to make his affirmations no longer provisional but sufficient. But what *Harmonium* establishes, as clearly as Eliot's early work and with a more optimistic courage, is the nature of the enemy.

5

'Harmonium'

Harmonium suggests the nature of the enemy. It also suggests the nature of something which Eliot, for reasons buried in the obscurity of his temperament, could never contemplate without evasion and equivocation: the power or the gift which is the poet's, and perhaps not only the poet's, one resource against the waste land. This power or gift Stevens calls 'imagination', though his adequate definitions of it are to be found in his poems and not in a single word featureless with use. What Stevens means by 'imagination' is the human ability to make from reality significance that will satisfy human need for significance. Both the similarities and the differences between Eliot and Stevens may be sketched by the thought that Eliot might conceivably have accepted this formulation as a description of something recognisable to himself if the words 'find in' had been substituted for the words 'make from'. The same nuance has already been suggested in the phrase 'power or gift'. It will be obvious that we are here on very difficult ground indeed. In a matter which touches the deepest level of conviction it may seem merely tendentious to call a division of opinion which separates a Christian from a non-Christian a nuance. But the question begged is ultimately the most interesting question that can be asked about these two most central of modern poets. It is the question whether what Stevens would have called the imagination's ability to construct is or is not closely related to what Eliot would have called the humble spirit's ability to receive. And evidence to support the suggestion that this question can be answered in the affirmative is there in the early work of both poets.

Let us look, first, at the *Harmonium* poem which contains most completely the full complexity of Stevens's poetic moods and ideas at this time. 'Le Monocle de Mon Oncle' matches 'Sunday Morning' in scale and in the grandeur of its rhetoric, but it is a much more difficult poem and demands elucidation in a way that 'Sunday Morning' does not. It was all very well for Stevens to write to an early commentator on 'Le Monocle': 'I am sure that I never had in mind the many abstractions that appear in your analysis. I had in mind simply a man fairly well along in life, looking back and talking in a more or less personal way about life.'[1] The warning is salutary. But whatever Stevens had in mind, his poem is far from simple: the 'man looking back and talking' is a man of immense and painstaking subtlety, like the poet who created him.

'Le Monocle de Mon Oncle' is about the waste land, and about the search of a man confronting it for something that will reconcile him to it, for a value that will justify his existence in it. This is Stevens's most fundamental theme, as it is Eliot's; and one indication of the distance between both of them and Pound is that the search they undertake is any man's search, rather than a quest confined to the poet *qua* poet. The two, in Eliot and Stevens, are inseparable. 'These fragments I have shored against my ruins': the despair is the poet's, but also a man's. The bird in 'Credences of Summer' is the poet in the modern world, but also 'simply a man' in the modern world. Here he is in an earlier manifestation regarding the decay 'of the arranged and of the spirit of the arranged'. And here, also, is the figure of what may reconcile him to his poverty. These are the first three stanzas of 'Le Monocle de Mon Oncle':

I

'Mother of heaven, regina of the clouds,
O sceptre of the sun, crown of the moon,
There is not nothing, no, no, never nothing,
Like the clashed edges of two words that kill.'
And so I mocked her in magnificent measure.
Or was it that I mocked myself alone?
I wish that I might be a thinking stone.
The sea of spuming thought foists up again
The radiant bubble that she was. And then
A deep up-pouring from some saltier well
Within me, bursts its watery syllable.

[1] Letter to L. W. Payne, 31 March 1928.

II

A red bird flies across the golden floor.
It is a red bird that seeks out his choir
Among the choirs of wind and wet and wing.
A torrent will fall from him when he finds.
Shall I uncrumple this much-crumpled thing?
I am a man of fortune greeting heirs;
For it has come that thus I greet the spring.
Those choirs of welcome choir for me farewell.
No spring can follow past meridian
Yet you persist with anecdotal bliss
To make believe a starry *connaissance.*

III

Is it for nothing, then, that old Chinese
Sat tittivating by their mountain pools
Or in the Yangtse studied out their beards?
I shall not play the flat historic scale.
You know how Utamaro's beauties sought
The end of love in their all-speaking braids.
You know the mountainous coiffures of Bath.
Alas! Have all the barbers lived in vain
That not one curl in nature has survived?
Why, without pity on these studious ghosts,
Do you come dripping in your hair from sleep?

It is useless to attempt to identify too closely the figure that is addressed here. To strip her of the poetry in which she exists in the expectation of disclosing a bare and manageable abstraction is only to destroy her. The most that can be said of her as she appears in 'Le Monocle' is that she is a figure of hope and a figure of frustration, and that she is the object of a love which is 'the great moving power and spring' of all Stevens's poetry. It is she, or, rather, whatever it is of which she is no more than one image, that is to be addressed in the epigraph to 'Notes toward a Supreme Fiction':

And for what, except for you, do I feel love?
Do I press the extremest book of the wisest man
Close to me, hidden in me day and night?
In the uncertain light of single, certain truth,
Equal in living changingness to the light

> In which I meet you, in which we sit at rest,
> For a moment in the central of our being,
> The vivid transparence that you bring is peace.

In other *Harmonium* poems we find the object of this love in the same image as that of 'Le Monocle'. In 'Homunculus et La Belle Etoile', the poet guesses that the philosophers' 'mistress'

> ...might, after all, be a wanton,
> Abundantly beautiful, eager,
>
> Fecund,
> From whose being by starlight, on sea-coast,
> The innermost good of their seeking
> Might come in the simplest of speech.

(One remembers the sea imagery of 'Le Monocle' 's first stanza, and the 'starry *connaissance*'.) In 'To the One of Fictive Music', a poem of extraordinary compression and emotional force, the relation between this figure and the poet who seeks her is defined with meticulous care. She is addressed just as she is in 'Le Monocle', though here she first appears free of the sadness and doubt that there surrounds her:

> Sister and mother and diviner love,
> And of the sisterhood of the living dead
> Most near, most clear, and of the clearest bloom,
> And of the fragrant mothers the most dear
> And queen, and of diviner love the day
> And flame and summer and sweet fire, no thread
> Of cloudy silver sprinkles in your gown
> Its venom of renown, and on your head
> No crown is simpler than the simple hair.

Later in this poem of four magnificent stanzas the peculiar beneficence which this image for the moment represents is described as plainly as it ever is in Stevens. The 'one of fictive music' answers human need, her perfection 'out of our imperfections wrought'. She comes of the real, the observable particular:

> That music is intensest which proclaims
> The near, the clear;

but she comes with something else as well:

Yet not too like, yet not so like to be
Too near, too clear, saving a little to endow
Our feigning with the strange unlike, whence springs
The difference that heavenly pity brings.

And the poem ends on a note of desolation which it is not inappropriate to the nature of Stevens's emotion to call, also, a note of prayer:

Unreal, give back to us what once you gave:
The imagination that we spurned and crave.

The figure of Susanna in 'Peter Quince at the Clavier', one of the earliest poems in *Harmonium*, is perhaps the original of 'the one of fictive music', the saving image of 'Le Monocle'. In 'Peter Quince at the Clavier' the story of Susanna and the elders is used as a parable to embody the relation between the poet and the object of his love. The poem opens:

Just as my fingers on these keys
Make music, so the selfsame sounds
On my spirit make a music, too.

Music is feeling, then, not sound;
And thus it is that what I feel,
Here in this room, desiring you,

Thinking of your blue-shadowed silk,
Is music. It is like the strain
Waked in the elders by Susanna.

Susanna flees the elders' lust; their momentary vision of her passes. But she herself survives as an image whose life is in what it contains of the real and mortal. Stevens's notebook remark written years later: 'Reality is the indispensable element of each metaphor' unlocks the paradox with which the poem ends:

Beauty is momentary in the mind –
The fitful tracing of a portal;
But in the flesh it is immortal...
Susanna's music touched the bawdy strings
Of those white elders; but, escaping,
Left only Death's ironic scraping.

Now, in its immortality, it plays
On the clear viol of her memory,
And makes a constant sacrament of praise.

There is in this poem, and in 'To the One of Fictive Music', a
deeper and simpler metaphor than that of the saving figure herself.
This is a knot of thought which, properly loosened, greatly helps the
reader towards domestication in the world of Stevens's poetry. It is
nothing more elaborate than the use of music as a metaphor for the
kind of significance which poetry also can create. 'Peter Quince at
the Clavier' – the title, the yokel at the delicate instrument, suggests
the inadequacy of the elders before Susanna, of the poet before his own
poetic concept, though it is perhaps not too extravagant to guess that
Theseus's speech about 'the lunatic, the lover, and the poet' was also
at the back of Stevens's mind. Shakespeare's lines about the imagination do perfectly describe the genesis of Stevens's Susanna:

And as imagination bodies forth
The forms of things unknown, the poet's pen
Turns them to shapes, and gives to airy nothing
A local habitation and a name.
Such tricks hath strong imagination,
That, if it would but apprehend some joy,
It comprehends some bringer of that joy.

In any case, the presence of the clavier is quite as important as the
presence of Shakespeare's carpenter-producer, for it is the clavier
which provides Stevens with his 'local habitation' for the complex of
thought and feeling expressed in the poem's opening.

Music is feeling, then, not sound;
And thus it is that what I feel,
Here in this room, desiring you,

Thinking of your blue-shadowed silk
Is music.

Throughout Stevens's poetry blue is the colour associated with the
imagination, as green is with reality. And 'music' here expresses
both a need and the fulfilment of that need, as it also does in 'To the
One of Fictive Music,' where Stevens writes of

74

> the music summoned by the birth
> That separates us from the wind and sea.

Music in this double aspect – as the expression of a specifically human need and as a constructed, 'fictive', answer to need – is a recurring metaphor in Stevens for what poetry at its highest can be and do. We have already seen examples of this in later poems, in, for instance, 'Extracts from Addresses to the Academy of Fine Ideas':

> to pierce the heart's residuum
> And there to find music for a single line,
> Equal to memory, one line in which
> The vital music formulates the words.

And in 'Esthétique du Mal':

> Yet we require
> Another chant, an incantation, as in
> Another and later genesis, music
> That buffets the shapes of its possible halcyon
> Against the haggardie.

In a short paper 'The Whole Man: Perspectives, Horizons', written a few months before he died, Stevens made a remark which goes far towards explaining his poetic use of the idea of music – for it is as an idea, without reference to any facile notion of 'the music of poetry', that he uses it.

The principle of poetry is not confined to its form however definitely it may be contained therein. The principle of music would be an addition to humanity if it were not humanity itself, in other than human form, and while this hyperbole is certain to be repulsive to a good many people, still it may stand. This is the life of the arts which the all-round man thinks of in relation to life itself.

If we go back more than half a century to *Interpretations of Poetry and Religion*, which, as we have seen, Stevens almost certainly read as an undergraduate, we find Santayana writing of 'harmony' and poetry in phrases which must have remained at the back of Stevens's mind for many years:

The good man is a poet whose syllables are deeds and make a harmony in nature. The poet is a rebuilder of the imagination, to make a harmony in that.

And he is not a complete poet if his whole imagination is not attuned and his whole experience composed into a single symphony.

(In 1954 Stevens wanted to call his *Collected Poems* 'The Whole of Harmonium', but was persuaded against it by his publisher.) A little further on in this, the extraordinary closing passage of *Interpretations of Poetry and Religion*, Santayana says:

If we drop the limitation to verbal expression, and think of poetry as that subtle fire and inward light which seems at times to shine through the world and to touch the images in our minds with ineffable beauty, then poetry is a momentary harmony in the soul amid stagnation or conflict, – a glimpse of the divine and an incitation to a religious life.

At no time would Stevens have committed himself to the incautious terms of Santayana's conclusion; but his word 'portal' in 'Peter Quince' surely carries similar implications:

> Beauty is momentary in the mind –
> The fitful tracing of a portal.

One of the strengths of 'Sunday Morning' is that it is an expression of confidence in the sufficiency of reality which Stevens came only later to see as provisional. One of the strengths of 'Le Monocle de Mon Oncle' is the opposite quality: the poem expresses lack of confidence, 'stagnation or conflict' in which the 'momentary harmony' that does appear is surrounded by equivocation and doubt. Here is the stagnation of disillusion with ordinary human love – the stanza is, incidentally, an apt comment on the weary revulsions of the *Prufrock* poems:

> If men at forty would be painting lakes
> The ephemeral blues must merge for them in one,
> The basic slate, the universal hue.
> There is a substance in us that prevails.
> But in our amours amorists discern
> Such fluctuations that their scrivening
> Is breathless to attend each quirky turn.
> When amorists grow bald, then amours shrink
> Into the compass and curriculum
> Of introspective exiles, lecturing.
> It is a theme for Hyacinth alone.

But even in this bitter mood Stevens retains his devotion to the 'ephemeral blues' of the saving imagination, and the next stanza opens with an image of startling beneficence:

> The mules that angels ride come slowly down
> The blazing passes, from beyond the sun.

As the complexities of the poem accumulate, sadness and disgust alternate with a strange calm, a calm that has something to do with the figure to whom the poem is addressed, and with her relation to reality. This is the end of stanza v:

> The measure of the intensity of love
> Is measure, also, of the verve of earth.
> For me, the firefly's quick, electric stroke
> Ticks tediously the time of one more year.
> And you? Remember how the crickets came
> Out of their mother grass, like little kin,
> In the pale nights, when your first imagery
> Found inklings of your bond to all that dust.

And the poem ends with a stanza (XII) on the same theme which explains much of what has gone before:

> A blue pigeon it is, that circles the blue sky,
> On sidelong wing, around and round and round.
> A white pigeon it is, that flutters to the ground,
> Grown tired of flight. Like a dark rabbi, I
> Observed, when young, the nature of mankind,
> In lordly study. Every day, I found
> Man proved a gobbet in my mincing world.
> Like a rose rabbi, later, I pursued,
> And still pursue, the origin and course
> Of love, but until now I never knew
> That fluttering things have so distinct a shade.

So the poem comes not to a conclusion, but to a subtly suggested declaration of intent. The pigeon, like the 'casual flocks of pigeons' at the end of 'Sunday Morning', is part of the real world in which the imagination must find a satisfying value. It is through the real world, in other words, that 'the origin and course of love' is to be pursued, and this thought lies behind the earlier stanza too, where:

> The measure of the intensity of love
> Is measure, also, of the verve of earth.

The rabbi, a figure who recurs frequently in Stevens's poetry, has an obvious relevance to the task Stevens set himself. 'The figure of the rabbi', he wrote in a letter of 1953, 'has always been an exceedingly attractive one to me because it is the figure of a man devoted in the extreme to scholarship and at the same time to making some use of it for human purposes.' (To R. Poggioli, 1 July 1953.)

The love which is the central subject of 'Le Monocle de Mon Oncle' is of course to be distinguished absolutely from sexual emotion, and this Stevens does, with some harshness, in the course of the poem:

> If sex were all, then every trembling hand
> Could make us squeak, like dolls, the wished-for words.

Nor does the love which is the 'moving power and spring' of Stevens's poetry have anything to do with the love of one individual for another, with what might be called personal devotion as opposed to sexual feeling. With the single exception of Santayana in 'To an Old Philosopher in Rome', other people as individuals play no part whatever in Stevens's pursuit of 'the origin and course of love' in poetry. He wrote no 'love poetry' in the ordinary sense of the phrase. Yet the emotion which fired the work of this remote and solitary man, whose detachment had nothing about it of the artist-as-outsider's self-dramatised alienation, can only be called love. In another age it would have been called 'the love of God', and although to use these words is at once to exceed the limits of caution set for himself by Stevens's rigorous honesty, he would have agreed to at least some of their implications.

His starting-point is the real world bereft of the sanction that men used to find in a God believed in as truly existing, believed in, that is, as children believe in ghosts and fairies. This bereft-ness is what Stevens called 'poverty', and it is there at the very centre of 'Sunday Morning':

> The tomb in Palestine
> Is not the porch of spirits lingering.
> It is the grave of Jesus, where he lay.

Many other poems in *Harmonium*, among them some of the best, are
concerned with this bereftness of man in a world without God, and
particularly with the desolating finality of death. 'The Emperor of
Ice-Cream', for instance, which has become for no obvious reason[1]
the most widely-known of all Stevens's poems, is about the bleak
fact of death with no god to give it saving significance:

> Let be be finale of seem.
> The only emperor is the emperor of ice-cream.
>
> Take from the dresser of deal
> Lacking the three glass knobs, that sheet
> On which she embroidered fantails once
> And spread it so as to cover her face.
> If her horny feet protrude, they come
> To show how cold she is, and dumb.
> Let the lamp affix its beam.
> The only emperor is the emperor of ice-cream.

(The pigeons are once again, however indirectly, vitality and move-
ment: the woman who is now dead alive, sewing.) Several other
Harmonium poems share with 'The Emperor of Ice-Cream' this un-
sentimental and at the same time profoundly uncynical realism on
the subject of death. 'Another Weeping Woman', 'From the Misery
of Don Joost', 'The Worms at Heaven's Gate' and 'Cortège for
Rosenbloom' are fine examples. But perhaps the best of these poems
about death are two that happen also to show how wide the range of
Stevens's poetic method already was in this, his first collection.

'The Death of a Soldier' was one of a group of war poems written
in 1917 and based on a collection of letters home from a French
soldier on the Western Front that had been published in 1916. These
poems do not appear in anthologies of First World War poetry,
presumably because they are by an American and a non-combatant,
but one or two of them, and certainly this one, deserve to stand beside
the best work of Owen and Herbert Read.

> Life contracts and death is expected,
> As in a season of autumn.
> The soldier falls.

[1] Possibly the explanation is Stevens's particular affection for it, which earned it
early anthology places.

He does not become a three-days personage,
Imposing his separation,
Calling for pomp.

Death is absolute and without memorial,
As in a season of autumn,
When the wind stops.

When the wind stops and, over the heavens,
The clouds go, nevertheless,
In their direction.

There is nothing the critic can usefully say about this, except that its simplicities gain subtlety with each re-reading, and that the faint Christian resonance evoked by the 'three-days personage' adds a particular sadness to the silence surrounding the soldier's own death. This silence, and this sadness, are also there in the very different and much more elaborate poem, 'Of Heaven Considered as a Tomb'.

What word have you, interpreters, of men
Who in the tomb of heaven walk by night,
The darkened ghosts of our old comedy?
Do they believe they range the gusty cold,
With lanterns borne aloft to light the way,
Freemen of death, about and still about
To find whatever it is they seek? Or does
That burial, pillared up each day as porte
And spiritous passage into nothingness,
Foretell each night the one abysmal night,
When the host shall no more wander, nor the light
Of the steadfast lanterns creep across the dark?
Make hue among the dark comedians,
Halloo them in the topmost distances
For answer from the·r icy Elysée.

The grand rhetoric of this richly modulated blank verse, with its mannered diction and far-fetched vocabulary, contrasts so strongly with the simple stressed lines and plain words of 'The Death of a Soldier' that no 'practical critic' would ever guess these two poems to have been written by the same poet in the same period. What they have in common is completely achieved quality, that sureness of technique and integrity of feeling that Stevens's best work possesses to a degree unsurpassed in modern poetry. In 'Of Heaven Considered as a Tomb' every device, every word, tells. The three questions that take up twelve of the poem's fifteen lines increase steadily in length and in intensity, only to be answered by the desolate chill of the last three lines. The forlornness of the phrase 'whatever it is they seek' is thrown into relief by the grandiloquence of the French 'porte' and the obsolete 'spiritous', as is the weary length of 'nothingness' coming at the end of the line. The lanterns that earlier seem frail against 'the gusty cold' become strong, even noble, with the use of the adjective 'steadfast' when they are extinguished, while the ambiguity of 'hue' against the dark, the silence surrounding 'halloo', and the white cold of 'icy' has the force of extreme compression.[1]

Winter and the north, with their associations of bareness, bereftness, and poverty in Stevens's personal sense, recur many times throughout his poetry, as do summer and the south, with their associations of richness and possible fulfilment. These are fundamental bearings in Stevens's world, and they are already firmly present in *Harmonium*. At this period summer and the south meant in particular Florida, where Stevens used to go for holidays, and which in *Harmonium* represents flourishing reality in consoling abundance:

> A few things for themselves,
> Convolvulus and coral,
> Buzzards and live-moss,
> Tiestas from the keys,
> A few things for themselves,
> Florida, venereal soil,
> Disclose to the lover ('O Florida, Venereal Soil').

In 'Nomad Exquisite', which Stevens placed last in the first edition of *Harmonium*, prolific Florida is associated with the prolific imagination:

> As the immense dew of Florida
> Brings forth
> The big-finned palm
> And green vine angering for life...

---

[1] Years later, in a note on another poem, Stevens wrote to a friend: 'When I first began to think of the past, as a child, I saw it as dark. People groped in it, carrying lights...' (to Simons, 30 August 1940).

> So, in me, come flinging
> Forms, flames, and the flakes of flames.

But the promises of Florida are in the end no more sufficient to the need that underlies *Harmonium* than the proposed satisfactions of 'Sunday Morning', and it is the poetry of winter, of death, of reality faced in its utmost bleakness with a courage that refuses all provisional comfort, that is the strongest poetry in the book. 'The Snow Man' is the supreme poem of Stevens's starting-point:

> One must have a mind of winter
> To regard the frost and the boughs
> Of the pine-trees crusted with snow;
>
> And have been cold a long time
> To behold the junipers shagged with ice,
> The spruces rough in the distant glitter
>
> Of the January sun; and not to think
> Of any misery in the sound of the wind,
> In the sound of a few leaves,
>
> Which is the sound of the land
> Full of the same wind
> That is blowing in the same bare place
>
> For the listener, who listens in the snow,
> And, nothing himself, beholds
> Nothing that is not there and the nothing that is.

This is poetry of the waste land, of 'the sadness and the discipline of the truth', and this, for all the exuberant richness composed above it, is the note that repeatedly sounds among *Harmonium*'s lavish splendours, even those of 'Sunday Morning' and 'Le Monocle de Mon Oncle'. Two lines from a strange poem called 'Palace of the Babies' catch this note exactly:

> The walker in the moonlight walked alone,
> And in his heart his disbelief lay cold.

It is from the desolation of unbelief and 'nothingness' that Stevens sets out to discover what will suffice, and already in *Harmonium* it is the imagination through which he feels he will gain his end. We have seen his use, in this connexion, of the mysterious saving figure, 'the one of fictive music', who against all the harsh evidence of reality persists 'to make believe a starry *connaissance*'. In two other, very short, poems the power of the imagination and the courage that it involves are celebrated in different terms. 'Anecdote of the Jar' has been much written about;[1] it has to do with human triumph, and also with the impermanence and unreality of that triumph:

> I placed a jar in Tennessee,
> And round it was, upon a hill.
> It made the slovenly wilderness
> Surround that hill.
>
> The wilderness rose up to it,
> And sprawled around, no longer wild.
> The jar was round upon the ground
> And tall and of a port in air.
>
> It took dominion everywhere.
> The jar was gray and bare.
> It did not give of bird or bush,
> Like nothing else in Tennessee.

'Valley Candle', an even shorter poem on the same theme, needs no critical comment:

> My candle burned alone in an immense valley.
> Beams of the huge night converged upon it,
> Until the wind blew.
> Then beams of the huge night
> Converged upon its image,
> Until the wind blew.

In spite of the many poems of great distinction in *Harmonium* and the whole volume's extraordinary assurance and definiteness – there is hardly a failure in it – Stevens was right to think of it, from his own point of view, as a collection of 'preliminary minutiae'. The

---

[1] Winters, with a characteristic and wilfully factious use of the word 'romantic' which hardly strengthens his case against Stevens, says that this poem 'would appear to be primarily an expression of the corrupting effect of the intellect upon natural beauty, and hence a purely romantic performance' (*In Defense of Reason* p. 437).

poems are certainly not immature: Stevens was, after all, forty-four when the book came out and there was little of the impatient youthful genius in his character. Nevertheless, however complete in themselves, these are tentative beginnings in an enterprise of whose full implications Stevens himself was not yet aware. As he gradually understood and met these implications over the last thirty years of his life, many of the *Harmonium* themes were to recur in his work with an ever-increasing density of significance. *Harmonium* is, as it were, a book of intuitions, the most accurate of which were in the course of time to become convictions as Stevens himself filled them out, made them heavy with his own thought and feeling. For the moment he was far from clear as to the ultimate direction his work was to take.

In the summer of 1922, when with considerable dissatisfaction he was collecting the poems for *Harmonium*, he finished his first long poem, 'The Comedian as the Letter C'. Of the poems that eventually appeared in *Harmonium*'s first edition this was the last to be written and it reflects both the uncertainty and the resolute exploratory persistence of Stevens at this period. The long poem was later to become the means of some of Stevens's greatest achievements and 'The Comedian as the Letter C' first gave him the feel of its possibilities. 'I find that this prolonged attention to a single subject has the same result that prolonged attention to a senora has according to the authorities', he wrote to Harriet Monroe on 23 September 1922. 'All manner of favors drop from it. Only it requires a skill in the varying of the serenade that occasionally makes one feel like a Guatemalan when one particularly wants to feel like an Italian. I expect that after a while..."The Comedian as the Letter C" will become rudimentary and abhorrent.' He turned out to be right in both respects. He was indeed to elicit 'all manner of favors' from the form; but his wholly successful long poems were written as cycles of short poems, variations on a central theme. 'The Comedian as the Letter C', on the other hand, while hardly 'rudimentary and abhorrent', is an allegorical narrative performed with almost ferocious virtuosity and is more exhausting than exhilarating to read straight through. Stevens's later (1935) account of it makes it sound easier than it is: 'The long and the short of it is simply that I deliberately took the sort of life that millions of people live, without embellishing it except by the embellishments in which I was interested at the moment: words and sounds.'[1] In fact the poem, composed (according to Stevens) as a kind of fantastic rhapsody on the sounds of the letter C, is a lengthy enquiry into the possibility of establishing a satisfactory relation between the imagination and reality, and the career of Crispin, the poem's hero, cannot help having more in common with the lives of the limited number of people who are consciously aware of the imagination's reconciling powers than with 'the sort of life that millions of people live'. This is not to say that Crispin 'is' Stevens in any direct sense. He is no more than a characterless questing figure, a clown at large in the daunting world; but for the poem's purposes he is lent, as it were, the poet's preoccupations and the poet's equipment.

The enquiry begins with an assumption that poems like 'Anecdote of the Jar' must sometimes have led Stevens to:

> Nota; man is the intelligence of his soil,
> The sovereign ghost.

But the assumption is quickly shattered by the sea (Crispin is on a voyage from Bordeaux to Yucatan). The sea, as often in Stevens, is finally intractable reality, that which the imagination cannot subdue to its devices. Crispin's realisation of his inability to make sense of his relation to this 'polyphony beyond his baton's thrust' appals him but is at the same time good for him. The closing passage of the poem's first section, 'The World without Imagination', reflects both Stevens's feeling of weakness and his resolution in the face of bare, meaningless, wintry reality, 'nothing that is not there and the nothing that is':

> Here was no help before reality.
> Crispin beheld and Crispin was made new.
> The imagination, here, could not evade,
> In poems of plums, the strict austerity
> Of one vast, subjugating, final tone.
> The drenching of stale lives no more fell down.
> What was this gaudy, gusty panoply?
> Out of what swift destruction did it spring?

[1] To Latimer, 15 November 1935.

> It was caparison of wind and cloud
> And something given to make whole among
> The ruses that were shattered by the large.

In the second section, 'Concerning the Thunderstorms of Yucatan', Crispin arrives, humbled and inspired by his experience of the sea, in a region of the south, of summer and the fecund jungle. This 'new reality' appears for a while to appease his need, the 'destitution' that the sea has brought him to; but a thunderstorm, which sends him into the cathedral 'with the rest', again unsettles his provisional assumptions, its violence shaking him into a new, yet still humble, realisation of his own ambition:

> This was the span
> Of force, the quintessential fact, the note
> Of Vulcan, that a valet seeks to own,
> The thing that makes him envious in phrase.
>
> And while the torrent on the roof still droned
> He felt the Andean breath. His mind was free
> And more than free, elate, intent, profound...

The third section is perhaps the best in the poem. It is verbally the least aggressively extravagant, and it comes closest to the centre of Stevens's deep concern with the problem of reality and the imagination. Crispin sails for Carolina: 'America was always north to him', and, after a beautiful passage of New England wintriness, Stevens describes the peculiar imaginative attraction that the ideas of winter and the north had for him – the moon is one of his figures for the imagination:

> How many poems he denied himself
> In his observant progress, lesser things
> Than the relentless contact he desired...
> Perhaps the Arctic moonlight really gave
> The liaison, the blissful liaison
> Between himself and his environment.

But this in turn is rejected as a conclusion; the claims of the sun (reality), the south, all that 'Florida' meant for Stevens at this period, are given their balancing due:

Thus he conceived his voyaging to be
An up and down between two elements,
A fluctuating between sun and moon.

These theoretical speculations are brought literally down to earth
with Crispin's actual arrival in Carolina. The 'antiquated seaport'
(Stevens's phrase in a letter[1] about a visit to Charleston made in
July 1922 when this poem was half-written) is described in all its
rank detail. It gives Crispin another sense of reality and this, one feels,
is the most satisfactory yet:

It made him see how much
Of what he saw he never saw at all.
He gripped more closely the essential prose
As being, in a world so falsified,
The one integrity for him, the one
Discovery still possible to make,
To which all poems were incident, unless
That prose should wear a poem's guise at last.

This passage is a kind of inner manifesto. In all the complexities of
his later work Stevens never dismantled this simple vision and its
courage underlies the whole of his achievement. For the moment, it
is the conclusion of Crispin's travels and the second half of the poem
(three more sections) is really no more than an extended elaboration
of the discovery made here, beginning with a significant reversal of
the poem's first premise:

Nota: his soil is man's intelligence.
That's better. That's worth crossing seas to find.

After this announcement the slender narrative thread of Crispin's
adventures is obscured by an increasing extravagance of idea and
language. The topographical actuality of the poem's first half is, of
course, used for its metaphorical implications; but 'reality is the
indispensable element of each metaphor', and the metaphorical
structure of the poem's second half does not have enough reality in it.
Crispin's four daughters of the last section, for instance, are symbolic
figures who may or may not represent the seasons; what they do not
have is the quality of daughters, as the sea or Yucatan had the quality

[1] To Harriet Monroe, 24 August 1922.

of the sea and Yucatan. Stevens ends the whole poem on a note of doubt and dissatisfaction, ornamented with wry self-deprecation:

> Or if the music sticks, if the anecdote
> Is false, if Crispin is a profitless
> Philosopher, beginning with green brag,
> Concluding fadedly, if as a man
> Prone to distemper he abates in taste,
> Fickle and fumbling, variable, obscure,
> Glozing his life with after-shining flicks,
> Illuminating, from a fancy gorged
> By apparition, plain and common things,
> Sequestering the fluster from the year,
> Making gulped potions from obstreperous drops,
> And so distorting, proving what he proves
> Is nothing, what can all this matter since
> The relation comes, benignly, to its end?
>
> So may the relation of each man be clipped.

This, the conclusion of the last *Harmonium* poem, reflects accurately enough, we may presume, Stevens's view of himself as a poet just before *Harmonium* was published. It recalls the letter of that autumn of 1922: 'The reading of these outmoded and debilitated poems does make me wish rather desperately to keep on dabbling and to be as obscure as possible until I have perfected an authentic and fluent speech.' And it contains also the self-mocking irony of the sentence that follows this: 'By that time I should be like Casanova at Waldheim with nothing to do except to look out of the windows.' The 'green brag' of the Florida poems and the positive assurances of 'Sunday Morning' have faded into the melancholy, the uncertainty, the fits and starts of Crispin and 'Le Monocle de Mon Oncle', 'fickle and fumbling, variable, obscure'. But both these remarkable poems have among their restless discontents signposts pointing the way that Stevens's later poetry was to follow. The last half of 'The Comedian as the Letter C' has, for instance, those aphorisms insisting on recognition of essential reality which were to remain the foundation of all the later work: 'The natives of the rain are rainy men'; 'The plum survives its poems'; 'For realist, what is is what should be'. It also contains a short passage which describes as well as anything

in Stevens both the object of his brave endeavour, and his own
humble view of the *Harmonium* poems:

> What was the purpose of his pilgrimage,
> Whatever shape it took in Crispin's mind,
> If not, when all is said, to drive away
> The shadow of his fellows from the skies
> And, from their stale intelligence released,
> To make a new intelligence prevail?
> Hence the reverberations in the words
> Of his first central hymns, the celebrants
> Of rankest trivia, tests of the strength
> Of his aesthetic, his philosophy,
> The more invidious, the more desired:
> The florist asking aid from cabbages,
> The rich man going bare, the paladin
> Afraid, the blind man as astronomer,
> The appointed power unwielded from disdain.

This is not, as we have seen, the whole truth about *Harmonium*. The
florist in Stevens could not always confine his attention to cabbages,
nor the rich man to bareness. The point is both illustrated and
proved by the beautiful 'Monocle' couplet:

> Why, without pity on these studious ghosts,
> Do you come dripping in your hair from sleep?

The imagination's beneficent power, symbolised in 'the one of
fictive music', haunts Stevens's 'first central hymns' with a persistence
no less significant than the persistence of plain, bereft reality; and
'what will suffice' had eventually to be found in the marriage of one
with the other, that 'blissful liaison' first referred to in 'The Comedian
as the Letter C'. But twenty years were to pass before this liaison
was finally achieved, in Stevens's greatest poem 'Notes toward a
Supreme Fiction'.

Meanwhile it is interesting to observe how accurately the long
passage above from 'The Comedian' describes Eliot's early poetry.
Here indeed was a 'celebrant of rankest trivia', a poet who began by
using his creative gift almost entirely 'to drive away the shadow of
his fellows from the skies', 'the paladin afraid', 'the appointed power

unwielded from disdain'. But though this is nearer the mark as a complete description of Eliot's early poetry than it is of Stevens's, it is not the whole truth about Eliot either. Eliot at this period, as we have seen, would never have committed himself to aspirations so firm as those of 'Peter Quince' and 'To the One of Fictive Music', or even as those, darker and more uncertain, of 'Le Monocle' or 'The Comedian'. Nevertheless there are in Eliot's early poetry hints, however guarded, of a figure of consolation that bears a striking resemblance to the figure that in Stevens brings with her the imagination's benediction. Her first and fullest appearance is in the poem that came last in *Prufrock*, 'La Figlia Che Piange', and here she is unequivocally a real person. This poem stands out among Eliot's early work because the emotion that informs it is positive rather than negative and can even, if one dares to use the word, be described as love. There is a farewell, a garden, a girl with sunlit hair and flowers, the whole composing a picture that even in the poem Eliot recognises the power of. The poem ends:

> She turned away, but with the autumn weather
> Compelled my imagination many days,
> Many days and many hours:
> Her hair over her arms and her arms full of flowers.
> And I wonder how they should have been together!
> I should have lost a gesture and a pose.
> Sometimes these cogitations still amaze
> The troubled midnight and the noon's repose.

The directness, the wistfulness, most of all the use of the phrase 'compelled my imagination' are highly uncharacteristic of the early Eliot. The obvious conclusion – that this figure, this incident, held a particular weight of significance and even of consolation for Eliot – is fully borne out by its recurrence, and the way in which it recurs, in the rest of his work. In the first section of *The Waste Land* the girl appears framed by the nostalgic love of the first quotation from *Tristan* and the desolation of the second:

> *Frisch weht der Wind*
> *Der Heimat zu*
> *Mein Irisch Kind,*
> *Wo weilest du?*

'You gave me hyacinths first a year ago;
'They called me the hyacinth girl.'
– Yet when we came back, late, from the hyacinth garden.
Your arms full, and your hair wet, I could not
Speak, and my eyes failed, I was neither
Living nor dead, and I knew nothing,
Looking into the heart of light, the silence.
Oed' und leer das Meer.[1]

These two are our only glimpses of this figure in the desert of irony and revulsion that is Eliot's early poetry. When she appears again, in the poems written after Eliot's religious crisis and conversion, she herself is unchanged. But from the old structure of belief newly accepted by Eliot she has gathered a new significance. She is the figure whom the poet sees 'At the first turning of the third stair' in *Ash-Wednesday,* and here the consolation and frustration that she represents are made explicitly religious by the last lines of the section (III):

Blown hair is sweet, brown hair over the mouth blown,
Lilac and brown hair;
Distraction, music of the flute, stops and steps of the mind
    over the third stair,
Fading, fading; strength beyond hope and despair
Climbing the third stair.
Lord, I am not worthy
Lord, I am not worthy
        but speak the word only.

And by the end of *Ash-Wednesday* she has become almost completely identified with Mary:

Blessed sister, holy mother, spirit of the fountain,
    spirit of the garden,
Suffer us not to mock ourselves with falsehood
Teach us to care and not to care
Teach us to sit still
Even among these rocks,
Our peace in His will...

---

[1] On the MS. of *The Waste Land,* Pound wrote the word 'Marianne' beside this passage. No one now knows whether this refers to a real person or not.

She is there as a mysterious presence amid the bleak sea imagery (remember '*Oed' und leer das Meer*') of 'Marina', and, less mysteriously, in 'The Dry Salvages':

> Lady, whose shrine stands on the promontory,
> Pray for all those who are in ships...

And, though she herself does not appear, it is surely her garden that is the garden in 'Burnt Norton', the garden of frustration and consolation where the lotos rose from the dry pool and, in a phrase from the *Waste Land* passage quoted above 'The surface glittered out of heart of light.'

To say that she reminds one irresistibly of Stevens's One of Fictive Music, 'Sister and mother and diviner love', 'Mother of heaven, regina of the clouds' is certainly not to impose a facile and external Christian interpretation upon Stevens's search through poetry for what would suffice – a search that was in any case still at a preliminary stage in *Harmonium*. But nor is it merely to point to a curious coincidence. It is, rather, to say that this image, associated for both poets with love and with possible rescue from the sea of desolate reality, suggests again that Eliot and Stevens are closer together in their quest and in their achievement than the division between Christian and non-Christian in most people's minds would lead them to suppose. The fact that this division was strongly present in the minds of both Eliot and Stevens themselves does not help to clarify the issue. But the final evidence is their poetry, and what is there made or found. Made or found, created or discovered: some apparently relevant problems profitably disappear if it is accepted that it does not matter very much which of these terms is used. In other words, there are areas – and areas of central and infinite interest – in human thought and feeling where it can be helpful rather than dangerous to forget the ancient, fierce distinction between fiction and truth. This is the ultimate issue raised by Stevens's (and Eliot's) mature poetry, and we shall return to it later.

Meanwhile it is enough to repeat that study of the work, early and late, of Eliot and Stevens reveals in each case the record of a persistent, patient and above all honest journey through the waste land of the bereft modern world towards what is in the end perhaps the same thing: 'what will suffice', 'a new intelligence', 'the origin and course of love'; or, in Eliot's words at the end of his last poem 'Little Gidding':

> The drawing of this Love and the voice of this Calling...
> A condition of complete simplicity
> (Costing not less than everything)

6
'Ideas of Order'

Harmonium was greeted with little critical acclaim and less public enthusiasm. Ten months after its publication Stevens wrote to Harriet Monroe: 'My royalties for the first half of 1924 amounted to $6.70. I shall have to charter a boat and take my friends around the world.'[1] 1922-3 was the *annus mirabilis* of modern literature: *Ulysses*, *The Waste Land*, Valéry's *Charmes* and the *Duino Elegies* appeared within a few months of each other, and the fact that a volume of poetry by an unknown middle-aged American businessman deserved a place in this list escaped nearly everyone's notice for several decades. In England at least, and perhaps still partly because *Harmonium* came out at the right time in the wrong continent, it is even yet not generally recognised. Among those to whom Joyce, Eliot, Valéry and Rilke are familiar spirits or, at any rate, familiar points of reference, Stevens's name often evokes only puzzled frowns and faintly ringing bells. And yet – or perhaps this is also part of the reason for his comparative lack of fame – of all the great writers of his generation he was producing his best work the most recently. Possibly it is just that while in English poetry the political 'thirties were followed by the hysterical 'forties and the drab 'fifties, this remote, prosperous, sane old man, having failed to be noticed as part of the great 'twenties, thereafter simply failed at every turn to be where most people were looking. Had they looked a little further they might have followed the whole course of a remarkable creative achievement in their own language.

As we have seen, Stevens was thoroughly, if unreasonably, dispirited about *Harmonium* before it was even published. In the years immediately following its appearance he wrote almost nothing: the fourteen additional poems he produced for *Harmonium*'s second

---

[1] *Letters*, p. 243; July 1924 probable date.

edition in 1931 had almost all been composed,[1] and the best published before 1923; and the four poems that appeared in magazines between 1923 and 1930 he rightly thought too insignificant to reprint.[2] One gathers from snatches of evidence in poems and letters that a combination of instinct, decision and external circumstances was reponsible for this long fallow period. The eight or so years of poetic effort that *Harmonium* represents had ended with the ambitious and not very satisfactory 'Comedian as the Letter C'. Its fantastic devices and moments of splendour do not conceal an irresolution and a staleness that are explicit in a poem written the year before (1921), 'The Man Whose Pharynx was Bad':

> The time of year has grown indifferent.
> Mildew of summer and the deepening snow
> Are both alike in the routine I know.
> I am too dumbly in my being pent.

Neither summer nor winter, always for certain purposes the poles of Stevens's imagination, can reach an acme, a timeless finality that will cure 'The malady of the quotidian'. If they could:

> One might in turn become less diffident,
> Out of such mildew plucking neater mould
> And spouting new orations of the cold.
> One might. One might. But time will not relent.

The futile hope expressed in flat, rhyming lines, the dreary sense of disillusion with that reality of place, time and weather which was at this period the basis of his most positive affirmations against the waste land, perhaps reflect no more than a passing moment. But one cannot help suspecting that some such dissatisfaction with what had seemed in 'Sunday Morning' the infinite promise of the real world lay behind the silence of the years following *Harmonium*. His intuition must have told him to wait for something new to emerge from within himself. It is impossible to believe that, if the poems had been there, the circumstances given by his daughter[3] as the reasons for his silence

---

[1] The exception is the rather empty virtuoso piece 'Sea Surface Full of Clouds' (1924); possibly also 'Sonatina to Hans Christian', 'Two at Norfolk', and 'In the Clear Season of Grapes'.

[2] They appear in *Opus Posthumous,* pp. 28–32.

[3] *Letters,* pp. 242, 256.

– domestic concerns, a noisy house, hard work at the insurance company – would have prevented them from being written.

When, some time in 1932–3, Stevens returned seriously to poetry, he at first found it hard going. 'I do not much like the new things that I write', he said in a letter of March 1933.[1] 'Writing again after a discontinuance seems to take one back to the beginning rather than to the point of discontinuance.' Nearly two years later, while collecting and adding to the poems that were to make up his new book *Ideas of Order*, he was writing regretfully of his long abstinence from poetry: 'If one does not write poetry more or less constantly, it seems to fade, or to receive its impulse from circumstances which more often than not would be cheerless to anyone except the poet.'[2] 'One of the essential conditions to the writing of poetry is impetus. That is a reason for thinking that to be a poet at all one ought to be a poet constantly... Writing poetry is a conscious activity. While poems may very well occur, they have very much better be caused.'[3] For the remaining twenty years of his life – he was already fifty-five – Stevens was indeed 'a poet constantly'. But he had no reason to regret the fallow period that had produced fruits of the quality of the best poems in *Ideas of Order*. As he wrote himself in his notebook, 'Thought tends to collect in pools'; and, 'cheerless' though these poems may seem in comparison with the variegated richness of *Harmonium*, they represent a major advance in both thought and feeling.

The less interesting poems in the book are written in the lighter, more extravagant vein of the less interesting poems in *Harmonium*. The suspicion that some of them are actually pieces left over from the *Harmonium* period is confirmed by Stevens's remark in a letter[4] of March 1935: 'The more recent poems have been spread more or less through the manuscript', and by the fact that the longest and least successful of them 'Academic Discourse at Havana' was in fact published in a magazine in 1923. The best poems in *Ideas of Order*, on the other hand, are far removed from the prodigious and provisional atmosphere of *Harmonium*. They are bound together by a new firmness, a new resolution, indicated in the book's title. The poet's attitude to the waste land has changed. Instead of sad prayers to 'the

[1] To M. D. Zabel, 13 March 1933. [2] To Latimer, 10 December 1934.
[3] To Latimer, 8 January 1935. [4] To Latimer, 26 March 1935.

one of fictive music', or Crispin's indecisions, there is a new bleak courage, an explicit acceptance of bareness and bereftness as an essential foundation in the mind without which nothing positive can be constructed. This is what Stevens surely meant by 'circumstances which...would be cheerless to anyone except the poet'. The poems are about the absence of God, the fact of death, above all about man's self-reliance. They are classic statements of the human condition in the modern world.

Stevens would have shuddered at the phrase, and indeed one of the most admirable qualities of these poems is the distance they keep from the dead weight of grandiloquent abstraction. A fine example is the short poem 'How to Live. What to Do', of which Stevens wrote[1] at this time: 'I like it most, I suppose, because it so definitely represents my way of thinking.' Here is the whole of it:

> Last evening the moon rose above this rock
> Impure upon a world unpurged.
> The man and his companion stopped
> To rest before the heroic height.
>
> Cold the wind fell upon them
> In many majesties of sound:
> They that had left the flame-freaked sun
> To seek a sun of fuller fire.
>
> Instead there was this tufted rock
> Massively rising high and bare
> Beyond all trees, the ridges thrown
> Like giant arms among the clouds.
>
> There was neither voice nor crested image,
> No chorister, nor priest. There was
> Only the great height of the rock
> And the two of them standing still to rest.
>
> There was the cold wind and the sound
> It made, away from the muck of the land
> That they had left, heroic sound
> Joyous and jubilant and sure.

In its plainness and restraint, and the range of its implications, this is a very considerable feat. The economy of the language – the weight

---

[1] Letter to Latimer, 15 November 1935.

carried, for instance, by the monosyllable at the end of each stanza and by the hinge-word 'instead' – and the bold simplicity of the conception, seem to bring into the clear light of day thoughts and feelings that in *Harmonium* found expression only fitfully through layers of rhetoric. Even 'The Snow Man', the *Harmonium* poem that has most in common with 'How to Live. What to Do', has a note of panic in it that here has been altogether transcended. One must

> have been cold a long time
> ...not to think
> Of any misery in the sound of the wind.

The listener in 'How to Live. What to Do' hears the same wind but it has now become, with exultant emphasis, 'Joyous and jubilant and sure', and he beholds, instead of 'Nothing that is not there and the nothing that is', the rock that comforts him. It is as real and as bereft as the snow in the January sun but it is not nothing.

'A Fading of the Sun' is a poem that Stevens called[1] 'in a way, a companion piece to "How to Live. What to Do".' Again the poem must be quoted in full:

> Who can think of the sun costuming clouds
> When all people are shaken
> Or of night endazzled, proud,
> When people awaken
> And cry and cry for help?
>
> The warm antiquity of self,
> Everyone, grows suddenly cold.
> The tea is bad, bread sad.
> How can the world so old be so mad
> That the people die?
>
> If joy shall be without a book
> It lies, themselves within themselves,
> If they will look
> Within themselves
> And cry and cry for help[2]

---

[1] Letter to Latimer, 21 November 1935.
[2] In *Collected Poems* (p. 139), there is a question mark here – clearly a mistake.

Within as pillars of the sun,
Supports of night. The tea,
The wine is good. The bread,
The meat is sweet.
And they will not die.

In the letter quoted above Stevens continues:

For convenience, and in view of the simplicity of the large mass of people,
we give our good qualities to God, or to various gods, but they come from
ourselves. In 'A Fading of the Sun' the point is that, instead of crying for
help to God or to one of the gods, we should look to ourselves for help.
The exaltation of human nature should take the place of its abasement.
Perhaps I ought to say, the sense of its exaltation should take the place of its
abasement...Another point about looking to oneself is this; the fundamental
source of joy in life is the instinct of joy. If that is true, and a little difficult to
realize in life, it is infinitely more true in poetry and painting, and much more
easy to realize there.

This passage and the two poems upon which it comments are the
key to the new poetry in *Ideas of Order* and to the firmer sense of the
world and his own relation to it that emerged in Stevens after his
long silence.

'How to Live. What to Do' and 'A Fading of the Sun' are both
concerned with the positive aspect of brave self-dependence in a
world bereft of God and of the sanctions which used to form the
supporting structure of people's lives. They express not only acceptance but also optimism. The two most considerable poems in *Ideas
of Order* are also about this exhilarating side of a coin whose obverse is
desolate and terrifying. 'Evening without Angels' is a glowing celebration of the self alone with reality at that time of day which often
in Stevens's poetry was to be the most consoling. (In the passage from
'Extracts from Addresses to the Academy of Fine Ideas' quoted
earlier the return to the cold evening from the alien moon is the
'return to the subtle centre'.) The poem begins with a resolute
denial that there is any sustenance to comfort us or any ordering
words for us to hear but our own:

Why seraphim like lutanists arranged
Above the trees? And why the poet as
Eternal *chef d'orchestre*?

> Air is air,
> Its vacancy glitters round us everywhere,
> Its sounds are not angelic syllables
> But our unfashioned spirits realized
> More sharply in more furious selves.

The rest of the poem, in paragraphs of relaxed blank verse, revolves this thought with respect to both sound and light:

> the wind
> Encircling us, speaks always with our speech.
>
> Light, too, encrusts us making visible
> The motions of the mind...

And the meditation comes to its end with an exquisite fusion of the sense of human weakness with the sense of human strength:

> Bare night is best. Bare earth is best. Bare, bare,
> Except for our own houses, huddled low
> Beneath the arches and their spangled air,
> Beneath the rhapsodies of fire and fire,
> Where the voice that is in us makes a true response,
> Where the voice that is great within us rises up,
> As we stand gazing at the rounded moon.

'Evening without Angels' is a fine poem: 'The Idea of Order at Key West', more intense, more direct, bearing a massive weight of thought and feeling that cannot be separated from each other, is a great one. An extraordinary calm pervades it, and an atmosphere of clarity through which the lines move with absolute assurance and steadiness. A girl walked singing by the sea; the poet who observed her reflects, as in 'Evening without Angels' on 'our speech', which is all the speech that there is:

> The song and water were not medleyed sound
> Even if what she sang was what she heard,
> Since what she sang was uttered word by word.
> It may be that in all her phrases stirred
> The grinding water and the gasping wind;
> But it was she and not the sea we heard.

As the poem gathers weight (it is too long to quote entire) the issues raised by the solitary figure of the girl become wider. A question is asked:

> Whose spirit is this? we said, because we knew
> It was the spirit that we sought...

But the poet continues warily, the course of his meditation traced with the utmost exactness and delicacy. Reality cannot give him his answer, but nor can even the figure of the girl herself:

> If it was only the dark voice of the sea
> That rose, or even colored by many waves;
> If it was only the outer voice of sky
> And cloud...
>   But it was more than that,
> More even than her voice, and ours, among
> The meaningless plungings of water and the wind...

In the end the question is not answered at all; but the poem's marvellous conclusion, suggests in its triumphant but still calm cadences a glimpsed victory over poverty that could be the poet's or could be any man's. 'The spirit that we sought' is not defined, but it is found, and found in human sense made of non-human senseless reality:

>   Then we,
> As we beheld her striding there alone,
> Knew that there never was a world for her
> Except the one she sang and, singing, made.
>
> Ramon Fernandez,[1] tell me, if you know,
> Why, when the singing ended and we turned
> Toward the town, tell why the glassy lights,
> The lights in the fishing boats at anchor there,
> As the night descended, tilting in the air,
> Mastered the night and portioned out the sea,
> Fixing emblazoned zones and fiery poles,
> Arranging, deepening, enchanting night.
>
> Oh! Blessed rage for order, pale Ramon,
> The maker's rage to order words of the sea,
> Words of the fragrant portals, dimly-starred,
> And of ourselves and of our origins,
> In ghostlier demarcations, keener sounds.

[1] A name, Stevens later asserted, chosen at random, though he knew of the Spanish critic and had read some of his work. (Letter to Poggioli, 4 March 1954.)

Unlike some of the poems of Stevens's later years, this meditation is no more difficult, in the manner people have come to expect from 'modern poetry', than 'Tintern Abbey'; and it deserves as early and as automatic a place in the educated mind as the acknowledged Wordsworth masterpieces. The best comment on it is a sentence from a Stevens letter[1] of November 1935 (a year or so after it was written): 'In "The Idea of Order at Key West" life has ceased to be a matter of chance.' To which can be added a passage from a letter written ten days earlier:

We are not beginning to get out of the world what it will ultimately yield through poets. If poetry introduces order, and every competent poem introduces order, and if order means peace, even though that particular peace is an illusion, is it any less an illusion than a good many other things that everyone high and low now-a-days concedes to be no longer of any account? Isn't a freshening of life a thing of consequence? It would be a great thing to change the status of the poet.[2]

The point of these rather obscure remarks, that an illusion may be 'a thing of consequence' and yet still an illusion, was the crucial discovery of this period of Stevens's life and the idea to which he was later to devote the grandest poetic effort of his career, in 'Notes toward a Supreme Fiction'. Meanwhile the order and peace both created and described in some of the poems in *Ideas of Order* are balanced in others not by confusion and strife but by the loneliness and sense of mortal weakness that are the black side of self-dependence. The poet, in 'The Sun this March', feels abandoned by the summer confidence he once possessed:

> Cold is our element and winter's air
> Brings voices as of lions coming down.
>
> Oh! Rabbi, rabbi, fend my soul for me
> And true savant of this dark nature be.

The same wintry cold pervades a beautiful short poem 'The Reader':

> No lamp was burning as I read,
> A voice was mumbling, 'Everything
> Falls back to coldness...'

---

[1] To Latimer, 15 November 1935.   [2] To Latimer, 5 November 1935.

And in the remarkable 'Anglais Mort à Florence', a sad and frightening picture is drawn of a man who has left behind his ability to make newly for himself 'what will suffice':

> His spirit grew uncertain of delight,
> Certain of its uncertainty...
> But he remembered the time when he stood alone,
> When to be and delight to be seemed to be one,
> Before the colors deepened and grew small.

Stevens was no proselytiser, no 'lunatic of one idea in a world of ideas' as he later put in 'Esthétique du Mal'. But nor was he merely, as one critic has called him 'a moody poet: a poet given to his moods, on the assumption that a man's life is only the sum of his moods'.[1] Behind the individual poems of *Ideas of Order*, and indeed behind all his work, lies neither a philosophical system nor a set of random states of mind, but a search. The poems record the course of the search, its moments of resolution and repose, its moments of fear, desolation and bleak irony. At the same time the poems are the object of the search, as Stevens, who had before him a vision of the whole of his work before he had written even half of it, was always aware. In the letters he wrote in 1935 to Latimer, the mysterious publisher of *Ideas of Order*, one sees these two, the course of his search and its object, what his poems are about and the poems themselves, inextricably fused in his mind. The very remark 'In "The Idea of Order at Key West" life has ceased to be a matter of chance' is one case in point, and there are several others. In letters only a fortnight apart he can say on the one hand: 'What I am after in all of this is poetry, and I don't think that I have ever written anything with any other objective than to write poetry.' And on the other (in the same letter as his passage about order, peace and 'a freshening of life'): 'There is no reason why any poet should not have the status of the philosopher, nor why his poetry should not give up to the keenest minds and the most searching spirits something of what philosophy gives up and, in addition, the peculiar things that only poetry can give.'[2] These two sentences appear to conflict, the second disclosing precisely that 'other objective' whose existence is denied by the first. But there is no conflict in

---

[1] Denis Donoghue in *New York Review of Books*, 1 February 1968.
[2] To Latimer, 22 October, 5 November 1935.

Stevens's mind, only two ways of looking at what was for him one thing: his own poetry and what he might attain by means of it for himself and for others.

At this period and in these informal letters Stevens did not think his way through these issues with the clarity of his later lectures. He was not yet trying to argue a case for the task he had embarked upon. But his sense of its seriousness and immense interest, a feeling that was greatly to increase in the next few years, was already strong. 'I think that the real trouble with poetry', he wrote to Latimer a few weeks later (10 December 1935),

is that poets have no conception of the importance of the thing. Life without poetry is, in effect, life without a sanction. Poetry does not only mean verse; in a way it means painting, it means the theatre and all the rest of it...The poet as a character has to be defined; poetry has to be defined. The world never moves at a very high level, but a few men should always move at a very high level.

Here we have another intimation of the 'other objective', the fulfilment of need, the assuagement of poverty, that was always at the back of Stevens's mind. But it was not until four years later in letters to Hi Simons[1] that he described it explicitly:

Of course, what one is after in all these things is the discovery of a value that really suffices.

I ought to say that it is a habit of mind with me to be thinking of some substitute for religion. I don't necessarily mean some substitute for the church, because no one believes in the church as an institution more than I do. My trouble, and the trouble of a great many people, is the loss of belief in the sort of God in Whom we were all brought up to believe. Humanism would be the natural substitute, but the more I see of humanism the less I like it. A thing of this kind is not to be judged by ideal presentations of it, but by what it really is. In its most acceptable form it is probably a baseball game with all the beer signs and coca cola signs, etc. If so, we ought to be able to get along without it.

This, though Stevens could have juxtaposed the church and the baseball game in such a way at any time, was written nearer to the composition of 'Notes toward a Supreme Fiction' than to *Ideas of*

[1] 29 December 1939; 9 January 1940.

Order. But it is in fact part of a comment on a strange *Ideas of Order* poem called 'Winter Bells'. This is a wry reflection, in Stevens's lightest ironic manner, on 'a world without religion, life without a sanction':

> It was the custom
> For his rage against chaos
> To abate on the way to church,
> In regulations of his spirit.
> How good life is, on the basis of propriety,
> To be followed by a platter of capon!

Next to 'Winter Bells' in *Ideas of Order* is an even stranger poem, lit with nostalgia instead of spiked with irony, but a variation on the same theme. Its title is 'Gray Stones and Gray Pigeons' and it begins:

> The archbishop is away. The church is gray.
> He has left his robes folded in camphor
> And, dressed in black, he walks
> Among fireflies.

Everything has stopped because he, whoever he is, is away, but the poem ends with the possibility of his return:

> A dithery gold falls everywhere.
> It wets the pigeons,
> It goes and the birds go,
> Turn dry,
>
> Birds that never fly
> Except when the bishop passes by,
> Globed in today and tomorrow,
> Dressed in his colored robes.

Of 'Gray Stones and Gray Pigeons' Stevens very properly wrote in the same letter to Simons:

This is a perfect instance of destroying a poem by explaining it. I suppose that there is an abstraction implicit in what is actually on the page, and that it would be something like this: everything depends on its sanction; and when its sanction is lost that is the end of it. But the poem is precisely what is printed on the page.

This poem is, in other words, no more than a graceful little skirmish with a huge and daunting subject; but as such, like all the best poems in *Ideas of Order*, and like the volume itself, it has a place and a point in the long history of Stevens's war with the waste land.

There is one *Ideas of Order* poem, 'Sad Strains of a Gay Waltz,' in which the fundamental issue of a world without 'a value that really suffices' and the challenge that such a world presents to the poet is explicitly faced. Here the waltz in Stevens's language of 'fictive music' is a metaphor for dead forms, for structures that have lost their sanction and their meaning:

> There comes a time when the waltz
> Is no longer a mode of desire, a mode
> Of revealing desire and is empty of shadows.

Later in the poem there is a vision of the human waste land that reminds one irresistibly of the Santayana passage already quoted (see p. 53), about 'the after-effects of supernaturalism' and 'children escaped from school' who 'find their whole happiness in freedom... They do not know what they want...They have discarded the machinery in which their ancestors embodied the ideal....' etc. Here is Stevens, thirty years later:

> There is order in neither sea nor sun.
> The shapes have lost their glistening.
> There are these sudden mobs of men,
>
> These sudden clouds of faces and arms,
> An immense suppression, freed,
> These voices crying without knowing for what,
>
> Except to be happy, without knowing how,
> Imposing forms they cannot describe,
> Requiring order beyond their speech.

At the end of the poem the figure of the poet appears, as he who, accepting the new bare world, will endow it with a new sufficient meaning, will make it once more three-dimensional:

> Too many waltzes – The epic of disbelief
> Blares oftener and soon, will soon be constant.
> Some harmonious skeptic soon in a skeptical music
>
> Will unite these figures of men and their shapes
> Will glisten again with motion, the music
> Will be motion and full of shadows.

Stevens himself considered 'that *Harmonium* was a better book than *Ideas of Order*, notwithstanding the fact that *Ideas of Order* probably contains a small group of poems better than anything in *Harmonium*.'[1] This is a fair assessment: the second volume does not have the prodigal richness, the extraordinary midsummer brilliance of the first, but the handful of poems I have singled out are marked by a firmness, an austerity and a compassion that do indeed make them 'better than anything in *Harmonium*'. Stevens did not fulfil the promise of future achievement that these poems hold for several more years. It was in 'Notes toward a Supreme Fiction', which appeared in 1942, that the 'harmonious skeptic' found his full voice, in a long poem of astonishing range and scale whose music is at last 'motion and full of shadows'. Meanwhile there was no fallow period such as had succeeded *Harmonium* but a torrent of new poems, long ones and short ones, failures and successes, trials and errors.

These seven years (1935-42) of prolific experiment are the hardest part of Stevens's poetic career to plot. Like a river split by swamps into many nameless streams before emerging as its single self, his course seems for a time diffuse and uncertain of its proper direction. *Owl's Clover*, a group of five large and luxuriant poems more or less political in intention, appeared in 1936, to be followed by a dry exercise in aesthetics, 'The Man With the Blue Guitar', in 1937; and both were preceded, accompanied and followed by a mass of shorter compositions, only some of which appeared as the sixty-three poems of *Parts of a World* in 1942. The whole period is prefigured in the oddest piece in *Ideas of Order*. 'Like Decorations in a Nigger Cemetery', written in 1934, looks like a long poem of fifty very short sections. In fact the sections make up no ordered whole, but simply coexist, with the random glitter and random pathos suggested by their title. The most that they have as a common theme is nothing more definite than the sense of human poverty and frailty which underlies all the positive 'ideas of order' in the book, and indeed all the positive and eventually much more complex affirmations that Stevens was ever to make. The very last section would make an epigraph to the whole of Stevens's work:

[1] Letter to Latimer, 5 November 1935.

Union of the weakest develops strength
Not wisdom. Can all men, together, avenge
One of the leaves that have fallen in autumn?
But the wise man avenges by building his city in snow.

Other sections gleam with the distinctive lustre of the Stevens
aphorism: one feels that these fragments are only one step removed
from the self-addressed pronouncements of his notebook. Here are
two about poetry and one about the poet:

XXV

From oriole to crow, note the decline
In music. Crow is realist. But, then,
Oriole, also, may be realist.

XXXII

Poetry is a finikin thing of air
That lives uncertainly and not for long
Yet radiantly beyond much lustier blurs.

XLVII

The sun is seeking something bright to shine on.
The trees are wooden, the grass is yellow and thin.
The ponds are not the surfaces it seeks.
It must create its colors out of itself.

'Like Decorations in a Nigger Cemetery' is not a poem, but it is a
fine if peculiar achievement; and it provides much evidence both of
the multifarious vitality of Stevens's mind at this time, and of his
own feeling, at an age when most poets have abandoned the struggle,
that most of what he had to do was still to come:

XLVIII

Music is not yet written but is to be.
The preparation is long and of long intent...

When a trade edition of *Ideas of Order* was published by Knopf in
1936, Stevens added three poems to the original Alcestis Press edition
of the year before. 'Farewell to Florida' Stevens placed at the beginning of the new book as if to emphasise his departure from the south,
the beguiling summer, of *Harmonium*: 'My North is leafless and lies
in a wintry slime...' This rather desperate and, for Stevens, un-

usually personal poem is, however, accompanied by a piece in
complete contrast to it, an exquisite appeal to 'the one of fictive
music', 'Ghosts as Cocoons', which Stevens placed second in the new
Ideas of Order. If reality, in all the dreariness of its poverty, must be
kept in mind, so must the possibility of the imagination's benediction,
'the bride' who answers need, 'a freshening of life'. Both are present
in the best of these three poems, and one of the best in the whole of
Ideas of Order, 'A Postcard from the Volcano'. This is Stevens's
'Afterwards', as beautiful as Hardy's poem, and even sadder. It is
about mortal imagination and mortal poetic effort in the face of ever-
lasting reality; it is also about the simple sadness of any man's death.
It deserves quotation in full not only because to cut it up is to destroy
it but because, like other short poems of rare excellence that stud
Stevens's career, it serves to refute two conclusions that are easily
jumped to. The first is that his real greatness is only to be found in
his long, difficult poems. The second, more pernicious, and common
among his American critics, is that the whole of his work constitutes
an amorphous body of ideas which it is permissible to treat as an
indivisible lump, and in which individual poems have no significant
identity and chronology no relevance. Partly to blame for both these
views is the fact that throughout his writing life Stevens published
poems which, though second-rate, have some bearing on his central
themes. But he also at all stages published more than enough first
rate short poems to make both conclusions untenable, and 'A Postcard
from the Volcano' is one of these:

> Children picking up our bones
> Will never know that these were once
> As quick as foxes on the hill;
>
> And that in autumn, when the grapes
> Made sharp air sharper by their smell
> These had a being, breathing frost;
>
> And least will guess that with our bones
> We left much more, left what still is
> The look of things, left what we felt
>
> At what we saw. The spring clouds blow
> Above the shuttered mansion-house,
> Beyond our gate and the windy sky

Cries out a literate despair.
We knew for long the mansion's look
And what we said of it became

A part of what it is...Children,
Still wearing budded aureoles,
Will speak our speech and never know,

Will say of the mansion that it seems
As if he that lived there left behind
A spirit storming in blank walls,

A dirty house in a gutted world,
A tatter of shadows peaked to white,
Smeared with the gold of the opulent sun.

The frailty of human significance, of the 'finikin thing of air', and the love with which the poet 'builds his city in snow' are as perfectly expressed here as anywhere in Stevens.

7
1935-1942

The pressure of the contemporaneous from the time of the beginning of the World War to the present time has been constant and extreme. No one can have lived apart in a happy oblivion...We are preoccupied with events, even when we do not observe them closely. We have a sense of upheaval. We feel threatened. We look from an uncertain present toward a more uncertain future. One feels the desire to collect oneself against all this in poetry as well as in politics.

This passage comes from 'The Irrational Element in Poetry', a short paper which Stevens, who called it 'a more or less casual commentary', read at Harvard in December 1936,[1] filling it out with readings from *Owl's Clover*. Both the lecture, Stevens's first effort of this kind, and the poems, which had appeared as a slim volume earlier in the year, attempt to face squarely the bleak and violent realities of the mid-thirties, apparently so unpropitious for the poet and for poetry. The first and best of the poems, he explained in the lecture, was prompted directly by 'the effect of the depression on the interest in art'.

I wanted a confronting of the world as it has been imagined in art and as it was then in fact. If I dropped into a gallery I found that I had no interest in what I saw. The air was charged with anxieties and tensions. To look at pictures there was the same thing as to play the piano in Madrid this afternoon.

Like the poem, 'The Old Woman and the Statue', to which they refer, these remarks are much more concerned with the plight of poetry in unfavourable circumstances than with the horrors of the circumstances themselves. But in Stevens's mind the two were not separable. In a world beset by social and political disintegration it did not seem to him that the collapse of the response to art was an insignificant

---

[1] It is wrongly dated 1937 in *Opus Posthumous*.

phenomenon, or one that the poet might ignore in favour of other, more obvious collapses. For, as usual with Stevens, a stock phrase like 'the response to art' does no more than brush the surface of what he meant by, what he hoped for, poetry. 'Art [is] a word that I have never used and never can use without some feeling of repugnance', he wrote with reference to this poem; and the statue which he called in the same letter[1] 'a symbol for art' becomes in the poem something larger, vaguer and more charged with meaning than his definition suggests. A group of marble horses in an autumn park, it is confronted by an old woman who is one of Stevens's most vivid figures of poverty:

> She was that tortured one,
> So destitute that nothing but herself
> Remained and nothing of herself except
> A fear too naked for her shadow's shape.

Her poverty is more than her own, more even than that of the grim American 'thirties. It is also the poverty of reality bare of sanctions and values. In her presence all that the statue held within itself dissolves:

> The mass of stone collapsed to marble hulk,
> Stood stiffly, as if the black of what she thought
> Conflicting with the moving colours there
> Changed them, at last, to its triumphant hue,
> Triumphant as that always upward wind
> Blowing among the trees its meaningless sound.

The desolation of this moment is the most successful thing in the whole of *Owl's Clover*. At this distance it does not seem hard to see that although 'The Old Woman and the Statue' is on one level 'about' the plight of poetry, its deeper levels of significance have directly to do with political and social menace and with the absence of sufficing belief. It is no less easy to see that the same is true of most of the best poems in *Ideas of Order* and one or two of the best poems in *Harmonium*. There were, nevertheless, those who did not see it at the time (there have been others since), and one or two of them certainly succeeded in upsetting Stevens.

[1] To Latimer, 5 November 1935.

Stanley Burnshaw, a young Marxist critic, reviewed *Ideas of Order* in a left-wing periodical *New Masses* in October 1935. Saying that *Harmonium* contained 'the kind of verse that people concerned with the murderous world collapse can hardly swallow today except in tiny doses', he called *Ideas of Order* 'the record of a man who, having lost his footing, now scrambles to stand up and keep his balance'. Stevens responded to this onslaught with 'Mr. Burnshaw and the Statue', the poem that became the second part of *Owl's Clover*. He wrote it with 'a good deal of trouble' that same October, intending in it to 'apply the point of view of a poet to Communism', and insisting nonetheless that his principal concern was 'not so much with the ideas as with the poetry of the thing'.[1] This last remark holds good for all his poems: it is as poems they were written and as poems they should be read. And if they fail, as 'Mr. Burnshaw and the Statue' fails, they fail as poems. Here for once the chosen subject, and perhaps also the heat of the moment, clouded Stevens's usual clarity of thought and feeling; 'Mr. Burnshaw' is turgid, obscure and incoherent. Written in thick rhetorical verse that recalls the worst passages of the first *Hyperion*, it achieves nothing whatever in the way of a satisfactory answer to Mr Burnshaw's complaints. Stevens was never happy about it and cut it drastically for the revised version of *Owl's Clover* which appeared in *The Man with the Blue Guitar* in 1937.

Meanwhile Mr Burnshaw was not alone in failing to see that his answer was in front of him, in work Stevens had already done. In March 1936 when Stevens was working on the last three *Owl's Clover* poems, Geoffrey Grigson attacked *Ideas of Order* in *New Verse* in a piece called 'The Stuffed Goldfinch'. Here the left-wing sledgehammer is garlanded with literary frills: Stevens is 'still the finicking privateer [of *Harmonium*], prosy Herrick, Klee without rhythm, observing nothing, single artificer of his own world of mannerism...He is dated between the two realities of the past and the future; that means, he is an 'imagist' emanation of a *dies non* we do not remember and do not bother to recall'. (This was the best that English criticism could do with Stevens in what is supposed to have been one of its finest hours.) Stevens produced no public reaction to these gems of perception, and his private comments on them reveal nothing more

[1] Letter to Latimer, 31 October 1935.

unexpected than that he was aware of his own inability to write 'political' poetry of the kind then fashionable in England. 'I am not a propagandist. Conceding that the social situation is the most absorbing thing in the world today...it is not possible for me, honestly, to take the point of view of a poet just out of school.'[1]

The trouble with *Owl's Clover* – and the three poems which complete it show no sustained improvement on 'Mr. Burnshaw' – is not in the least that it is written from a naive point of view. Rather the opposite: a highly sophisticated point of view and a technique of prolific subtlety are applied to subjects which one feels have been chosen rather than found and which are essentially too simple not to fall apart under the weight of Stevens's whole poetic intelligence. His own self-admonition: 'While poems may very well occur, they had very much better be caused', written early in 1935 just before *Owl's Clover* was begun, has been carried too far, into areas in which his particular gifts could only be misused. He thought at the time, for instance, that 'the specific subject' of the third poem, 'The Greenest Continent', was 'the white man in Africa...What I have been trying to do in the thing is to apply my own sort of poetry to such a subject. To What one reads in the papers.'[2] What happens in the poem is that the subject disappears almost completely beneath 'his own sort of poetry'; and when, four years later, he comes to explain this poem to Simons, one sees why:

It concerns the difficulty of imposing the imagination on those that do not share it. The idea of God is a thing of the imagination. We no longer think that God was, but was imagined. The idea of pure poetry, essential imagination, as the highest objective of the poet, appears to be, at least potentially, as great as the idea of God, and, for that matter, greater, if the idea of God is only one of the things of the imagination.[3]

In other words, the whole force of Stevens's central preoccupation was brought to bear on a subject which could not withstand its pressure (as the girl singing at Key West had withstood its pressure), and the result was a muddle. For – and this is the important point – in 1935–6 Stevens had not yet reached a stage at which he could

---

[1] Letter to Latimer, 17 March 1936.   [2] To Latimer, 6 February 1936.
[3] To Simons, 28 August 1940.

formulate this preoccupation with the clarity he had achieved by 1940, when he was working towards 'Notes toward a Supreme Fiction'. The occasional passage in *Owl's Clover* points forward to the distinctive world of 'Notes'. One such is the third section of 'The Greenest Continent', 'There was a heaven once':

> It was
> The spirit's episcopate, hallowed and high,
> To which the spirit ascended, to increase
> Itself, beyond the utmost increase come
> From youngest day or oldest night and far
> Beyond thought's regulation. There each man,
> Through long cloud-cloister-porches walked alone,
> Noble within perfecting solitude...

But this of course has left 'the white man in Africa... What one reads in the papers' far behind, and is not as yet part of a whole poem that can support and frame it.

In the long poetic journey that was to be 'The Whole of Harmonium' *Owl's Clover* is, then, an aberration, an almost fruitless detour that Stevens momentarily mistook for the right path. (He eventually realised this himself: it was the only major piece of work that he left out of his *Collected Poems* in 1954.) The nature of his mistake can be traced in 'The Irrational Element in Poetry'. Here he produces the following argument:

If it is true that the most abstract painters paint herrings and apples, it is no less true that the poets who most urgently search the world for the sanctions of life, for that which makes life so prodigiously worth living, may find their solutions in a duck in a pond or in the wind on a winter night... The only possible resistance to the pressure of the contemporaneous is a matter of herrings and apples or, to be less definite, the contemporaneous itself.

The flaw in this is the suggestion that herrings and apples, ducks and the wind, can be identified with 'the contemporaneous' in any political sense. They are part of reality: they are not part of that order of reality which in 1936 was represented by, say, the Depression and the Spanish Civil War. Herrings and apples, a girl singing by the sea, poverty itself, war itself (as 'Notes' was to show) could take the weight of Stevens's poetic preoccupations; war as a political issue, poverty as a political issue, 'what one reads in the papers' could not. Stevens must at some level have known this to have chosen herrings and apples as his examples of 'the contemporaneous itself'. And in the very next sentence after his duck and his winter wind he reverts suddenly to what is after all, and despite the justifications for *Owl's Clover*, the central theme of 'The Irrational Element in Poetry' as of his whole career: 'It is conceivable that a poet may arise of such scope that he can set the abstraction on which so much depends to music.'

On 12 December 1936, four days after this lecture was delivered, Stevens, in a letter to a sympathetic critic (Ben Belitt), came close to acknowledging his failure: 'What I tried to do in *Owl's Clover* was to dip aspects of the contemporaneous in the poetic. You seem to think that I have produced a lot of Easter eggs, and perhaps I have. We shall both have to wait to see what happens next.' What happened next was that three months later Stevens had almost finished a new long poem, completely different from *Owl's Clover* in both conception and execution. 'The Man with the Blue Guitar' marks a return to Stevens's central path, to the problem of setting 'the abstraction on which so much depends to music' – hence the guitar, and hence its blue, the blue of the imagination. 'What one reads in the papers' is abandoned in favour of herrings and apples, politics in favour of the whole real world with which the man without belief must struggle to construct a satisfactory relation. With this drastic paring and refining of ends, in the direction of the fundamental, goes an equally drastic paring and refining of means. 'The Man with the Blue Guitar', a series of thirty-three short poems in couplets with four stresses to the line, is written entirely without the luxuriant rhetoric of *Owl's Clover*. It is a poem of experiment and enquiry, its language economical and braced with careful thought, and it rises beside the ornate Gothic ruins of *Owl's Clover* like the steel skeleton of a clean new building. The building itself was not to be completed until 'Notes toward a Supreme Fiction': there is a fleshlessness about 'The Man with the Blue Guitar' that prevents it from being, as a whole, one of Stevens's best poems. But it is a remarkable piece of work in itself, and, one feels, an essential part of Stevens's preparation for the supreme poetic effort that was 'in limbo still'.

While he was writing it he told Latimer that the poems 'deal with the relation or balance between imagined things and real things, which...is a constant source of trouble to me...I have been trying to see the world about me both as I see it and as it is. This means seeing the world as an imaginative man sees it' (17 March 1937). In other words, as is almost always the case with Stevens, 'poetry is the subject of the poem', as a fine section already quoted begins. But, again characteristically, this by no means limits the poem's interest and significance to an area which some people would call that of 'mere aesthetics'. When Stevens glosses a section of 'The Man with the Blue Guitar' with the sentence: 'In short, the dull world is either its poets or nothing',[1] he seems to be being extravagant to the point of silliness. A gloss on another section makes the real situation clearer and shows how much more is involved in the poem's subject than reflection on the poet himself and his immediate problems. 'Poetry is the spirit, as the poem is the body...The validity of the poet as a figure of prestige to which he is entitled, is wholly a matter of this, that he adds to life that without which life cannot be lived, or is not worth living, or is without savor, or, in any case, would be altogether different from what it is today.'[2] And when we add to this the notebook remark: 'To study and to understand the fictive world is the function of the poet', it becomes plain once again that the poet's role, for Stevens, committed him to an enormous responsibility, and that in the shouldering of this responsibility 'the relation between imagined things and real things' inevitably became for him a matter of crucial importance. 'Poetry does not only mean verse...'

> The man bent over his guitar,
> A shearsman of sorts. The day was green.
>
> They said, 'You have a blue guitar,
> You do not play things as they are.'
>
> The man replied, 'Things as they are
> Are changed upon the blue guitar.'
>
> And they said then, 'But play, you must,
> A tune beyond us, yet ourselves,
>
> A tune upon the blue guitar
> Of things exactly as they are.'

[1] Letter to Simons, 9 August 1940.   [2] To Simons, 10 August 1940.

This, the first poem of the sequence, states the theme of the thirty-two poems that follow in the baldest possible terms. Reality unlit, untuned by the imagination is not enough: the green day must be played by a blue guitar. But the imagination must remain faithful to things as they are. As Stevens said in his notebook: 'The real is only the base. But it is the base.' In the rest of the poems this theme is revolved, enlarged upon, once or twice obscured by writing so economical that its density is impenetrable without the help of Stevens's own notes made for Simons in 1940.[1] The best sections have an astonishing firmness and clarity, as, for instance, here in section V:

> Day is desire and night is sleep.
> There are no shadows anywhere.
>
> The earth, for us, is flat and bare.
> There are no shadows. Poetry
>
> Exceeding music must take the place
> Of empty heaven and its hymns,
>
> Ourselves in poetry must take their place,
> Even in the chattering of your guitar.

(Observe the sharp effect of the word 'poetry' in the second couplet where the ear is expecting 'anywhere'.) The desolation of this earth to which poetry must restore its shadows, its third dimension of sufficient meaning, is echoed in the very last section (XXXIII) where poverty is contrasted with the blue guitar's tuning of apparently insignificant reality:

> Here is the bread of time to come,
>
> Here is its actual stone. The bread
> Will be our bread, the stone will be
>
> Our bed and we shall sleep by night.
> We shall forget by day, except
>
> The moments when we choose to play
> The imagined pine, the imagined jay.

---

[1] Simons was a critic whose essay on 'The Comedian as the Letter C' Stevens found so sympathetic that he was prepared to annotate both *Owl's Clover* and 'The Man with the Blue Guitar' for him in correspondence. Simons died in 1945.

The claim made for the imagination in the whole of 'The Man with the Blue Guitar' is vast; but it is also humble. What it can achieve is a matter not of extreme people in extreme situations but of what Stevens called 'the normal'.[1] A fine poem (XIV) sets the individual imagination confronting ordinary things beside the grandeurs of the reason. In his gloss[2] Stevens said: 'I don't know that one is ever going to get at the secret of the world through the sciences...It may be that the little candle of the imagination is all we need. In the brilliance of modern intelligence, one realizes that, for all that, the secret of the world is as great a secret as it ever was.'

> First one beam, then another, then
> A thousand are radiant in the sky...
>
> One says a German chandelier –
> A candle is enough to light the world.
>
> It makes it clear. Even at noon
> It glistens in essential dark.
>
> At night, it lights the fruit and wine,
> The book and bread, things as they are,
>
> In a chiaroscuro where
> One sits and plays the blue guitar.

In this section there is an intimation of comfort, a glimpse of the reconciliation between the imagination and reality, blue and green, that gleams fitfully throughout the poem. Only once does the underlying search, and the deep emotion with which Stevens pursues 'whatever it is he seeks', emerge fully. This is in the short section XX:

> What is there in life except one's ideas,
> Good air, good friend, what is there in life?
>
> Is it ideas that I believe?
> Good air, my only friend, believe,
>
> Believe would be a brother full
> Of love, believe would be a friend,

---

[1] 'For myself, the inaccessible jewel is the normal and all of life, in poetry, is the difficult pursuit of just that'. Letter to Church, 21 January 1946.
[2] To Simons, 10 August 1940.

Friendlier than my only friend,
Good air. Poor pale, poor pale guitar...

And the next section reiterates in a new way that it is 'ourselves in poetry' that must take the place 'of empty heaven and its hymns'.

A substitute for all the gods:
This self, not that gold self aloft...

One's self and the mountains of one's land,

Without shadows, without magnificence,
The flesh, the bone, the dirt, the stone.[1]

It is not surprising to find Stevens saying of these sections: 'Only the ones over which I take a great deal of trouble come through finally.'[2] To have written this long poem of spare exactness so soon after the even longer and not at all exact *Owl's Clover* must have cost him a considerable effort of concentration and reorientation. 'The Man with the Blue Guitar' itself was not the only fruit of this effort. The return to the central path of his poetry and the making explicit of so much that had been latent in *Harmonium* and *Ideas of Order* resulted at first in this skeletal announcement of a theme and some of its implications. But 'The Man with the Blue Guitar' was the framework upon which much of what was to follow was built and, bare as it was, the difficult writing of it pulled Stevens's mind together in preparation for the full blooded poetic enterprise of 'Notes toward a Supreme Fiction'.

'Notes' was completed and published in the summer of 1942. In the five years that elapsed between 'The Man with the Blue Guitar' and this, his next long poem, Stevens wrote a large number of shorter poems, most of which were published as *Parts of a World* in the same year as 'Notes'. Many of these poems can be read as preliminary sketches for 'Notes', although the best of them of course have a self-contained life of their own. The familiar themes recur: poverty and the search for a reconciling belief, obdurate reality with its moments of consolation and its lasting insufficiency, the great demand made on the imaginative man and his poetry. And from this last theme is

[1] This seems to me one of the rare occasions on which Kermode misreads Stevens (*Wallace Stevens*, p. 69).
[2] To Latimer, 17 March 1937.

developed, tentatively and from a variety of directions, a new one, the idea of the hero who in 'Notes' is called 'major man'. This figure has caused almost as much confusion among Stevens's critics as the supreme fiction itself. But unless one wishes on Stevens some sort of philosophical rigour that he would never have dreamed of taking upon himself, there need be no fearsome problem about either. In this middle period of Stevens's career, when he was experimenting with the poetry of his ideas in a multitude of different ways, it is more than ever necessary to allow each poem its own identity and not to look for rational, paraphrasable consistency where nothing of the kind was intended. This being said and borne in mind, it neverthe-less remains true that Stevens is, more than most, a poet whose poems almost infinitely throw light upon each other, and also that, in the fundamentals of his work, some tactful critical help may circumvent for the reader one or two serious misunderstandings.

The most important thing to realise about Stevens's idea of the hero is that it has very little to do with the heroic in any ordinary sense. The indistinct vision that occupied the centre of Stevens's mind in these years was not an image of a concrete superhuman individual but rather an intuition of something abstract, human and universal, something to do with the self, each self, ourselves, and yet something not at all implying solipsism, for Stevens could not have been more strongly conscious of the absolute existence of the real world outside the self. These terms are deliberately vague: more harm than good is done to the poems by attempts to define what Stevens was so careful to create without definition. The first mani-festation of this vision is one of the vaguest. It is the passage already quoted from the third poem of *Owl's Clover* where:

> each man,
> Through long cloud-cloister-porches, walked alone...
> And there he heard the voices that were once
> The confusion of men's voices, intricate
> Made extricate by meanings, meanings made
> Into music never touched to sound.

In his gloss on this, written (like the others on *Owl's Clover*) four years later when his vision had become clearer, Stevens said: 'The extreme poet will produce a poem equivalent to the idea of God.

The extreme poet will be as concerned with a knowledge of man as people are now concerned with a knowledge of God.'[1] The gloss announces that the heaven described in *Owl's Clover*, the heaven of the knowledge of God, must be replaced with the knowledge of man, on earth; but the words of the poem disclose that the one is, as it were, the model for the other. The passage in *Owl's Clover*, that is to say, hardly refers to 'empty heaven and its hymns' but to something human that can perhaps be found again. The order in its words is echoed in an image that closes a poem in *Parts of a World*, 'Connoisseur of Chaos':

> The pensive man...He sees that eagle float
> For which the intricate Alps are a single nest.

Only man and his own world are suggested here.

In 'The Man with the Blue Guitar' we have seen a different fore-shadowing of the idea of the hero, but one that also connects each man walking alone with a reconciling belief. 'Believe would be a brother full of love'; and the section is joined by Stevens's dots...to the beginning of the next:

> A substitute for all the gods:
> This self, not that gold self aloft.

The strange and not wholly successful poem 'A Thought Revolved', which was published with 'The Man with the Blue Guitar' in 1937, turns upon a firmer conception of the hero, one that is indeed perhaps too explicit for the poem's good:

> He sought an earthly leader who could stand
> Without panache, without cockade,
> Son only of man and sun of men,
> The outer captain, the inner saint.

But earlier in the same poem there is a fine passage concerning the modern poet and his need for the idea of the hero; and this passage stresses both the abstract nature of the 'earthly leader' and his ambiguous relation to 'empty heaven'. ('He' is the poet.)

> One man, the idea of man, that is the space,
> The true abstract in which he promenades.

[1] To Simons, 28 August 1940.

The era of the idea of man, the cloak
And speech of Virgil dropped, that's where he walks,
That's where his hymns come crowding, hero-hymns...
Hymns of the struggle of the idea of god
And the idea of man, the mystic garden and
The middling beast, the garden of paradise
And he that created the garden and peopled it.

The poet walking in a world no longer divinely ordered, attempting to
make of it music that will somehow bring meaning into its poverty;
paradoxical man, the 'middling beast' who created paradise and
peopled it: these ideas with their vast and various implications were
often to recur in later and better poems.

In *Parts of a World*, next to the great 'Of Modern Poetry' quoted
at the beginning of this book, is a poem rather obscurely called 'Man
and Bottle' which gives these ideas another and more haunting shape:

> The mind is the great poem of winter, the man,
> Who, to find what will suffice,
> Destroys romantic tenements
> Of rose and ice
>
> In the land of war. More than the man, it is
> A man with the fury of a race of men,
> A light at the centre of many lights,
> A man at the centre of men.

Parts of a World is, among other things, Stevens's book of war poems
(although his best war poem is 'Notes toward a Supreme Fiction'
itself). Here is no direct confrontation with political issues such as
he attempted without success in *Owl's Clover*. It is rather that the
presence of the war is everywhere felt as a terrible accentuation of
the meaningless poverty that had for so long been the constant background to the workings of Stevens's imagination. Those who com-
plain that he should have taken more notice of the horrifying events
that were shaking the world at this time have failed to see that behind
all his work, behind his search for a saving belief and the perseverance
with which he used his mind and his imagination to find or make
'what will suffice', lay a compassion and an honesty that were the
very opposite of complacent. The miseries of the Depression and of

Europe in 1940 did not have to jolt Stevens out of one set of ideas
and into another; they confirmed him in a sadness and a resolution
that he had long ago arrived at from within himself. It should not be
forgotten that in 1939 he was sixty years old, and a sane and wise man
by any standards. His response to the war was not something new
but something evolved from what was already old and familiar in
his way of thought. When he wrote a short poem called 'Idiom of
the Hero' in a time mangled by dictators and deafened by their
hysterical simplicities this is what emerged:

> I heard two workers say, 'This chaos
> Will soon be ended'.
>
> This chaos will not be ended,
> The red and the blue house blended,
>
> Not ended, never and never ended,
> The weak man mended,
>
> The man that is poor at night
> Attended
>
> Like the man that is rich and right.
> The great men will not be blended...[1]
>
> I am the poorest of all.
> I know that I cannot be mended,
>
> Out of the clouds, pomp of the air,
> By which at least I am befriended.

This hero, whose idiom is the language of humility and anonymity,
is the very antithesis of the political hero

> of him whom none believe,
> Whom all believe that all believe,

as Stevens had written in the tenth section of 'The Man with the
Blue Guitar'. 'In the land of war' it is not in the world of action and
politics that Stevens seeks his hero, his figure of hope, but in the
mind, and the mind must be closed to nothing.

Again and again in different poems in *Parts of a World* the questing

---

[1] Stevens's ellipsis.

mind, 'Tired of the old descriptions of the world' as Stevens puts it in 'The Latest Freed Man', is seen struggling towards a relation with reality that will satisfy its need for meaning and yet will exclude nothing. The moments when reality by itself appears at its most beneficent no longer satisfy because they do exclude something. The water, the bowl, the flowers of 'The Poems of Our Climate' do not suffice because 'There would still remain the never-resting mind'; the promise of the beautiful poem 'The Well Dressed Man with a Beard', 'One thing remaining, infallible', quails before the desolation of its final line: 'It can never be satisfied, the mind, never.' And in 'Landscape with Boat' there is a remarkable portrait of Stevens's private anti-hero, 'An anti-master-man, floribund ascetic', who reaches what he supposes to be the truth by excluding not 'the never-resting mind' but reality itself,

> By rejecting what he saw
> And denying what he heard. He would arrive.
> He had only not to live, to walk in the dark,
> To be projected by one void into
> Another...
>   He never supposed
> That he might be truth, himself, or part of it,
> That the things he rejected might be part
> And the irregular turquoise, part, the perceptible blue
> Grown denser, part, the eye so touched, so played
> Upon by clouds, the ear so magnified
> By thunder, parts, and all these things together,
> Parts, and more things, parts. He never supposed divine
> Things might not look divine, nor that if nothing
> Was divine then all things were, the world itself...

'Landscape with Boat' is not a distinguished poem. It is as if Stevens, having arrived with sudden clarity at an idea of immense importance to himself, had simply allowed himself to write it down as fast and as lucidly as possible. But it is one of the key poems of *Parts of a World*. From it the book's title is derived, and in it Stevens makes his most explicit denial that the object of his own search is 'the truth' in any exclusive or strictly philosophical sense. What he was looking for in his poems, in all his attempts to find a satisfactory relation, a balance, between the imagination and reality, was not 'the truth' but something else, 'what will suffice' or, as we have seen him calling this something in another *Parts of a World* poem,[1] 'the chants of final peace...the acutest end of speech'. In this search the dual realisation that exclusive truth was not its object, and that in its course 'things as they are' should never be transcended in the supposition that beyond them lies some ultimate end, was crucial; and its momentousness accounts for the air of excitement that pervades 'Landscape with Boat'. In a much better poem with the title 'On the Road Home', this excitement is controlled and subdued, but given more moving form:

> It was when I said,
> 'There is no such thing as the truth',
> That the grapes seemed fatter.
> The fox ran out of his hole.
>
> You...You said,
> 'There are many truths,
> But they are not parts of a truth.'
> Then the tree, at night, began to change,
>
> Smoking through green and smoking blue.
> We were two figures in a wood.
> We said we stood alone.
>
> It was when I said,
> 'Words are not forms of a single word.
> In the sum of the parts, there are only the parts.
> The world must be measured by eye';
>
> It was when you said,
> 'The idols have seen lots of poverty,
> Snakes and gold and lice,
> But not the truth';
>
> It was at that time, that the silence was largest
> And longest, the night was roundest,
> The fragrance of the autumn warmest,
> Closest and strongest.

[1] 'Extracts from Addresses to the Academy of Fine Ideas'.

The 'anti-master-man, floribund ascetic' of 'Landscape with Boat' recalls Emerson, or at least Emerson as criticised by Santayana for supposing that 'The lights of life must be extinguished that the light of the absolute may shine, and the possession of everything in general must be secured by the surrender of everything in particular.' ('He had only not to live, to walk in the dark...'). This passage, like others in *Interpretations of Poetry and Religion*, may well have lain permanently in Stevens's mind at a level too deep for the word 'influence' to apply. It is perhaps not too far-fetched to suggest that, on a similarly obscure level, the person addressed in 'On the Road Home' may be, however remotely, Santayana. When, as we have seen in 'To an Old Philosopher in Rome', Stevens finally reached the end of his road, it was certainly Santayana whom he found there.

In any case, by defining as they do what the object of Stevens's search was not, these two poems help us to see more clearly not, yet, what that object was, but that it was in the poems about his hero, the anonymous human figure immersed in things as they are, that Stevens was tentatively feeling his way towards it. 'Feeling' is the right word: feeling in Stevens's work is not often without some element of thought, but thought is never without a strong element of feeling. If one can bear this in mind when considering his idea of the hero, one is more than half way towards grasping it. The longest poem in *Parts of a World* and the one with which Stevens chose to end the volume, is a meditation on this idea called 'Examination of the Hero in a Time of War'. This is not as a whole one of the most successful of Stevens's longer poems: the promise of clarity in the title is not fulfilled, and several of the sixteen sections are marred by the same kind of arbitrary, almost perverse extravagance of language that had been carried to extremes in 'The Comedian as the Letter C' and *Owl's Clover*. There are passages, nevertheless, when the right words are found, when the complex of thought and feeling surrounding the figure of the hero comes to order and is simultaneously expressed and described:

> It is not an image. It is a feeling.
> There is no image of the hero.
> There is a feeling as definition.
> How could there be an image, an outline,

A design, a marble soiled by pigeons?
The hero is a feeling, a man seen
As if the eye was an emotion...
        Instead of allegory,
We have and are the man, capable
Of his brave quickenings, the human
Accelerations that seem inhuman. (XII)

And the last section has, in an image of peculiar and memorable grandeur, a sudden touch of Stevens at his most powerful and assured:

Each false thing ends. The bouquet of summer
Turns blue and on its empty table
It is stale and the water is discolored.
True autumn stands then in the doorway.
After the hero, the familiar
Man makes the hero artificial.
But was the summer false? The hero?
How did we come to think that autumn
Was the veritable season, that familiar
Man was the veritable man? So
Summer, jangling the savagest diamonds and
Dressed in its azure-doubled crimsons,
May truly bear its heroic fortunes
For the large, the solitary figure.

These lines, which were written in 1941, close *Parts of a World*. The next year, in 'Notes toward a Supreme Fiction', Stevens was to bring together many of the discoveries he had made in the course of writing all his previous poems. Of these discoveries his idea of the hero was one of the most important in the path that led to 'Notes', despite the fact that in the whole of that poem this idea plays only a subsidiary part. It is only destructive of the poems in which he exists to attempt too close a description of Stevens's hero, as Stevens very well knew: 'There is a feeling as definition'. It may nevertheless throw a little light on a much misunderstood idea to suggest that what is recorded in the last section of 'Examination of the Hero' is at least akin to something that in the past would have been called a moment of grace, a moment, even of revelation. It is a moment of perception that brings with it a sense of certainty and a sense of comfort, and both are found, if only for a moment, in the course of a search that is nothing if not a search for belief. We are here in an area calling for the utmost tact, where anything firmer than a suggestion would be out of place. But the reader of Stevens cannot afford to forget altogether the size of the issues at stake in this extraordinary poet's work. What I am suggesting, and no more than suggesting, is that it may not be inappropriate to relate the significance of Stevens's figure of the hero to the significance once contained in a figure that Stevens had rejected for himself long ago when the woman in 'Sunday Morning' heard

> A voice that cries, 'The tomb in Palestine
> Is not the porch of spirits lingering.
> It is the grave of Jesus, where he lay.'

The suggestion is strengthened by a remarkable passage in 'Extracts from Addresses to the Academy of Fine Ideas'. This, written the year before 'Examination of the Hero', is the poem which we have already seen to contain one of Stevens's most exquisite descriptions of the blessed balance between imagination and reality, the mind and things as they are. In an earlier section of the poem, a female figure, perhaps *Harmonium*'s 'one of fictive music', and the figure of the hero are placed side by side, almost as interchangeable alternatives. They are nothing more definite than figures of hope in the frightening confusion of the bereft world. But behind them, as the close of the passage reveals, is the nostalgia, the overwhelming sadness, with which Stevens looks back to the sustaining figures of the old world:

> The lean cats of the arches of the churches,
> That's the old world. In the new, all men are priests.
>
> They preach and they are preaching in a land
> To be described. They are preaching in a time
> To be described. Evangelists of what?
> If they could gather their theses into one,
> Collect their thoughts together into one,
> Into a single thought, thus: into a queen,
> An intercessor by innate rapport,
> Or into a dark-blue king, *un roi tonnerre*,

Whose merely being was his valiance,
Panjandrum and central heart and mind of minds –
If they could! Or is it the multitude of thoughts,
Like insects in the depths of the mind, that kill
The single thought? The multitudes of men
That kill the single man, starvation's head,
One man, their bread and their remembered wine?

Nostalgia means the pain of longing for the return home; but Stevens knew that the road home lay for him not backwards towards the arches of the churches, but forwards and in his own poems. 'There is no difference between god and his temple' he wrote in his notebook; and also 'Poetry is a purging of the world's poverty and change and evil and death. It is a present perfecting, a satisfaction in the irremediable poverty of life.' If sometimes one is reminded by Stevens's own poems that for many centuries something else would have stood as the subject of these sentences, one is recognising only that these poems were written from and for a part of himself that man perhaps ignores at his peril.

8
'Notes toward a Supreme Fiction'
(1)

Make-belief is an enervating exercise of fancy not to be confused with imaginative growth. The saner and greater mythologies are not fancies; they are the utterance of the whole soul of man and, as such, inexhaustible to meditation. They are no amusement or diversion to be sought as a relaxation and an escape from the hard realities of life. They are these hard realities in projection, their symbolic recognition, co-ordination and acceptance... Without his mythologies man is only a cruel animal without a soul – for a soul is a central part of his governing mythology – he is a congeries of possibilities without order and without aim. . .

The waning of any one mode of order – a traditional morality, or a religious sanction or symbolization for it – is not the loss of all possibilities of order. The traditional schemas by which man gave an account of himself and the world in which he lived were made by him, and though they have lost their power to help him as they formerly helped him, he has not lost his power to make new ones...

To put the burden of constituting an order for our minds on the poet may seem unfair. It is not the philosopher, however, or the moralist who puts it on him, but birth. And it is only another aspect of the drift by which knowledge in all its varieties – scientific, moral, religious – has come to seem a vast mythology with its sub-orders divided according to their different pragmatic sanctions, that the poet should thus seem to increase so inordinately in importance...For while any part of the world-picture is regarded as not of mythopoeic origin, poetry – earlier recognized as mythopoeic – could not but be given a second place. If philosophic contemplation, or religious experience, or science gave us Reality, then poetry gave us something of less consequence, at best some sort of shadow. If we grant that all is myth, poetry, as the myth-making which most brings 'the whole soul of man into activity'...becomes the necessary channel for the reconstitution of order.

...the study of poetry, for those born in this age, is more arduous than we suppose. It is therefore rare. Many other things pass by its name and are encouraged to its detriment...[Its positive task should be] to recall that poetry is the supreme use of language, man's chief co-ordinating instrument, in the service of the most integral purposes of life; and to explore, with thoroughness, the intricacies of the modes of language as working modes of the mind.

These passages are from I. A. Richards's book *Coleridge on Imagination*[1] which was published in 1934. Stevens certainly read this book, and almost certainly read it in the winter of 1941 when he was preparing his lecture 'The Noble Rider and the Sound of Words'.[2] Stevens took immense pains over this task. 'No one would suppose', he wrote to Simons afterwards (8 July 1941), 'from that paper what a lot of serious reading it required preceding it, and how much time it took.' In it he collected together and ordered in his idiosyncratic luminous prose much of the thought and feeling that had been variously developing in his poems since *Owl's Clover* and that in the following year were to find a new and more complete form in 'Notes toward a Supreme Fiction'. Though Richards's book is not mentioned by name in 'The Noble Rider' it is four times referred to indirectly and twice actually quoted. The phrases 'inexhaustible to meditation' and 'poetry is the supreme use of language' are attributed to Richards and can come from nowhere else. It is clear, even from the brief samples quoted above, that the book was the most appropriate possible grist to Stevens's mill at this time, not so much for its analyses of Coleridge's abstruse disquisitions, which were probably quite unfamiliar to Stevens, as for the attention it drew to the poet's use of words in relation to 'the truth' and for the vast breadth of the challenge it threw down for the modern poet.

In Stevens's letters of 1940, the year before 'The Noble Rider', one can see him moving towards the very ideas that he found formulated in more elaborate and cautious but no less fundamental terms in Richards's book. As a by-product of a gloss on an obscure section of *Owl's Clover* he wrote to Simons:

If one no longer believes in God (as truth), it is not possible merely to disbelieve; it becomes necessary to believe in something else. Logically, I ought to believe in essential imagination, but that has its difficulties. It is easier to believe in a thing created by the imagination...In one of [my

[1] Pages 171–2, 226–8, 230.   [2] Delivered at Princeton in May 1941.

recent poems] I say that one's final belief must be in a fiction. Yet the state-
statement seems a negation, or, rather, a paradox. (28 August 1940.)

The poem referred to is 'Asides on the Oboe', one of the best pieces
in *Parts of a World*, where Stevens's hero is God himself, as a manifestation of the paradox of belief in a fiction, and as a figure of the
supreme poet who gives, by accurate making, what human significance it has to the meaningless world.

> If you say on the hautboy man is not enough,
> Can never stand as god, is ever wrong
> In the end, however naked, tall, there is still
> The impossible possible philosophers' man,
> The man who has had the time to think enough,
> The central man, the human globe, responsive
> As a mirror with a voice, the man of glass,
> Who in a million diamonds sums us up.
>
> He is the transparence of the place in which
> He is and in his poems we find peace.
> He sets this peddler's pie and cries in summer,
> The glass man, cold and numbered, dewily cries,
> 'Thou art not August unless I make thee so.'

One can guess with what delighted recognition Stevens must have
read Richards's book, with its insistence upon the soul as 'a central
part of a man's mythology' and on poetry as 'the supreme use of
language, man's chief co-ordinating instrument'. Here he found a long
and careful discussion of the nature of words and the nature of the
poet's use of them, starting from Coleridge's remark: 'The sense of
musical delight, with the power of producing it, is a gift of the
imagination', and culminating in a quotation from Coleridge's letter
of 1827 to the young James Gillman:

It is the fundamental mistake of grammarians and writers on the philosophy
of grammar and language, to suppose that words and their syntaxis are the
immediate representatives of *things*, or that they correspond to *things*. Words
correspond to thoughts, and the legitimate order and connection of words,
to the *laws* of thinking and to the acts and affections of the thinker's mind.

Or, one might say, 'He sets this peddler's pie[1] and cries in summer, . . .
"Thou art not August unless I make thee so." '

When, in another letter of 1940 (15 October), Stevens was setting
out for his friend Henry Church his ideas about the Chair of Poetry
Church was considering founding, he used this line from 'Asides on
the Oboe' to illustrate what he meant by 'the subject-matter of
poetry'. This subject-matter, he went on,

> is the aspects of the world and of men and women that have been added to
> them by poetry...While aesthetic ideas are commonplaces in this field, its
> import is not the import of the superficial. The major poetic idea in the world
> is and always has been the idea of God. One of the visible movements of the
> modern imagination is the movement away from the idea of God. The poetry
> that created the idea of God will either adapt it to our different intelligence,
> or create a substitute for it, or make it unnecessary. These alternatives prob-
> ably mean the same thing, but the intention is not to foster a cult. The
> knowledge of poetry is a part of philosophy, and a part of science; the import
> of poetry is the import of the spirit. The figures of the essential poets should
> be spiritual figures.

In his private turning over of these ideas Stevens must have found in
Richards a kindred mind with a kindred view of reality and the
imagination and a kindred hope for poetry. Indeed it is Richards's
absence from Stevens's suggestions as to possible holders of Church's
Chair – a project which eventually came to nothing – that leads one
to suppose that he read *Coleridge on Imagination* after rather than before
he wrote this memorandum. (The people he does suggest are
Santayana, 'although in him the religious and the philosophic are
too dominant', and Eliot, 'except that I regard him as a negative
rather than a positive force'.)

A few months later in 'The Noble Rider and The Sound of Words'
itself, the corroborative presence of Richards, and Coleridge as
interpreted by Richards, is obvious. Stevens first explores the loss of
meaning in the modern world of old figures of nobility. These are
symbols that he uses to narrow and reveal what Richards calls
'waning modes of order'. The examples Stevens chooses are Plato's
winged horses, and 'the noble rider' himself, Verrocchio's Bartolomeo

---

1 'Peddler's pie' cf. Pedlar's French: 'rogues' and thieves' cant, hence unintelligible
jargon' – *OED*.

Colleoni, who is a further appearance of the heroic statue of *Owl's Clover* and the 'Examination of the Hero in a Time of War' which was written in this same year.

> How could there be an image, an outline,
> A design, a marble soiled by pigeons?

Towards the end of the lecture, when Stevens reaches the second aspect of his subject, 'the sound of words', what he has to say has clearly been given strength and form by his reading of Richards's book, as even the two short Coleridge quotations above show. Here is Stevens; and the personal commitment and passion that one feels everywhere behind his prose are none the weaker for the support he has received.

I do not know of anything that will appear to have suffered more from the passage of time than the music of poetry and that has suffered less. The deepening need for words to express our thoughts and feelings which, we are sure, are all the truth that we shall ever experience, having no illusions, makes us listen to words when we hear them, loving them and feeling them, makes us search the sound of them, for a finality, a perfection, an unalterable vibration, which it is only within the power of the acutest poet to give them. Those of us who may have been thinking of the path of poetry, those who understand that words are thoughts and not only our own thoughts but the thoughts of men and women ignorant of what it is that they are thinking, must be conscious of this: that, above everything else, poetry is words...A poet's words are of things that do not exist without the words.

This view of words, and of the poet's use of them, of course does not at all imply either a neglect of reality's absolute existence or a denial of the imagination's dependence on it. Indeed, one of the most important themes of 'The Noble Rider', as of 'Notes' itself, is the interdependence, the proper balance or marriage, of reality and the imagination. Once this theme, by now a highly-developed axiom of Stevens's mind, is fully grasped, many of the hardest passages of 'Notes' lose their difficulty and 'a supreme fiction' itself is seen to be something whose very fabrication depends upon this balance or marriage. Here is the theme as it appears in 'The Noble Rider': The 'possible poet', Stevens says, will have 'to come to a decision regarding the imagination and reality; and he will find that it is not a choice of one over the other and not a decision that divides them, but something subtler, a recognition that here, too, as between these poles, the universal interdependence exists, and hence his choice and his decision must be that they are equal and inseparable.' Enlarging upon this as the lecture progresses, Stevens insists that 'the subject-matter of poetry' is not non-human reality in its barren poverty but 'the life that is lived in the scene that it composes', or, as he had put it in the memorandum to Church, 'what comes to mind when one says of the month of August "Thou art not August, unless I make thee so." ' The example he uses in 'The Noble Rider' is Wordsworth's 'Upon Westminster Bridge', saying of it, 'This illustration must serve for all the rest. There is, in fact, a world of poetry indistinguishable from the world in which we live.'

The choice of Wordsworth to demonstrate how, by achieving a perfect balance between reality and his own imagination, the poet may 'help people to live their lives', was more appropriate than perhaps Stevens realised. There is no evidence to show that he was particularly well acquainted with the work of either Wordsworth or Coleridge, except through Richards's book, and no cause to disbelieve his own denial of 'influence' by either of them. They, and no other poet so fully as they, had nevertheless covered much of the same ground as Stevens had covered for himself, and they had covered it for the same reasons. Though each of them in quite different ways later adopted a Christian structure for his thought and feeling, each had once observed himself as a solitary modern poet exerting like Stevens his own imagination against the pressure of reality to make some sufficient sense of the world in which he found himself. Stevens's notion of 'a supreme fiction' would probably have struck each of them as blasphemous or incomprehensible or in some other way intolerable. But Stevens's foundation for his supreme fiction, the interdependence, the marriage, of reality and the imagination, was an idea at which each of them had arrived by a personal process parallel to Stevens's own. And because the words they chose to express their discovery are already familiar, it is worth recalling them to show not only that Stevens was not isolated in speculation bearing only on his own poetry, but also that he was right to attribute to the poet the power of creating in his words 'things that do not exist without the words'.

How much of what everyone since has felt to be the substance of the word 'imagination' was put into existence by such a passage as this:

> O Lady! we receive but what we give
> And in our life alone does Nature live:
> Ours is her wedding garment, ours her shroud!
>   And would we aught behold, of higher worth,
> Than that inanimate cold world allowed
> To the poor loveless ever-anxious crowd,
>   Ah! from the soul itself must issue forth
> A light, a glory, a fair luminous cloud
>   Enveloping the Earth –
> And from the soul itself must there be sent
>   A sweet and potent voice, of its own birth,
> Of all sweet sounds the life and element!...
>
> Joy, Lady! is the spirit and the power,
> Which wedding Nature to us gives in dower
> A new Earth and a new Heaven...[1]

This marriage, the image Coleridge here uses to explain to his beloved Sara Hutchinson what he means by his 'shaping spirit of Imagination', now lost, was an idea of central importance to Wordsworth. He developed it, no doubt partly under Coleridge's influence, throughout the great years of his poetic career. One can see it fore-shadowed in 'Tintern Abbey' (1798), where his 'sense sublime' of a mysterious power that 'rolls through all things' has to do with his contemplating nature not by itself but in conjunction with 'The still, sad music of humanity', and yet does not lead him to abandon reality but rather to renew his devotion to it:

> Therefore am I still
> A lover of the meadows and the woods,
> And mountains; and of all that we behold
> From this green earth.

Seven years later Wordsworth devoted two whole books of *The Prelude* (XI–XII 'Imagination, How Impaired and Restored') to describing how he pulled himself out of an exclusive infatuation with reality in which he 'rejoiced To lay the inner faculties asleep', and eventually

---

[1] From 'Dejection: An Ode' (1802).

achieved a state of mind from which he could feel, almost in Coleridge's words,

> That from thyself it is that thou must give,
> Else never canst receive.

He concludes Book XII with a direct reference to Coleridge's companionship, discovered at the end of 'that lonesome journey', and sums up his new-found optimism and sense of purpose for his poetry in these words:

> I seem'd about this period to have sight
> Of a new world, a world too, that was fit
> To be transmitted and made visible
> To other eyes, as having for its base
> That whence our dignity originates,
> That which both gives it being and maintains
> A balance, an ennobling interchange
> Of action from within and from without,
> The excellence, pure spirit, and best power
> Both of the object seen, and eye that sees.

If Stevens knew this passage, he could not have chosen an apter text to illuminate some crucial sentences in 'The Noble Rider' where he expresses his own sense of purpose, the purpose that he was to attempt to fulfil in 'Notes':

About nobility I cannot be sure that the decline, not to say the disappearance of nobility is anything more than a maladjustment between the imagination and reality. We have been a little insane about the truth. We have had an obsession. In its ultimate extension, the truth about which we have been insane will lead us to look beyond the truth to something in which the imagination will be the dominant complement. It is not only that the imagination adheres to reality, but, also, that reality adheres to the imagination and that the interdependence is essential. We may emerge from our *bassesse* and, if we do, how would it happen if not by the intervention of some fortune of the mind?

The parallel between Wordsworth and Stevens may be drawn even closer. *The Recluse* was intended to be in Wordsworth's career what 'Notes' was in fact in Stevens's, 'a philosophical Poem, containing views of Man, Nature, and Society', as Wordsworth put it. To it

The Prelude was to be 'as the Ante-chapel...to the body of a gothic Church' and 'his minor Pieces' as 'the little Cells, Oratories, and sepulchral Recesses, ordinarily included in those Edifices'.[1] In the event, the only part of *The Recluse* to be completed was its middle section 'The Excursion', and with this, as 'a philosophical poem', most of its readers have been as dissatisfied as Coleridge was at the time. Nevertheless, in the Preface to 'The Excursion' Wordsworth quotes a long passage from 'the first Book of the Recluse...as a kind of *Prospectus* of the design and scope of the whole Poem', and this passage alone would be enough to substantiate Coleridge's remark made years later: 'Wordsworth possessed more of the genius of a great philosophical poet than any man I ever knew, or, as I believe, has existed in England since Milton.'[2] But what particularly concerns us is that this 'Prospectus' for a whole poem that was never written serves as a prophetic programme for a poem that was written, a century and a quarter later and in another continent, Stevens's 'Notes toward a Supreme Fiction'. The quotation has to be a long one:

> Not Chaos, not
> The darkest pit of lowest Erebus,
> Nor aught of blinder vacancy – scooped out
> By help of dreams, can breed such fear and awe
> As fall upon us often when we look
> Into our Minds, into the Mind of Man,
> My haunt, and the main region of my Song.
> – Beauty – a living Presence of the earth,
> Surpassing the most fair ideal Forms
> Which craft of delicate Spirits hath composed
> From earth's materials – waits upon my steps;
> Pitches her tents before me as I move,
> An hourly neighbour. Paradise, and groves
> Elysian, Fortunate Fields – like those of old
> Sought in the Atlantic Main, why should they be
> A history only of departed things,
> Or a mere fiction of what never was?
> For the discerning intellect of Man,
> When wedded to this goodly universe

---

[1] Preface to 'The Excursion' 1814. [2] *Table Talk*, 21 July 1832.

In love and holy passion, shall find these
A simple produce of the common day.
– I, long before the blissful hour arrives,
Would chant, in lonely peace, the spousal verse
Of this great consummation: – and, by words
Which speak of nothing more than what we are,
Would I arouse the sensual from their sleep
Of Death, and win the vacant and the vain
To noble raptures; while my voice proclaims
How exquisitely the individual Mind
(And the progressive powers perhaps no less
Of the whole species) to the external World
Is fitted: – and how exquisitely, too,
Theme this but little heard of among Men,
The external world is fitted to the Mind;
And the creation (by no lower name
Can it be called) which they with blended might
Accomplish: this is our high argument.

It is not only that the imagination adheres to reality, but, also, that reality adheres to the imagination and that the interdependence is essential. We may emerge from our *bassesse*...

'Notes', in the short prologue, thirty separate poems and coda which make it up, is at all times humbler and more oblique than it was Wordsworth's poetic habit to be. It is not called 'Notes' for nothing, and Stevens, from the time of its composition to the end of his life was content to leave his greatest poem's relation to its subject humble and oblique. 'I ought to say that I have not defined a supreme fiction', he wrote to Simons on 12 January 1943, adding, 'In principle there appear to be certain characteristics of a supreme fiction *and the "Notes" is confined to a statement of a few of those characteristics*. As I see the subject, it could occupy a school of rabbis for the next few generations.' And in 1954 he was firmer still:[1] 'That a man's work should remain indefinite is often intentional. For instance, in projecting a supreme fiction, I cannot imagine anything more fatal than to state it definitely and incautiously... We are dealing with poetry, not with philosophy. The last thing in the world that I should want to do

[1] Letter to Robert Pack, 28 December 1954.

would be to formulate a system.' (As Wordsworth said of *The Recluse*: 'It is not the Author's intention formally to announce a system: it was more animating to him to proceed in a different course'.) Nevertheless what Wordsworth, in the remarkable lines above, meant by 'the creation' which the imagination and reality 'with blended might accomplish', is no more than another word for Stevens's 'supreme fiction', though Stevens, with a clearer, more ruthless and yet more cautious mind than Wordsworth's, was able to travel much further in its direction.

The three sections of 'Notes', each containing ten poems, approach the central subject from three different qualifying ideas. The first section, entitled *It Must Be Abstract*, concerns the vanishing of a personal, a non-abstract god, the loss of old certainties and the search for something to replace them, the difficulty of achieving a satisfactory adjustment, a balance, between the mind and reality, the part that can be played in this adjustment by Stevens's idea of the hero, by an abstraction that is of man himself. All these, of course, are old Stevens themes; but now they have a new unity, a new drive and purpose, given them by their subordinate relation to the central subject itself, and by the extraordinary measured confidence of the writing. Here is part of the first poem:

> You must become an ignorant man again
> And see the sun again with an ignorant eye
> And see it clearly in the idea of it.
>
> Never suppose an inventing mind as source
> Of this idea nor for that mind compose
> A voluminous master folded in his fire.
>
> How clean the sun when seen in its idea,
> Washed in the remotest cleanliness of a heaven
> That has expelled us and our images...[1]
>
> The death of one god is the death of all.
> Let purple Phoebus lie in umber harvest,
> Let Phoebus slumber and die in autumn umber,
>
> Phoebus is dead, ephebe. But Phoebus was
> A name for something that never could be named.

---

[1] Stevens's ellipsis.

The admission at the end of this quotation catches at once the immense scope and the immense difficulty of the task Stevens set himself in 'Notes'. His subject is precisely 'something that never could be named'. Yet he is a poet: words are his only tools, his only bricks; and 'a poet's words are of things that do not exist without the words'. This paradox is the reason for the poem's method, for its obliqueness and humility. It is also the reason for its very existence. It is referred to in the second poem, which is about the transience of structures of truth and hence the necessary remoteness and inaccessibility of what 'must be abstract':

> so poisonous
>
> Are the ravishments of truth, so fatal to
> The truth itself, the first idea becomes
> The hermit in a poet's metaphors.
>
> And not to have is the beginning of desire.
> To have what is not is its ancient cycle. . .
>
> It knows that what it has is what is not
> And throws it away like a thing of another time,
> As morning throws off stale moonlight and shabby sleep.

As Stevens had said in 'The Noble Rider', 'We have been a little insane about the truth.' And 'Notes' now moves, as 'The Noble Rider' had moved, 'beyond the truth to something in which the imagination will be the dominant complement'. In the fourth poem, reality, separate and non-human, is seen as from the other side of a frightening chasm which only 'the mind of man' with its words can bridge:

> From this the poem springs: that we live in a place
> That is not our own and, much more, not ourselves
> And hard it is in spite of blazoned days.

This thought is one which Coleridge had expressed in formal philosophical terms in the very difficult Essay XI of *The Friend*, probably unknown to Stevens in its entirety, although Richards quotes from it. 'All speculative disquisition must begin with postulates, which the conscience alone can at once authorize and substantiate: and from whichever point the reason may start, from the things which are seen to the one invisible, or from the idea of the absolute one to the things that are seen, it will find a chasm, which the moral being only, which the spirit and religion of man alone, can fill up.' Once it is realised that it is precisely in this chasm that 'Notes' consciously and deliberately exists, its not being 'true' comes to seem a less important characteristic of the 'supreme' fiction than its quality of being supreme. There is perhaps finally very little to be gained by distinguishing it too sharply from what Coleridge, for instance, means here by 'the idea of the absolute one'.

In any case in 'Notes' what we have to deal with is not formal philosophy but poetry, and when Stevens, in the fifth poem, suggests the barrenness, 'the disappearance of nobility' which is 'a maladjustment between the imagination and reality', he does so not with abstract discourse but with imagery drawn, with his own combination of surprisingness and perfect appropriateness, from 'the things which are seen'. The great beasts, lion, elephant and bear, their natural adjustment to reality marvellously displayed in the spontaneous noises they make, roaring, blaring, snarling, are contrasted with man when 'the sound of words', music that is his own, fails him.

> The bear
> The ponderous cinnamon, snarls in his mountain
>
> At summer thunder and sleeps through winter snow.
> But you, ephebe, look from your attic window,
> Your mansard with a rented piano. You lie
>
> In silence upon your bed. You clutch the corner
> Of the pillow in your hand. You writhe and press
> A bitter utterance from your writhing, dumb,
>
> Yet voluble dumb violence.

Man, unable to find his proper voice, unable even to sleep, like the bear, at the proper time, can only wage distorting war upon reality. The end of this poem turns its imagery to sudden new account with stunning irony:

> These are the heroic children whom time breeds
> Against the first idea – to lash the lion,
> Caparison elephants, teach bears to juggle.

After this tremendous poem 'Notes' moves into a quieter phase, and its first 'spousal verse', in Wordsworth's phrase, for the marriage of imagination and reality, the human adjustment, happens in poem VII quietly and swiftly, as befits, again in Wordsworth's phrase, 'a simple produce of the common day'.

> ...not balances
> That we achieve but balances that happen,
>
> As a man and woman meet and love forthwith.
> Perhaps there are moments of awakening,
> Extreme, fortuitous, personal, in which
>
> We more than awaken, sit on the edge of sleep,
> As on an elevation, and behold
> The academies like structures in a mist.

In the last three poems of 'It Must Be Abstract' Stevens returns to his figure of the hero, the 'major man' who is not man but a mysterious and powerful abstraction of man, now appearing as a manifestation of that balance between imagination and reality out of which alone the supreme fiction can be approached. The connexion between this 'major abstraction...the idea of man' and what in 'The Noble Rider' was called 'nobility' is obvious. In poem VIII an individual, arbitrarily named MacCullough,[1] lies by the sea – the old image of disorderly reality – and his words combine with its waves to produce a magical example of the possible 'balances that happen':

> He might take habit, whether from wave or phrase,
>
> Or power of the wave, or deepened speech,
> Or a leaner being, moving in on him,
> Of greater aptitude and apprehension,
>
> As if the waves at last were never broken,
> As if the language suddenly, with ease,
> Said things it had laboriously spoken.

The 'leaner being', in all his indefiniteness, has something to do with 'the hermit in a poet's metaphors' of the second poem, as the very beautiful poem IX makes clear. He is:

---

[1] Stevens wrote of the name to Church 'They say that, in Ireland, God is a member of the family and that they treat Him as one of them.' (18 May 1943.)

the object of

The hum of thoughts evaded in the mind,
Hidden from other thoughts, he that reposes
On a breast forever precious for that touch...

My dame, sing for this person accurate songs.

He is and may be but oh! he is, he is,
This foundling of the infected past, so bright,
So moving in the manner of his hand.

Yet look not at his colored eyes. Give him
No names. Dismiss him from your images.
The hot of him is purest in the heart.

Here again we have the poet's dilemma, the fundamental paradox upon which 'Notes' is built and which finds its most concise expression in the poem's title. The figure celebrated in these lines, like the supreme fiction itself, cannot be named; he lurks behind the poet's images, the hermit of his metaphors, yet is in none of them, being an abstraction. Yet the idea of him exists only in words, in the 'accurate songs' which are to be sung for him. He is nevertheless not to be confused with the supreme fiction, being no more than 'part of the entourage of that artificial object', as Stevens explained in a letter[1] which insisted also that his heroic figures were 'neither exponents of humanism nor Nietzschean shadows'. This statement and these negatives are as near as we can profitably get to a description of what Stevens felt to be behind his phrase 'major man'. But the tenth and last poem of 'It Must Be Abstract', the climax of the section and one of the finest passages Stevens ever wrote, raises again an ancient, resonant connexion:

The major abstraction is the idea of man
And major man is its exponent...

The major abstraction is the commonal,
The inanimate, difficult visage. Who is it?

What rabbi, grown furious with human wish,
What chieftain, walking by himself, crying
Most miserable, most victorious,

[1] To the young Cuban poet José Rodríguez Feo, 26 January 1945.

145

Does not see these separate figures one by one,
And yet see only one, in his old coat,
His slouching pantaloons, beyond the town,

Looking for what was, where it used to be?
Cloudless the morning. It is he. The man
In that old coat, those sagging pantaloons,

It is of him, ephebe, to make, to confect
The final elegance, not to console
Nor sanctify, but plainly to propound.

This figure of manifold ambiguity, heroic, 'a man at the centre of men', and yet a figure of poverty and loss, to be discovered only out of need, by, for instance, a 'rabbi, grown furious with human wish' or a 'chieftain...most miserable, most victorious', is also an image of the ultimate demand that the bereft modern world makes upon the poet. What has been lost must be recovered, and its recovery is the poet's task. The complex of need and resolve that was at the centre of Stevens himself is behind the last three lines of the poem; and, deeply involved in his longing for a belief that would suffice, one can detect a nostalgia for what once sufficed. It is all this, united in the simplest words, that makes the line 'Looking for what was, where it used to be', together with the memory from the previous poem of 'This foundling of the infected past', indeed 'inexhaustible to meditation'. It was perhaps the composition of these marvellous concluding poems of 'It Must Be Abstract' that led Stevens to make, in his lecture of the following year,[1] some fascinating remarks about 'the experience of writing a poem that completely accomplishes the purpose of the poet'. He quotes Bergson on religious aspiration, noting 'that Bergson intended to include in aspiration not only desire but the fulfilment of desire, not only the petition but the harmonious decree', and goes on to say that the poet's experiences 'are of no less a degree than the experiences of the saints themselves'. He adds, to avoid confusion, 'It is a question of the nature of the experience. It is not a question of identifying or relating dissimilar figures; that is to say, it is not a question of making saints out of poets or poets out of saints.'

[1] 'The Figure of the Youth as Virile Poet' (1943).

For all his necessary caution, we cannot help observing that Stevens does ascribe the quality of religious aspiration, 'not only the petition but the harmonious decree' to a possible experience of the poet, and that this quality is exactly the quality of his own work at its highest. As he put a similar thought in a line from poem II of 'It Must Be Abstract': 'The monastic man is an artist'. And 'The Figure of the Youth' continues with a further description of the supreme poetic experience that adds still more verve and depth to the whole idea of 'looking for what was, where it used to be'. The experience, he says,

may be dismissed, on the one hand, as a commonplace aesthetic satisfaction; and, on the other hand, if we say that the idea of God is merely a poetic idea, even if the supreme poetic idea, and that our notions of heaven and hell are merely poetry not so called, even if poetry that involves us vitally, the feeling of deliverance, of a release, of a perfection touched, of a vocation so that all men may know the truth and that the truth may set them free – if we say these things and if we are able to see the poet who achieved God and placed Him in His seat in heaven in all His glory, the poet himself, still in the ecstasy of the poem that completely accomplished his purpose, would have seemed...a man who needed what he had created, uttering the hymns of joy that followed his creation.

This, like many other passages in Stevens's prose, helps one to see that his search for belief in and through his own poetry was not founded upon the idea of substituting poetry for religion but upon a dissolution of the traditional rigid frontier between the two. He felt, as Santayana had said at the end of *Interpretations of Poetry and Religion*, that:

when the poet enlarges his theatre and puts into his rhapsodies the true visions of his people and of his soul, his poetry is the consecration of his deepest convictions, and contains the whole truth of his religion. What the religion of the vulgar adds to the poet's is simply the inertia of their limited apprehension, which takes literally what he meant ideally, and degrades into a false extension of this world on its own level what in his mind was a true interpretation of it upon a moral plane. This higher plane is the sphere of significant imagination, of relevant fiction, of idealism become the interpretation of the reality it leaves behind. Poetry, raised to its highest power is then identical with religion grasped in its inmost truth.

'It Must', in other words, 'Be Abstract'. Stevens felt that 'the death of one god is the death of all'; but this feeling, far from leading him to despise what he might have called the great fictions of the past, what he in fact called 'our idea of God...the supreme poetic idea', produced in him, on the contrary, a profound sense of continuity and of responsibility. This sense finds expression in the deep echoes of old belief which reverberate through some of his best poems. His description of the seventeenth century imagination in 'The Figure of the Youth' could well be applied to his own:[1]

It is the imagination of the son still bearing the antique imagination of the father. It is the clear intelligence of the young man still bearing the burden of the obscurities of the intelligence of the old. It is the spirit out of its own self, not out of some surrounding myth, delineating with accurate speech the complications of which it is composed. For this Aeneas, it is the past that is Anchises.

[1] He used the Anchises image again and in the same way in a poem called 'Recitation After Dinner' (*Opus Posthumous*, p. 86) which he left out of *Collected Poems*.

9

'Notes toward a Supreme Fiction'
(2)

The middle section of 'Notes', 'It Must Change', lightens the poem's mood with a series of parables, some of them written with that glittering far-fetched gaudiness that was always a characteristic Stevens manner. Their theme is what in the first poem of the section is called 'a universe of inconstancy', the world of endless repetition and yet endless new beginnings, out of his relation with which man must make whatever sense he can. A sexual metaphor, the booming bee of spring, connects the first poem to the second, in which 'the President' for all his power powerless against change, is juxtaposed with the new spring, the new bee.

> The President ordains the bee to be
> Immortal. The President ordains.

But:

> This warmth is for lovers at last accomplishing
> Their love, this beginning, not resuming, this
> Booming and booming of the new-come bee.

The third poem revolves, with wit and precision, round the now familiar image of the noble rider, the great equestrian statue which has lost its force as an incarnation of nobility. It ends:

> Nothing had happened because nothing had changed.
> Yet the General was rubbish in the end.

After the mundane thud of this conclusion and the exuberant realism of these first three poems of the section, the fourth, a new 'spousal verse' celebrating what Stevens had called 'a decision regarding the imagination and reality...a recognition that here, too, as between these poles, the universal interdependence exists', comes upon the reader like a sunrise. By introducing the imagination into

his poem in this sudden, surprising way, Stevens creates as it were a
model of what he is writing about, of the transformation of reality that
the imagination, when wedded to it, itself brings about.

> Two things of opposite natures seem to depend
> On one another, as a man depends
> On a woman, day on night, the imagined
>
> On the real. This is the origin of change.
> Winter and spring, cold copulars, embrace
> And forth the particulars of rapture come.
>
> Music falls on the silence like a sense,
> A passion that we feel, not understand.
> Morning and afternoon are clasped together
>
> And North and South are an intrinsic couple
> And sun and rain a plural, like two lovers
> That walk away as one in the greenest body.
>
> In solitude the trumpets of solitude
> Are not of another solitude resounding;
> A little string speaks for a crowd of voices.
>
> The partaker partakes of that which changes him.
> The child that touches takes character from the thing,
> The body, it touches. The captain and his men
>
> Are one and the sailor and the sea are one.
> Follow after, O my companion, my fellow, my self,
> Sister and solace, brother and delight.

The splendour and beauty of this, coming as it does almost exactly
in the middle of the whole poem and referring both backwards to the
'balances that happen' of the first section and forward, as we shall see,
to the last, make it in some ways the climax of 'Notes'. Here indeed
is 'la confiance que le poète fait, et nous invite à faire, au monde', the
'little string' of the imagination's blue guitar that does 'speak for a
crowd of voices'. It is pointless to inquire whether it is the imagination
or reality that is addressed in the last two lines: their unity is exactly
what the poem has achieved, and achieved by a combination of
thought and feeling for which the appropriate phrase is Wordsworth's
'intellectual love'. When Stevens writes on this level one wonders

whether there should be a new answer to Hopkins's question: 'Wordsworth's particular grace...has been granted in equal measure to so very few men since time was – to Plato and who else?' And Wordsworth's description, in the last book of *The Prelude*, of the qualities he felt to be essential to the modern poet seems to fit Stevens no less well than himself:

> Imagination having been our theme,
> So also hath that intellectual love,
> For they are each in each, and cannot stand
> Dividually. Here must thou be, O Man!
> Strength to thyself: no Helper hast thou here;
> Here keepest thou thy individual state:
> No other can divide with thee this work.

As Stevens said in a letter written while he was writing 'Notes': 'One has, after all, only one's own horn on which to toot, one's own synthesis on which to rely; one's own fortitude of spirit is the only "fester Burg"; without that fortitude one lives in chaos...The order of the spirit is the only music of the spheres: or, rather, the only music.'[1]

More parables, again lighter in tone, succeed the exquisite balances of poem IV. In the fifth poem, of which Stevens was particularly fond, a lonely planter lives and dies 'on a blue island'. 'Here keepest thou thy individual state: No other can divide with thee this work.' 'He is', Stevens noted for Simons (12 January 1943), 'the laborious human who lives in illusions and who, after all the great illusions have left him, still clings to one that pierces him'. What pierces the planter in his mortal solitude between 'an island beyond him' and 'the land from which he came' is the little string of the blue guitar:

> An unaffected man in a negative light
> Could not have borne his labor nor have died
> Sighing that he should leave the banjo's twang.

In all the grandeur and large courage of Stevens's poetic undertaking, this note of humility is never absent from his work. It comes from his sanity, his sense of the essential tether between the poet and ordinary life. 'Eventually', he wrote in his notebook, 'an imaginary

---

[1] To Simons, 18 February 1942.

world is entirely without interest'. And he also wrote, 'Poetry is a
health.'

The last five poems of 'It Must Change' concern, each from its
separate direction, the poet's labour, the struggle of his imagination
to find or make what will answer his need. Poem VI, a fantasia on the
meaningless monotony of birdsong on a summer afternoon, is followed
by a difficult meditation on 'the easy passion' with which the lover
of beauty responds to the world again and again but never adequately.
One is reminded once more of *The Prelude* and Wordsworth's personal
history of his efforts to recover from what Stevens here calls

> the ever-ready love
> Of the lover that lies within us.

But in poem VIII, with one of the sudden lifts that makes 'Notes'
apart from everything else a masterpiece of large-scale composition,
Stevens achieves an embodiment of one of his most central ideas
that would have been for a number of reasons quite beyond Wordsworth. 'Embodiment' is the right word:

> On her trip around the world, Nanzia Nunzio
> Confronted Ozymandias. She went
> Alone and like a vestal long-prepared.
>
> I am the spouse. She took her necklace off
> And laid it in the sand. As I am, I am
> The spouse. She opened her stone-studded belt.
>
> I am the spouse, divested of bright gold,
> The spouse beyond emerald or amethyst,
> Beyond the burning body that I bear.

The powerful sexual emotion is, as often in Stevens's work, no more
than the only appropriate image for love and desire of another kind.
The transposition is a natural one which, for not dissimilar reasons,
was once common in Christian mystical writing. This is not 'the easy
passion' of the previous poem, and Stevens allows it no simple
climax:

> I am the woman stripped more nakedly
> Than nakedness, standing before an inflexible
> Order, saying I am the contemplated spouse.

> Speak to me that, which spoken, will array me
> In its own only precious ornament.
> Set on me the spirit's diamond coronal.
>
> Clothe me entire in the final filament,
> So that I tremble with such love so known
> And myself am precious for your perfecting.
>
> Then Ozymandias said the spouse, the bride
> Is never naked. A fictive covering
> Weaves always glistening from the heart and mind.

Here, in the most haunting form that Stevens ever found for it, is, again, the central dilemma of 'Notes', the poet's temptation to name directly something of which it is only certain that it cannot be named directly, and the poet's victory over this temptation. Definition, finality, a hardening is offered – in all those words, 'I am', 'nakedness', 'inflexible order', 'only', 'diamond', 'entire', 'final', 'known', 'perfecting' – and then, in the poem's last three lines, at one stroke rejected. These three lines amount to a summary of the intention and the achievement of the whole of 'Notes', indeed of the whole of Stevens's work. They also, concluding as they do a poem that is itself a fabulous metaphor, a glistening fiction, fill the section's title 'It Must Change' with particular substance and vitality.

Poem IX takes the poet's struggle to marry what is peculiar to himself to the ordinary language of men as an image of the marriage that is his goal, the endowment of manifold changing reality with the imagination's meanings:

> It is the gibberish of the vulgate that he seeks.
> He tries by a peculiar speech to speak
>
> The peculiar potency of the general,
> To compound the imagination's Latin with
> The lingua franca et jocundissima.

(The superlatively deft making of the point by using a Latin phrase for 'the gibberish of the vulgate' is typical of Stevens's inventiveness.) The imagination's meanings are more directly treated in poem X, the last of the section. A man sits on a park bench, something Stevens was fond of doing in the Hartford park through which he walked to

work every day. He contemplates changing reality from his own
'Theatre of Trope', and realises that reality's endless renewals must
be met by human renewal, the human fictive power meeting the
transient challenge that is always presenting itself:

> There was a will to change, a necessitous
> And present way, a presentation, a kind
> Of volatile world, too constant to be denied,
>
> The eye of a vagabond in metaphor
> That catches our own. The casual is not
> Enough. The freshness of transformation is
>
> The freshness of a world. It is our own,
> It is ourselves, the freshness of ourselves...

The third and final section of 'Notes' is called 'It Must Give
Pleasure'. After the contemplative rigours of 'It Must Be Abstract'
and 'It Must Change', this last requirement made of the supreme
fiction may seem surprising; but it comes from something very deep
in Stevens's creative nature. His search for a belief that would suffice
was always simultaneously a search for something that at the deepest
level would please. He felt, as Santayana had put it in *Reason in Art*,
that: 'The value of art lies in making people happy, first in practising
the art and then in possessing its product', and it depressed him
considerably that among all the reviews of, for instance, *Parts of a
World*, there was not 'even so much as a suggestion that the book
gave the man who read it any pleasure.'[1] His desire for his poetry to
give pleasure cannot be disentangled from his proposition that 'a
supreme fiction' should do the same: we are back with the basic
key to 'Notes', that 'a poet's words are of things that do not exist
without the words'. If the supreme fiction, which is no more than the
supreme example of such 'things', is to give pleasure, it must do so
through the poet's words in which alone it exists. The difficulty with
which this task presents the lonely modern poet is the subject of the
first poem of the section, where the ancient religious forms that used
to bring common joy to those who were 'borne on the shoulders of
joyous men' are contrasted with the new meanings that the poet must

[1] Letter to Church, 8 December 1942.

speak for himself. 'Jubilas at exact, accustomed times' are harshly dismissed: 'This is a facile exercise'. But the backward look is not without nostalgia, for all the moving simplicity of the look forward:

> But the difficultest rigor is forthwith,
> On the image of what we see, to catch from that
>
> Irrational moment its unreasoning.
> As when the sun comes rising, when the sea
> Clears deeply, when the moon hangs on the wall
>
> Of heaven-haven. These are not things transformed.
> Yet we are shaken by them as if they were.

Poem II takes this 'as if' as its subject, enlarging upon it by means of one of Stevens's characters of the imagination. A 'blue woman' looks out of her window at things of the real world that are 'not transformed'. But she is 'shaken by them as if they were'. At the end of the poem it emerges that it is from herself that the satisfaction they give her comes: again we have, here most delicately suggested, the poet's marriage of the real and the imagined. The woman's naming of these things is closely bound up with her imaginative seeing and remembering:

> It was enough for her that she remembered.
> The blue woman looked and from her window named
>
> The corals of the dogwood, cold and clear,
> Cold, coldly delineating, being real,
> Clear and, except for the eye, without intrusion.

The deliberate lucidity of this – Stevens said of it to Simons:[1] 'One of the approaches to fiction is by way of its opposite: reality, the truth, the thing observed, the purity of the eye' – is followed by the obscure forcefulness of one of the most mysterious poems in the whole of 'Notes'. A terrifying Old Testament vision of God is evoked:

> A lasting visage in a lasting bush,
> A face of stone in an unending red,
> Red-emerald, red-slitted-blue, a face of slate...

The face dies away on a note of almost wistful sadness. But the poem

[1] Letter, 29 March 1943.

ends with one of those astonishing Stevens images whose power defies explanation:

> That might have been
> It might and might have been. But as it was,
> A dead shepherd brought tremendous chords from hell
>
> And bade the sheep carouse. Or so they said.
> Children in love with them brought early flowers
> And scattered them about, no two alike.

The splendour of this lies not so much in the shepherd's identity, which is obvious, as in the profound complexity of the emotion that has produced him exactly here, in these words and no others. Stevens admitted as much in his comment for Simons,[1] which is more revealing than directly helpful: 'This dead shepherd was an improvisation. What preceded it in the poem made it necessary, like music that evolved for internal reasons and not with reference to an external program. What the spirit wants it creates, even if it has to do so in a fiction.' It was shortly after this letter that Stevens wrote those sentences in 'The Figure of the Youth' that are the best gloss on the dead shepherd: 'It is the spirit out of its own self, not out of some surrounding myth, delineating with accurate speech the complications of which it is composed. For this Aeneas, it is the past that is Anchises.' Of the children and the flowers that accompany the shepherd it can only be said that they too are part of 'what the spirit wants' delineated with accurate speech.

After the extraordinary intensity of this poem which seems for a moment to recover for the supreme fiction its ancient imagery, we return to things as they are and what the imagination makes of them. Poem IV is a fable on the now familiar marriage theme, a new 'spousal verse' through which 'a great captain' and his bride move in steady ceremonious language to illustrate the statement made at the poem's beginning:

> ...we make of what we see, what we see clearly
> And have seen, a place dependent on ourselves.

It is, as usual, a mistake to pin down too firmly the 'significance' of the figures themselves; what matters is their love, their union in a

---

[1] Letter, 28 January 1943.

place that is the sufficient earth, and the sense of fulfilment created in the words in which they exist:

> The great captain loved the ever-hill Catawba
> And therefore married Bawda, whom he found there,
> And Bawda loved the captain as she loved the sun.
>
> They married well because the marriage-place
> Was what they loved. It was neither heaven nor hell.
> They were love's characters come face to face.

Here at last, one feels, is the simple image that catches perfectly and without philosophical fuss the essence of the 'great consummation' that Wordsworth and Coleridge thought to be the fundamental fact of modern poetry.

This consummation is also the subject of the next two poems, though now it is approached not through simple imagery but from thought-processes of elaborate sophistication. The figure whose story is told in these two poems is not a fabulous personage like Ozymandias or Bawda and her captain but only a representative man, 'Canon Aspirin', whose name shows roughly what he represents. He is, Stevens explained,[1] 'the man who has explored all the projections of the mind, his own particularly'. In poem v he contemplates his sensible sister who, her widowhood implies, is without imagination, and who accepts her poverty only 'by rejecting dreams'. She is confined to 'rigid statement' and 'simple names'. This poem is one of the few comparative failures in 'Notes', as if the dreariness of the sister had cast a temporary blight on Stevens himself. The Canon's midnight meditation is described in poem VI. He rejects his sister's world of fact as leading in the end to 'nothingness', but then finds that thought by itself leads no further. Finally he abandons either exclusion and is driven to accept the essential balance:

> He had to choose. But it was not a choice
> Between excluding things. It was not a choice
>
> Between, but of. He chose to include the things
> That in each other are included, the whole,
> The complicate, the amassing harmony.

[1] To Simons, 29 March 1943.

This poem suffers, in its turn, from the Canon's somewhat dry and formal cast of mind. Both he and his sister have a schematic, an almost merely illustrative quality that denies them the glowing vitality of the other figures Stevens uses in 'Notes', from MacCullough and the President to the planter and the blue woman. Perhaps Stevens somewhere felt this himself, for poem VII begins with a description of a certain kind of inadequacy that may refer back to the Canon:

> He imposes orders as he thinks of them,
> As the fox and snake do. It is a brave affair.

With this as a method of dealing with reality is contrasted the irrational spontaneity, the love, by means of which the imagination may achieve the sufficiency that is the poet's longed-for goal. After the laborious tribulations of Canon Aspirin, the second part of this poem reminds us that the section's title was 'It Must Give Pleasure':

> But to impose is not
> To discover. To discover an order as of
> A season, to discover summer and know it,
>
> To discover winter and know it well, to find,
> Not to impose, not to have reasoned at all,
> Out of nothing to have come on major weather,
>
> It is possible, possible, possible...

And the poem ends on an immense promise that is the promise of 'Notes' itself:

> To find the real,
> To be stripped of every fiction except one,
>
> The fiction of an absolute – Angel,
> Be silent in your luminous cloud and hear
> The luminous melody of proper sound.

Stevens has now, nearly at the end of the whole poem, reached its supreme moment. One might expect that 'the luminous melody of proper sound' is at last to take the form of words that approach 'the fiction of an absolute' more directly than has as yet been possible. On the other hand one knows that such an approach is, in the nature of the enterprise, always to be impossible. 'The spouse, the bride is never naked.' The dilemma that underlies every poem of 'Notes' is here felt at its keenest. Stevens resolves it with a device whose effect is breathtaking. After twenty-seven poems of 'fictive covering' he breaks for the first time into the first person singular and describes not, of course, the supreme fiction itself, but his own relation to this 'thing created by the imagination'.[1] The angel is no more than a new image, a new poetic covering for the 'thing': what becomes clear here is that it is not the thing, the fiction, that matters most, but the relation between it and the human individual who finds it in what will suffice.

> What am I to believe? If the angel in his cloud,
> Serenely gazing at the violent abyss,
> Plucks on his strings to pluck abysmal glory,
>
> Leaps downward through evening's revelations, and
> On his spredden wings, needs nothing but deep space,
> Forgets the gold centre, the golden destiny,
>
> Grows warm in the motionless motion of his flight,
> Am I that imagine this angel less satisfied?
> Are the wings his, the lapis-haunted air?
>
> Is it he or is it I that experience this?
> Is it I then that keep saying there is an hour
> Filled with expressible bliss, in which I have
>
> No need, am happy, forget need's golden hand,
> Am satisfied without solacing majesty,
> And if there is an hour there is a day,
>
> There is a month, a year, there is a time
> In which majesty is a mirror of the self:
> I have not but I am and as I am, I am.

This poem, more than any other in 'Notes', rings as the poem of 'a man who needed what he had created, uttering the hymns of joy that followed his creation'. It will be remembered that Stevens was to use these phrases of[2] 'the poet who achieved God and placed Him in His seat in heaven in all His glory'. The proper time to recall this,

---

[1] See letter to Simons above, p. 132.
[2] In 'The Figure of the Youth as Virile Poet'.

however, is not now – 'Notes' remains only 'notes toward', in spite of the shining affirmations of the poem just quoted – but in relation to some of the poems of Stevens's old age. For it is in those later poems and not in 'Notes' itself that he explored what might be called the otherness of the supreme fiction, an aspect of it that in 'Notes' appears only in the eight introductory lines:

> And for what, except for you, do I feel love?
> Do I press the extremest book of the wisest man
> Close to me, hidden in me day and night?
> In the uncertain light of single, certain truth,
> Equal in living changingness to the light
> In which I meet you, in which we sit at rest,
> For a moment in the central of our being,
> The vivid transparence that you bring is peace.

This sense of otherness is expressly denied in the forlorn three lines that close the angel poem:

> These external regions, what do we fill them with
> Except reflections, the escapades of death,
> Cinderella fulfilling herself beneath the roof?

Meanwhile 'Notes' ends in an atmosphere altogether milder and less intense. Poem IX returns to the repetitiousness of birdsong, finding in it a parallel for the repetitiousness of balances achieved between the imagination and reality:

> These things at least comprise
> An occupation, an exercise, a work,
>
> A thing final in itself and, therefore, good:
> One of the vast repetitions final in
> Themselves and, therefore, good, the going round
>
> And round and round, the merely going round,
> Until merely going round is a final good,
> The way wine comes at a table in a wood...
>
>   ...Perhaps,
> The man-hero is not the exceptional monster,
> But he that of repetition is most master.

The claim made here seems a humble one until we realise that it is the justification for the method and achievement, which cannot be separated, both of 'Notes' itself and of the whole poetic enterprise to which 'Notes' is the key but not the conclusion. It was not just of 'Notes' but of 'the author's work' ('an occupation, an exercise...a thing final in itself') that Stevens wrote at the end of his life that it: 'suggests the possibility of a supreme fiction, recognised as a fiction, in which men could propose to themselves a fulfilment. In the creation of any such fiction, poetry would have a vital significance.' In other words, in the simplest possible words, Stevens's work is

> the merely going round,
> Until merely going round is a final good.

In the last poem of 'Notes' the poet turns, suddenly and finally, to address not 'the bride' who 'is never naked' but beloved reality, 'the base' of all his repetitions: 'Fat girl, terrestrial, my summer, my night'. She is reality touched by the poet's imagination into significance:

> You
> Become the soft-footed phantom, the irrational
>
> Distortion, however fragrant, however dear.
> That's it: the more than rational distortion,
> The fiction that results from feeling. Yes, that.

Thus lightly, after the oblique splendours and many varied humours of his 'Notes', Stevens dismisses, for the moment, his great preoccupation, 'the irrational distortion' costing not less than everything. His last six lines cast an enigmatic glance, amused and a little sad, at the possible end of his 'merely going round':

> They will get it straight one day at the Sorbonne.
> We shall return at twilight from the lecture
> Pleased that the irrational is rational,
>
> Until flicked by feeling, in a gildered street,
> I call you by name, my green, my fluent mundo.
> You will have stopped revolving except in crystal.

Stevens added an epilogue to 'Notes', a poem the same shape and length as all the others but outside their three defining sections. It relates what he has tried to do in the whole of his poem to what in

'The Noble Rider' he had called 'the extraordinary pressure of reality', in particular to the war which was then, in the summer of 1942, in one of its darkest phases. There is of course no attempt in 'Notes', as there was in *Owl's Clover*, to deal with the horror and misery of contemporary events as such. Nevertheless it would be a mistake to suppose that 'Notes' is not in its way a war poem. 'The war is only a part of a war-like whole', Stevens had written;[1] and if the war was a colossal and terrifying intensification of the violence, poverty and meaninglessness of modern reality, then 'Notes' was an answering intensification of the poet's effort to confront that reality. The war against Hitler was a war that, as Stevens had put it, involved 'the concepts and sanctions that are the order of our lives'; and, Stevens's sense of poetic responsibility being what it was, it is not at all surprising that that moment of greatest threat should have drawn from him his greatest poem. His epilogue is addressed to the soldier. It places side by side the soldier's war and the poet's:

> The two are one...
> Two parallels that meet if only in
>
> The meeting of their shadows or that meet
> In a book in a barrack, a letter from Malay.

And it ends by making, again and most memorably, that connexion between the poet's words and the 'sanctions that are the order of our lives' which is the *raison d'être* of the whole of 'Notes':

> The soldier is poor without the poet's lines,
>
> His petty syllabi, the sounds that stick,
> Inevitably modulating, in the blood.
> And war for war, each has its gallant kind.
>
> How simply the fictive hero becomes the real;
> How gladly with proper words the soldier dies,
> If he must, or lives on the bread of faithful speech.

[1] Also in 'The Noble Rider and the Sound of Words'.

10
'Transport to Summer'

Stevens was fully aware of the crucial place that 'Notes' was to occupy in his work as a whole. He felt for the rest of his life that his discovery or invention (the distinction is not important) of the idea of a supreme fiction, having life and force only in the poet's words, the poet's notes toward it, was not only the fruit of that marriage between reality and the imagination which had for so long pre-occupied him, but was also that which might satisfy modern man in his waste land of unbelief. Sometimes he felt even that his idea was only a new identification of what, variously named, in other words, other notes, had always sustained human belief. In any case, he knew that the vein he had revealed for himself in this extraordinary poem was for him an inexhaustible one. How the achievement of 'Notes' looked to him shortly after it was published can be seen in the letter he wrote to Henry Church on 8 December 1942:

It is only when you try to systematize the poems in the NOTES that you conclude that it is not the statement of a philosophic theory. A philosopher is never at rest unless he is systematizing: constructing a theory. But these are Notes; the nucleus of the matter is contained in the title. It is implicit in the title that there can be such a thing as a supreme fiction... The truth is that this ought to be one of only[1] a number of books and that, if I had nothing else in the world to do except to sit on a fence and think about things, it would in fact be only one of a number of books.

Stevens was now sixty-three and, as vice-president of a large company, certainly had plenty else to do apart from sitting on a fence and thinking about things. Nevertheless in the remaining twelve years of his life, during which he refused to retire from his job, he produced nearly half of his poetry (as well as almost all his prose).

[1] Obviously this should read 'only one of...', *Letters*, p. 431.

In this large and extremely impressive body of work there are in one sense no new themes. There are new perceptions, new starts, new directions, in a word, new poems. But each poem is an elaboration of the theory of which 'Notes' was the original statement, although, as with 'Notes' itself, 'when you try to systematize the poems' the theory disappears. Each of the many poems that followed 'Notes' is a new note or set of notes 'toward a supreme fiction', for it was in this phrase that Stevens had at last expressed to his own satisfaction what had always been, and was to remain, the object of his poetic effort. But at the same time it is the individuality, the uniqueness, of each poem that makes it a poem, and, as Stevens knew very well, without this quality of being a poem, no arrangement of words could have any part to play as a note toward a supreme fiction 'in the creation of [which] poetry would have a vital significance'. As he said of his method in the composition of 'Notes' itself, 'I very soon found that, if I stuck closely to a development, I should lose all of the qualities that I really wanted to get into the thing, and that I was likely to produce something that did not come off in any sense, not even as poetry.'[1]

In the three new collections that Stevens was to publish before his death, *Transport to Summer* (1947), *Auroras of Autumn* (1950) and *The Rock* (the last section of the *Collected Poems* which he finally allowed to appear in 1954), there are poems which fail precisely because they stick too closely to the development of an idea and miss that rich singularity which so distinctly marks almost every poem in 'Notes'. This is particularly true of *Transport to Summer*, the largest of the three collections, and least true of *The Rock*, much the smallest. Stevens placed 'Notes', which until then had appeared only in the limited edition of 1942, at the end of *Transport to Summer*, and saw it as 'the most important thing in the book,'[2] which indeed it was. But in spite of, on the one hand, the pre-eminence of 'Notes', and, on the other, the presence of several pieces that do not 'come off in any sense, not even as poetry', the volume contained much new work of high quality and wide range.

The most ambitious poem in *Transport to Summer*, apart from

---

[1] To Church, 8 December 1942.
[2] Letter to Herbert Weinstock of Knopf's, 12 November 1946.

'Notes', is 'Esthétique du Mal'. This series of fifteen poems, varying in form and approach, is his complex and inventive attempt to reach 'in this bad...The last purity of the knowledge of good.' Written in 1944 and more directly a war poem than 'Notes', it emerged, one may guess, from the effort to test the idea of a supreme fiction against reality in its most adverse possible shape. The tone of its conclusion, which restates the essential sufficiency of the real world married to the imagination, seems oddly simple after the much more mysterious affirmations of 'Notes'. But the poem has travelled a far-flung and difficult path to reach its almost 'Sunday Morning'-like end, and some of its sections penetrate freshly and deeply into the problems of belief from which his idea of a supreme fiction had by no means absolved Stevens. The idea had indeed by its very nature increased rather than diminished his sense of the poet's responsibility and necessary involvement in these problems. Section III of 'Esthétique du Mal', with its seven three-line stanzas, might almost be a 'Notes' poem except that it confronts Stevens's ambivalent attitude to Christian belief with an explicitness that would have been circumvented in 'Notes':

> His firm stanzas hang like hives in hell
> Or what hell was, since now both heaven and hell
> Are one, and here, O terra infidel.
>
> The fault lies with an over-human god,
> Who by sympathy has made himself a man
> And is not to be distinguished, when we cry
>
> Because we suffer, our oldest parent, peer
> Of the populace of the heart, the reddest lord,
> Who has gone before us in experience.
>
> If only he would not pity us so much,
> Weaken our fate, relieve us of woe both great
> And small, a constant fellow of destiny,
>
> A too, too human god, self-pity's kin
> And uncourageous genesis...It seems
> As if the health of the world might be enough.
>
> It seems as if the honey of common summer
> Might be enough, as if the golden combs
> Were part of a sustenance itself enough,

As if hell, so modified, had disappeared,
As if pain, no longer satanic mimicry,
Could be borne, as if we were sure to find our way.

The 'over-human god' who is suddenly and movingly spoken of here in the present tense, cannot perhaps be firmly distinguished from Stevens's figure of the hero in some of his manifestations. And the rejection no more than half-suggested here is more resolutely announced elsewhere in *Transport to Summer*, most obviously in a little virtuoso piece called 'Crude Foyer' and in the two short poems that Stevens placed immediately after 'Esthétique du Mal'. In 'The Bed of Old John Zeller' the poet regrets the easy wish 'for another structure of ideas' seeing it as a disastrous habit of the past:

This is the habit of wishing, as if one's grandfather lay
In one's heart and wished as he had always wished...

(Zeller was Stevens's Pennsylvania Dutch grandfather.)

It is more difficult to evade
That habit of wishing and to accept the structure
Of things as the structure of ideas.

In the following poem, 'Less and Less Human, O Savage Spirit', the same idea appears in a completely different form. The poem, transfixed in an exquisite quietness, ends:

If there must be a god in the house, let him be one
That will not hear us when we speak: a coolness,

A vermilioned nothingness, any stick of the mass
Of which we are too distantly a part.

Neither of these poems, nor the section quoted from 'Esthétique du Mal', is without the sadness with which the figure of Jesus was abandoned in the last stanza of 'Sunday Morning'. It only 'seems as if the honey of common summer Might be enough': it is not a certainty, even in the marvellous glow of the 'physical world' in which 'Esthétique du Mal' ends, and hell, in 1944, had not disappeared, even if the word for it had lost its divine sanction. There are other poems in *Transport to Summer* which balance these by stressing the opposite side of the same issue: again Stevens compels one to remember that he was not a philosopher but a poet, and that a single exclusive truth was never the object of his search.

The beautiful 'Dutch Graves in Bucks County' is a case in point. This poem, which has a solemn formality unusual in Stevens, super-imposes upon the violent present the violence of a segment of the American past and by so doing gives an extra dimension to both. The device is one which has produced some of the best American poems of the century, Tate's 'Ode to the Confederate Dead', and Lowell's 'The Quaker Graveyard in Nantucket' and 'For the Union Dead'. ('Dutch Graves in Bucks County' is good enough to have taken its place beside these three well-known poems: if it had been the best poem in *Transport to Summer*, it probably would have.) Stevens looks at the apparent futility of the old violent idealism of religious conviction, tragic in its irrelevance to 'these violent marchers of the present'. There is an echo of 'A Postcard from the Volcano' in one of the finest stanzas:

> This is the pit of torment that placid end
> Should be illusion, that the mobs of birth
> Avoid our stale perfections, seeking out
> Their own, waiting until we go
> To picnic in the ruins that we leave.

In this poem Stevens does not resolve to detach himself from the John Zellers, his ancestors of the Christian past. On the contrary, he seems to identify himself with them: each stanza is followed by a couplet in which they are addressed as 'you, my semblables'. Yet he is himself, of course, of the present. And the ambiguity of the whole poem, which derives from Stevens's mixed feelings about both present and past, is brought to a perfectly pitched conclusion in the final couplet with its brilliant pun on the word 'temples':

> Time was not wasted in your subtle temples.
> No: nor divergence made too steep to follow down.

There are many other poems in *Transport to Summer* in which Stevens's yearning for the objects of belief which one part of his mind had long ago abandoned for ever is revealed more obviously than it was by the dense imagery of 'Notes'. The figure of the hero, in spite of the poems that seem to deny him value, reappears; and his connexion with the figure of Christ is allowed to emerge more clearly than before. The haunting little fable 'The Good Man Has No Shape' and the short poem 'Paisant Chronicle'[1] seem to assert that the hero may not after all be an abstraction; while the long and, for Stevens, rather dull meditation 'Chocorua to its Neighbor'[2] comes most alive when the 'fictive man' that is its subject is described in terms that almost seem to answer the bitter complaint against the God of Christianity that was made in 'Esthétique du Mal':

> He was more than an external majesty,
> Beyond the sleep of those that did not know,
> More than a spokesman of the night to say
> Now, time stands still. He came from out of sleep.
> He rose because men wanted him to be.
>
> They wanted him by day to be, image,
> But not the person, of their power, thought,
> But not the thinker, large in their largeness, beyond
> Their form, beyond their life, yet of themselves,
> Excluding by his largeness their defaults.

'A Pastoral Nun', one of the smallest and also one of the finest poems in the volume and a particular favourite of Stevens's, goes so far as to identify, with startling simplicity, the ancient images that bear the meaning of Christianity with the figures Stevens had for years been using in his own search for belief.

> Finally, in the last year of her age,
> Having attained a present blessedness,
> She said poetry and apotheosis are one.
>
> This is the illustration that she used:
> If I live according to this law I live
> In an immense activity, in which
>
> Everything becomes morning, summer, the hero,
> The enraptured woman, the sequestered night,
> The man that suffered, lying there at ease,
>
> Without his envious pain in body, in mind,
> The favourable transformations of the wind
> As of a general being or human universe.

---

[1] The word 'paisant' appears to be a Stevens coinage.
[2] Chocorua is a mountain in New Hampshire.

> There was another illustration, in which
> The two things compared their tight resemblances:
> Each matters only in that which it conceives.

It is significant that Stevens chose this poem, in May 1952, to intro-
duce one of his rare readings from his own work.

Behind 'A Pastoral Nun' lies Stevens's constant preoccupation with
the power of poetry, the power of words, the power that was, as it
were, both the subject and the object of 'Notes'. Stevens's still growing sense of this power makes itself felt many times in *Transport to
Summer*: one poem is actually called 'Men Made out of Words' and
ends:

> The whole race is a poet that writes down
> The eccentric propositions of its fate.

And a long conversational poem 'Description Without Place', is a
continuous enquiry into this 'writing down'. At its climax (sections
VI–VII) it is again to the possible unity of 'poetry and apotheosis'
that Stevens turns, this time with a reference to the beginning of the
Fourth Gospel:

> Description is revelation. It is not
> The thing described, nor false facsimile.
>
> It is an artificial thing that exists,
> In its own seeming, plainly visible,
>
> Yet not too closely the double of our lives,
> Intenser than any actual life could be,
>
> A text we should be born that we might read,
> More explicit than the experience of sun
>
> And moon, the book of reconciliation,
> Book of a concept only possible.
>
> In description, canon central in itself,
> The thesis of the plentifullest John.
>
> Thus the theory of description matters most.
> It is the theory of the word for those
>
> For whom the word is the making of world,
> The buzzing world and lisping firmament.

This was perhaps the clearest exposition Stevens ever made of a theme that had obsessed him all his life, and that had already found expression in the varied splendours of such poems as 'To The One of Fictive Music'. 'The Idea of Order at Key West' and parts of 'Notes'. It was to him of course far more than a mere theme: it was at once the claim he made for poetry and the many-coloured justification of that claim. He hoped that his own poems should be in the end, as 'The Whole of Harmonium', themselves a 'book of reconciliation', and with this hope in his mind, inextricably involved with his search for a tranquil belief, it was almost inevitable that he would have one day come to see St. John's *Logos* as in some way parallel to the poet's words through which alone the 'supreme fiction' could have any meaning or value. There is in this volume a beautiful short poem, 'The House was Quiet and the World was Calm', which describes the reading of a 'book of reconciliation':

> The house was quiet and the world was calm.
> The reader became the book; and summer night
>
> Was like the conscious being of the book.
> The house was quiet and the world was calm.
>
> The words were spoken as if there was no book,
> Except that the reader leaned above the page,
>
> Wanted to lean, wanted much most to be
> The scholar to whom his book is true, to whom
>
> The summer night is like a perfection of thought.
> The house was quiet because it had to be.
>
> The quiet was part of the meaning, part of the mind:
> The access of perfection to the page.
>
> And the world was calm. The truth in a calm world,
> In which there is no other meaning, itself
>
> Is calm, itself is summer and night, itself
> Is the reader leaning late and reading there.

This by itself is a fine poem. In the context of the rest of *Transport to Summer*, indeed of the whole of Stevens's work up to this time, it gains an extra significance, an extra depth. What the book was that 'the reader became' does not matter; what matters is the possibility that a book should be for the moment sufficient, should be one summer night 'the truth in a calm world'. Stevens is now able to use the phrase 'the truth' without the ironic misgivings that once would have surrounded it. The truth is now for him something that the writer may create between his book and its reader – 'One does not write for any reader except one', he said in his notebook. The truth is now for him something that may also and without violence be called a fiction. 'Thou art not August unless I make thee so'.

The intense peace of 'The House Was Quiet and World was Calm', reminding one of the line that ended the prologue to 'Notes': 'The vivid transparence that you bring is peace', has to do with the summer of this volume's title. 'Credences of Summer' (1946), the last long poem in the book to be written and, after 'Notes' and 'Esthétique du Mal', the most considerable, brings this peace and this intensity to a new peak of elaboration. Stevens rightly thought this one of his best poems. Its ten sections, each of three five-line blank verse stanzas, have a glowing rhetorical magnificence that makes each one of them a memorable achievement in his grandest manner. Beginning with a marvellous evocation of midsummer satiety in which 'the health of the world' and 'the honey of common summer' of 'Esthétique du Mal' are finally proclaimed as 'enough', the poem moves towards its great declaration about modern poetry which we have already had occasion to quote (see p. 66), by way of a description of the poet's task. Stevens said of it several years later that 'at the time when [it] was written my feeling for the necessity of a final accord with reality was at its strongest'.[1] But the 'final accord' of 'Credences of Summer' is by no means simply a matter of the exuberant rejoicing with which he had once celebrated the real world in the Florida poems of *Harmonium*. Now, after many years of thought and effort, and many more poems than years, his subject is not just reality itself, midsummer, 'green's green apogee', but what can be made of it, its marriage with the imagination, its created existence in the poet's words, how summer can become belief. The hinge of the poem is section VI, where the image of 'final accord' is a rock that recalls the mysterious rock of 'How To Live. What to Do':

[1] Letter to Charles Tomlinson, 19 June 1951.

The rock cannot be broken. It is the truth.
It rises from land and sea and covers them.
It is a mountain half way green and then,
The other immeasurable half, such rock
As placid air becomes. But it is not

A hermit's truth nor symbol in hermitage.
It is the visible rock, the audible,
The brilliant mercy of a sure repose,
On this present ground, the vividest repose,
Things certain sustaining us in certainty.

It is the rock of summer, the extreme,
A mountain luminous half way in bloom
And then half way in the extremest light
Of sapphires flashing from the central sky,
As if twelve princes sat before a king.

This, one of the supreme affirmations of Stevens's maturity, is impossible to paraphrase. Perhaps the most helpful thing that can be said of it is that it could not have been written if 'Notes' had not been written earlier. The truth it speaks, 'not a hermit's truth', has emerged into the light from what at the start of 'Notes' was 'the hermit in a poet's metaphors', and the confidence which attends it is a confidence Stevens had earned by himself and for himself. Immediately after this passage comes a difficult but powerful section about the modern poet's hard struggle 'to sing in face of the object' and finally to proclaim

> The meaning of the capture, this hard prize,
> Fully made, fully apparent, fully found.

It is not surprising that 'Credences of Summer' should turn out once again to be a poem about poetry. This is so of all Stevens's best poems after 'The Man with the Blue Guitar' and most of those before it, and it is so because the ends for poetry that he refused to lose sight of imposed upon his work a self-consciousness that forces his reader to share an awareness of those ends. Three consecutive entries in his notebook run: 'The theory of poetry is the life of poetry.' 'Feed my lambs (on the bread of living)...The glory of God is the glory of the world...To find the spiritual in reality...

To be concerned with reality.' 'The theory of poetry is the theory of life.' Behind such a view of poetry is neither arrogance nor naïveté, but a complex sense of responsibility and a profound humility. Together they produced in his work that constant preoccupation with poetry itself and what it may achieve, that self-consciousness, that some have seen as Stevens's great fault. But, when everything that needs saying about individual strengths and weaknesses has been said, this self-consciousness is the single decisive characteristic that distinguishes all modern poetry of real, central interest from the poetry of the past. It appeared with Blake, Wordsworth and Coleridge: it was they who first perceived that poetry, if anyone could be found to give its new potentiality adequate substance, had lost its innocence, had broken out of the marginal enclosure to which, however grand its glories, Christian certainties had confined it. Eliot, who, with his own certainties dictating his own priorities, would have disagreed with every word of this, nevertheless put it perfectly, in section v of 'East Coker':

> And what there is to conquer
> By strength and submission, has already been discovered
> Once or twice, or several times, by men whom one cannot hope
> To emulate – but there is no competition –
> There is only the fight to recover what has been lost
> And found and lost again and again: and now, under conditions
> That seem unpropitious. But perhaps neither gain nor loss.
> For us, there is only the trying. The rest is not our business.

This is the self-consciousness of modern poetry; and this courage and this honesty are the supreme qualities of 'Notes' and of all Stevens's other major poems, as they are of *Four Quartets* – which, like 'Notes', was finished in the dark summer of 1942.

11
1947-1950

In the spring of 1947 when *Transport to Summer* was published, Stevens was nearly sixty-eight. His eyesight, which had given him trouble since the 1920s, had lately grown worse and he had been told 'very much to cut down my reading and not read at night, which, after all, is the only time when I do read'.[1] Henry Church, the same age as himself and the closest friend he ever made, died on 4 April, his death drawing from Stevens one of the most exquisitely beautiful of all his longer poems 'The Owl in the Sarcophagus' (see pp.15–16). It is not surprising that some of the poems in *The Auroras of Autumn*, the new collection that appeared in 1950, should be shadowed by the sadness of old age and the consciousness of approaching death. What is surprising, even in a poet of Stevens's self-discipline and strength of character, is the freshness and vigour, the refusal to give up his openness of mind, the advances in thought and feeling that he was able to produce in this late period of his life. An old man, and at last in his own country beginning to be a famous one, he would not rest upon the tremendous positive achievement of 'Notes' and the later poems of *Transport to Summer*, but bore out to his last months the prescription he had laid down for the supreme fiction: It Must Change.

> The freshness of transformation is
> The freshness of a world. It is our own.

The best pieces in *The Auroras of Autumn*, in *The Rock*, the section of new poems that concluded *The Collected Poems* in 1954, and in the little group of poems written too late for *The Rock* and published in *Opus Posthumous*, move with the mastery of long experience, but there is nothing about them that is easy or lazy. The imaginative response to

[1] Letter to Feo, 19 December 1946.

reality is as unexpected and various as ever, and the scrupulousness, the tense caution which had always sustained Stevens in his search, is even now, after so many victories, not relaxed.

A case in point is the long title poem of *The Auroras of Autumn* which Stevens wrote in the summer or autumn of 1947 and three years later placed at the head of his new collection. In the poem's ten sections, written in Stevens's familiar three-line stanzas, a series of ideas, each a suggestion of fear or consolation indissolubly embodied in its particular imagery, is tried out in an atmosphere of loneliness and exhaustion. The cold lights of the aurora borealis 'which we have now and then in Hartford, sometimes quite strong enough to attract attention from indoors...symbolize a tragic and desolate background'.[1] This frightening background throws into new relief the frailty and impermanence of whatever it is that now and then, in one set of words or another, for a moment satisfies the poet's need. The northern lights make their first, terrifying appearance in the poem's second section. Then in section VI the poet himself is set against them:

> This is nothing until in a single man contained,
> Nothing until this named thing nameless is
> And is destroyed. He opens the door of his house
>
> On flames. The scholar of one candle sees
> An arctic effulgence flaring on the frame
> Of everything he is. And he feels afraid.

Images of transience and fear pervade the poem. There is a mysterious mother related to 'the one of fictive music', who 'gives transparence. But she has grown old...'

> The soft hands are a motion not a touch.
> The house will crumble and the books will burn.

And there is an even more mysterious father round whom no order will revolve.

In the poem's last three sections images of reconciliation appear against the background of menace, section VIII postulating 'a time of innocence' the idea of which transforms the poet's feeling towards the northern lights:

[1] Letter to M. Van Duyn, 29 November 1954.

So then, these lights are not a spell of light,
A saying out of a cloud, but innocence.
An innocence of the earth and no false sign

Or symbol of malice.

By the end of the poem the lights have themselves become an image
of warmth and frailty, of that temporary balance that the poet may
contrive, and that may give 'an unhappy people' a sufficient confidence
in their world:

In these unhappy he meditates a whole,
The full of fortune and the full of fate,
As if he lived all lives, that he might know,

In hall harridan, not hushful paradise,
To a haggling of wind and weather, by these lights
Like a blaze of summer straw, in winter's nick.

'The Auroras of Autumn' is one of Stevens's most difficult poems,
not least because it is the final flowering of his technique at its
densest and most elaborate. The long poems that came after this were
written in a more direct or more discursive manner, or both: here
the images carry in their strangeness a burden of meaning that seems
to withstand disengagement even as it demands it. Stevens may have
written in his notebook: 'Poetry must resist the intelligence almost
successfully', but the key word is 'almost' and his own poems were
certainly intended to satisfy his reader's intelligence as well as his
reader's emotions (insofar as these can be separated: not far, Stevens
thought). A similar 'almost' appears in a passage from the lecture
'Effects of Analogy' (1948), a passage which forms an apt comment on
'The Auroras of Autumn' and the powerfully individual atmosphere
which its impenetrable images create:

Poetry is almost incredibly one of the effects of analogy...It is almost
incredibly the outcome of figures of speech or, what is the same thing, the
outcome of the operation of one imagination on another through the instru-
mentality of the figures...There is always an analogy between nature and
the imagination, and possibly poetry is merely the strange rhetoric of that
parallel: a rhetoric in which the feeling of one man is communicated to
another in words of the exquisite appositeness that takes away all their
verbality.

The loneliness and sense of loss that lie behind the 'strange rhetoric' of 'The Auroras of Autumn' reappear several times in the shorter and more accessible poems of the volume. One group of four such poems, 'This Solitude of Cataracts', 'In the Element of Antagonisms', 'In a Bad Time' and 'The Beginning' leave an over- whelming impression of the sadness of old age, which is no more than a new accentuation of the sadness that had never been far from the centre of Stevens's poetry. As in 'The Auroras of Autumn', winter and the north haunt these poems, making more poignant the poet's desire for the transient benediction of summer. In 'The Beginning' the figure of vanished summer is a figure we recognise from far in Stevens's past:

> So summer comes in the end to these few stains
> And the rust and rot of the door through which she went.
>
> The house is empty. But here is where she sat
> To comb her dewy hair, a touchless light.

And in the saddest of these poems, 'In a Bad Time', there is a figure who recalls the slouching figure of 'Notes', 'Looking for what was, where it used to be'.

> But the beggar gazes on calamity
> And thereafter he belongs to it, to bread
> Hard found, and water tasting of misery...
>
> He has his poverty and nothing more.
> His poverty becomes his heart's strong core –
> A forgetfulness of summer at the pole.

There is, as usual, nothing negative about these bleak lines. The acceptance of poverty as the fundamental state, the recognition of winter and the north as the essential background without which the fulfilments of summer would lose their meaning – these are for Stevens 'his heart's strong core', the basis, in this volume as in all his others, of his positive affirmations. And the best poems in *The Auroras of Autumn* are neither tragic nor desolate but lit and warmed with a new love for the real world and a new humility in the definition of whatever it is in the real world that is finally the object of that love.

'Take the case of a man for whom reality is enough, as, at the end of his life, he returns to it like a man returning from Nowhere to his village and to everything there that is tangible and visible, which he has come to cherish and wants to be near. He sees without images. But is he not seeing a clarified reality of his own? Does he not dwell in an analogy?' These sentences, also from 'Effects of Analogy', describe perfectly the mood of 'Large Red Man Reading', a short poem written at about the same time. Stevens himself liked this poem 'very much'. It is certainly among the best dozen short poems of his entire career, finding as it does 'at the end of his life' the perfect words for the 'man for whom reality is enough' but who nevertheless, as a poet, 'dwells in an analogy'. Here is the whole poem:

> There were ghosts that returned to earth to hear his phrases,
> As he sat there reading, aloud, the great blue tabulae.
> They were those from the wilderness of stars that had expected more.
>
> There were those that returned to hear him read from the poem
>   of life,
> Of the pans above the stove, the pots on the table, the tulips among
>   them.
> They were those that would have wept to step barefoot into reality,
>
> That would have wept and been happy, have shivered in the frost
> And cried out to feel it again, have run fingers over leaves
> And against the most coiled thorn, have seized on what was ugly
>
> And laughed, as he sat there reading, from out of the purple tabulae,
> The outlines of being and its expressings, the syllables of its law:
> *Poesis, poesis,* the literal characters, the vatic lines,
>
> Which, in those ears and in those thin, those spended hearts,
> Took on color, took on shape and the size of things as they are
> And spoke the feeling for them, which was what they had lacked.

Here is celebrated again the marriage which had for so long been Stevens's image of sufficiency and his goal, the union, in 'the great blue tabulae' of poetry, of reality and the imagination, of 'the outlines of being and its expressings'. This union, in these late poems, has become closer than ever before. As Stevens put it in his lecture of 1947, 'Three Academic Pieces': 'What our eyes behold may well be the text of life but one's meditations on the text and the disclosures of these meditations are no less a part of the structure of reality.' The longest and most ambitious poem in *The Auroras of Autumn*, 'An Ordinary Evening in New Haven', is an extended meditation on this theme. One (section XII) of its thirty-one sections begins:

> The poem is the cry of its occasion,
> Part of the res itself and not about it.

This same section ends with a stanza that well summarises the whole poem:

> In the end, in the whole psychology, the self,
> The town, the weather, in a casual litter,
> Together, said words of the world are the life of the world.

When Stevens was writing 'An Ordinary Evening in New Haven', in 1949, he explained to a correspondent: 'Here my interest is to try to get as close to the ordinary, the commonplace and the ugly as it is possible for a poet to get. It is not a question of grim reality but of plain reality. The object is of course to purge oneself of anything false'.[1] Possibly Stevens carried too far the self-denial implicit in this explanation; in any case the poem, though it has fine and memorable moments, suffers from a certain lack of vitality and lack of impetus. 'The self, the town, the weather' are not by themselves, when expressed in such a deliberately low tone, enough to sustain the poem's life, and too much of it has the air of 'a casual litter'. But its best passages lead one to suppose that Stevens himself realised this, for all of them concern that need for something more than the ordinary, more than fact, which had always made him by no means a poet of plainness and the commonplace. The lines that end section v are surely self-descriptive:

> The self, the chrysalis of all men
>
> Became divided in the leisure of blue day
> And more, in branchings after day. One part
> Held fast tenaciously in common earth
>
> And one from central earth to central sky
> And in moonlit extensions of them in the mind
> Searched out such majesty as it could find.

[1] Letter to Bernard Heringman, 3 May 1949.

It is, precisely, the 'moonlit extensions' of the imagination's meanings, what in section IX is called 'the spirit's alchemicana' 'within' reality, that too much of this very long poem seems to lack. Nevertheless there are occasions when the new awareness of reality, the new love for it that had been the subject of 'Large Red Man Reading', is caught again with sharpness and clarity. One such is the second half of section XIII:

> It is a fresh spiritual that he defines,
> A coldness in a long, too-constant warmth,
> A thing on the side of a house, not deep in a cloud,
>
> A difficulty that we predicate:
> The difficulty of the visible
> To the nations of the clear invisible,
>
> The actual landscape with its actual horns
> Of baker and butcher blowing, as if to hear,
> Hear hard, gets at an essential integrity.

This chill freshness of perception was something that Stevens was to recapture in several of the short poems of *The Rock*. 'The Plain Sense of Things', a beautiful poem written in 1952 and suspended in an atmosphere of wintry melancholy, shows the unflagging self-discipline of Stevens's old age. Nothing here is easier, more self-indulgent than the honesties of 'The Snow Man', written more than thirty years earlier. Yet this winter is the winter after summer, not before; and in its forlornness, as the last two stanzas make clear, there is also a triumph:

> After the leaves have fallen, we return
> To a plain sense of things. It is as if
> We had come to an end of the imagination,
> Inanimate in a inert savoir.
>
> It is difficult even to choose the adjective
> For this blank cold, this sadness without cause.
> The great structure has become a minor house.
> No turban walks across the lessened floors...
>
> Yet the absence of the imagination had
> Itself to be imagined. The great pond,

The plain sense of it, without reflections, leaves,
Mud, water like dirty glass, expressing silence

Of a sort, silence of a rat come out to see,
The great pond and its waste of the lilies, all this
Had to be imagined as an inevitable knowledge,
Required, as a necessity requires.

Poems like this and 'Not Ideas About the Thing but the Thing Itself' (1954), which Stevens put at the end of his *Collected Poems* so that the last line of the whole book was 'A new knowledge of reality', were the latest and perhaps the most valuable fruits of the arduous experiment in thought and feeling about the real world that was 'An Ordinary Evening in New Haven'.

The closing sections of 'An Ordinary Evening' itself create an increasing sense that its new clean vision of reality should be recognised as a new victory for the imagination. In section XXV the imagination appears in a dramatic embodiment that might come from 'Notes' or much earlier in Stevens's poetry:

Nothing about him ever stayed the same,
Except this hidalgo and his eye and tune,
The shawl across one shoulder and the hat.

The sections that follow emphasise more and more strongly the imagination's part in the union that can make out of the most ordinary evening, out of the commonplace and the ugly, words that are 'the life of the world'. In the penultimate section (XXX), a poem very like 'The Plain Sense of Things', the gain won by the poet's resolution 'to purge oneself of anything false' is made explicit:

The barrenness that appears is an exposing.
It is not part of what is absent, a halt
For farewells, a sad hanging on for remembrances.

It is a coming on and a coming forth...

The glass of the air becomes an element –
It was something imagined that has been washed away.
A clearness has returned. It stands restored.

It is not an empty clearness, a bottomless sight.
It is a visibility of thought,
In which hundreds of eyes, in one mind, see at once.

What is described here is what in the lines already quoted from section XIII had been called 'a fresh spiritual'...

> A coldness in a long, too-constant warmth,
> A thing on the side of a house, not deep in a cloud.

The possible breadth and depth of the implications of both passages can be seen in some remarkable sentences using the same imagery which Stevens wrote nearly two years later in his lecture 'Two or Three Ideas'. Among other things, these sentences suggest very strongly that in 'An Ordinary Evening in New Haven' Stevens was not, as one might at first sight suppose, in any sense backing down from the high ambitions of 'Notes', but, rather, was for the moment deliberately concentrating on one aspect of them: the cleaned vision of the world which now in his old age he had renewed in himself.

In an age of disbelief, or, what is the same thing, in a time that is largely humanistic, in one sense or another, it is for the poet to supply the satisfactions of belief, in his measure and in his style...I think of it as a role of the utmost seriousness. It is, for one thing, a spiritual role...To see the gods dispelled in mid-air and dissolve like clouds is one of the great human experiences...It was as if they had never inhabited the earth. There was no crying out for their return. They were not forgotten because they had been a part of the glory of the earth. At the same time no man ever muttered a petition in his heart for the restoration of those unreal shapes...

One has to pierce through the dithyrambic impressions that talk of the gods makes to the reality of what is being said. What is being said must be true and the truth of it must be seen. But the truth about the poet in a time of disbelief is not that he must turn evangelist. After all, he shares the disbelief of his time. He does not turn to Paris or Rome for relief from the monotony of reality. He turns to himself and denies that reality was ever monotonous except in comparison. He asserts that the source of comparison having been eliminated, reality is returned, as if a shadow had passed and drawn after it and taken away whatever coating had concealed what lay beneath it.

It was the passing of this shadow, and the new revelation not only of the reality beneath it but of the possible 'satisfactions' of a relationship between the self and this reality, that were the real subjects of 'An Ordinary Evening in New Haven'. Here, as Stevens had always intended in his poetry as a whole, the consolations of dead orthodoxy,

whether aesthetic or religious ('Paris or Rome'), were to be resisted
and there was to be created what in 'Things of August', an obscure
and rather tired poem of this period, he called:

> A new text of the world...
> A text of intelligent men
> At the centre of the unintelligible.

For all the ambition of these phrases, there is nothing pretentious
or grandiose about Stevens's late poems. Indeed the wariness of
assertion in which Stevens had trained himself for years is here
stretched tauter than ever, and it was this wariness that now
produced the last of his great figures, the necessary angel after whom
he named the collection of his prose pieces that was published in
1951. The angel himself, who has nothing to do with the angel in the
closing poems of 'Notes', appears in only one poem, 'Angel Surrounded
by Paysans', the last piece in *The Auroras of Autumn* to be written and
one that particularly excited Stevens. Here he is, at the point of his
appearance and instant vanishing:

> I am the angel of reality,
> Seen for a moment standing in the door...
>
> I am one of you and being one of you
> Is being and knowing what I am and know.
>
> Yet I am the necessary angel of the earth,
> Since, in my sight, you see the earth again,
>
> Cleared of its stiff and stubborn, man-locked set,
> And, in my hearing, you hear its tragic drone
>
> Rise liquidly in liquid lingerings,
> Like watery words awash; like meanings said
>
> By repetitions of half-meanings. Am I not,
> Myself, only half of a figure of a sort,
>
> A figure half seen, or seen for a moment, a man
> Of the mind, an apparition apparelled in
>
> Apparels of such lightest look that a turn
> Of my shoulder and quickly, too quickly, I am gone?

'The Angel', said Stevens, commenting upon this later,[1] 'is the angel of reality. This is clear only if the reader is of the idea that we live in a world of the imagination, in which reality and contact with it are the great blessings. For nine readers out of ten, the necessary angel will appear to be the angel of the imagination and for nine days out of ten that is true, although it is the tenth day that counts.' This may appear to be in direct conflict with many of Stevens's pronouncements about reality and the imagination, and, in particular, with the tremendous claims for the imagination's power made in 'Notes'. But neither the imagination's angel of 'Notes' nor this angel of reality is meant to embody a final statement. 'I have no wish to arrive at a conclusion', Stevens wrote in another letter[2] of this time. 'Sometimes I believe most in the imagination for a long time and then, without reasoning about it, turn to reality and believe in that and that alone. But both of these things project themselves endlessly and I want them to do just that.' For the present, for the period of *The Auroras of Autumn*, this endless projection had resolved itself into a new belief in reality, but a belief of the most extreme and delicately suggested subtlety. The angel 'surrounded by paysans' bringing for a moment his sudden miraculous clarity, is here 'the necessary angel of the earth'. He is the wholly successful image that the poet has found for the slight and transient manifestations of meaning in reality which were evoked in the last section (XXXI) of 'An Ordinary Evening in New Haven':

> The less legible meanings of sounds, the little reds
> Not often realized, the lighter words
> In the heavy drum of speech, the inner men
>
> Behind the outer shields, the sheets of music
> In the strokes of thunder, dead candles at the window
> When day comes, fire-foams in the motions of the sea,
>
> Flickings from finikin to fine finikin...
>
> It is not in the premise that reality
> Is a solid. It may be a shade that traverses
> A dust, a force that traverses a shade.

[1] Letter to Sister M. Bernetta Quinn, 29 May 1952.
[2] To Heringman, 20 March 1951.

In a major poem of the previous year, 'A Primitive Like an Orb', the same slight and transient signs of meaning, of a vindicating value, seem to come not from reality itself but from something existing only in the imagination, 'the essential poem at the centre of things'.

> We do not prove the existence of the poem.
> It is something seen and known in lesser poems.
> It is the huge, high harmony that sounds
> A little and a little, suddenly,
> By means of a separate sense. It is and it
> Is not and, therefore, is. In the instant of speech,
> The breadth of an accelerando moves,
> Captives the being, widens – and was there.

And later the crucial role of the imagination in this 'difficult apperception' is confirmed by a paradox that echoes Theseus's speech on imagination in *A Midsummer Night's Dream*:

> One poem proves another and the whole,
> For the clairvoyant men that need no proof:
> The lover, the believer and the poet.

But in the next stanza it becomes clear that the swift vision described in this poem is not opposed to the vision for which the necessary angel was later to be the figure. For, just as in the sight of the necessary angel the earth is to be 'cleared of its stiff and stubborn, man-locked set', so here, for 'the clairvoyant men', the central poem will enlarge itself

> Until the used-to earth and sky, and the tree
> And cloud, the used-to tree and used-to cloud,
> Lose the old uses that they made of them.

Finally, at the climax of 'A Primitive Like an Orb', the distinction between reality and the imagination becomes quite lost in the great 'as if' of Stevens's old image of a marriage between the two:

> It is
> As if the central poem became the world,
>
> And the world the central poem, each one the mate
> Of the other...

In all these difficult and tentative poems of *The Auroras of Autumn*, even in the ones which, like 'Angel Surrounded by Paysans', seem most firmly to announce 'A new knowledge of reality', it is still the familiar and inexhaustible theme of the interdependence of reality and the imagination that Stevens is exploring, and the attempt to detach too definitely one from the other in any particular phase or moment of his thought is bound to fail. What was for him a matter of the utmost tact and caution, 'the breadth of an accelerando', 'the less legible meanings of sounds', 'repetitions of half-meanings', cannot in any case be grasped for inspection by the clumsy gloves of para- phrase. Nevertheless one can say of these poems that while whatever it is that they affirm seems, since 'Notes' and 'Credences of Summer', to have become more elusive, it has also become more certain. There is a suggestion of a separate existence from the poet's, of an 'otherness', about 'the central poem', the 'force that traverses a shade', 'the necessary angel', that the supreme fiction never, except in the pro- logue, had in 'Notes' itself, although Stevens said of the poem: 'It is implicit in the title that there can be such a thing as a supreme fiction.'[1] This 'otherness' of course does not involve any idea of a real being; the necessary angel is no more real than the one of fictive music or Keats's Moneta. What is suggested in these poems, with new conviction and new emphasis, is the existence of the ideal.

Several times in the lectures of these years Stevens struggled to find words for this sense of the ideal. In 'Three Academic Pieces' (1947), he has been speaking only of the possible perfection of resemblances when he suddenly concludes:

Metaphor has its aspect of the ideal. This aspect of it cannot be dismissed merely because we think that we have long since outlived the ideal. The truth is that we are constantly outliving it and yet the ideal itself remains alive with an enormous life.

In the following year, in 'Effects of Analogy' and still more in 'Imagination as Value', he made a sustained effort to explain what it was that the 'enormous life' of the ideal could mean for the poet, what kind of certainty it was that the imagination alone could per- ceive. Sometimes he seems defeated by the difficulty of this task, and his argument becomes merely circular:

[1] Letter to Church, 8 December 1942.

It is so easy for the poet to say that a learned man must go on being a learned man but that a poet respects no knowledge except his own and, again, that the poet does not yield to the priest. What the poet has in mind, when he says things of this sort, is that poetic value is an intrinsic value. It is not the value of knowledge. It is not the value of faith. It is the value of the imagination.

But in the next paragraph after this passage from 'Imagination as Value' a forceful clarity suddenly breaks through. The imagination, Stevens now says,

is part of our security. It enables us to live our own lives. We have it because we do not have enough without it. This may not be true as to each one of us, for certainly there are those for whom reality and the reason are enough. It is true of us as a race...If the imagination is the faculty by which we import the unreal into what is real, its value is the value of the way of thinking by which we project the idea of God into the idea of man.

In these attempts to describe 'the value of the imagination', the value which he himself had consciously taken to be supreme in the ordering of his own life, Stevens might have used a key text from *Interpretations of Poetry and Religion*:

Religion may falsely represent the ideal as a reality, but we must remember that the ideal, if not so represented, would be despised by the majority of men, who cannot understand that the value of things is moral, and who therefore attribute to what is moral a natural existence, thinking thus to vindicate its importance and value. But value lies in meaning, not in substance.

In this passage, and particularly in its last sentence, there is a more confident, a more unequivocal justification for the power of the supreme fiction and all the many and various figures of its 'entourage' than Stevens ever committed himself to in prose. But it was at this very time that, in his poetry, he was beginning for the first time to face the furthest implications of his own idea of the imagination's value. These implications are those contained in Santayana's word 'moral' in the passage above, and their first cautious appearance in Stevens's poetry is in the word 'good' as it appears in the first stanza of 'A Primitive Like an Orb':

The essential poem at the centre of things,
The arias that spiritual fiddlings make,
Have gorged the cast-iron of our lives with good
And the cast-iron of our works. But it is, dear sirs,
A difficult apperception, this gorging good,
Fetched by such slick-eyed nymphs, this essential gold,
This fortune's finding, disposed and re-disposed
By such slight genii in such pale air.

Twelve years before, in the less subtle days of *Ideas of Order*, Stevens had been able to write simply that 'while it can lie in the temperament of very few of us to write poetry in order to find God, it is probably the purpose of each of us to write poetry to find the good which, in the Platonic sense, is synonymous with God.'[1] Now, in the spring of 1948, just after 'A Primitive Like an Orb' and just before 'Imagination as Value', we find him writing with much more circumspection to Sister Bernetta Quinn, a nun and critic with whom he occasionally corresponded about his work. (From this reply one may guess that she had stressed some of the religious connotations of his poems.)

It is a relief to have a letter from some one that is interested in understanding. However, I don't want to turn to stone under your very eyes by saying 'This is the centre that I seek and this alone'. Your mind is too much like my own for it to seem to be an evasion on my part to say merely that I do seek a centre and expect to go on seeking it. I don't say that I shall not find it or that I do not expect to find it. It is the great necessity even without specific identification. (7 April 1948.)

These few remarks tell us a lot about Stevens's frame of mind in these last years of his life, and do much to explain the extraordinary spiritual force, a force that comes not from settled declaration but from restless feeling, of the great poems that were still to be written. Of these the first was 'The Rock', which was finished early in 1950 and from which Stevens took the title of the concluding section of his *Collected Poems*.

'The Rock' is a set of three poems, each revolving round the image that Stevens had used in 'How To Live. What To Do', and, with

---

[1] From 'The Irrational Element in Poetry' (1936).

glowing exhilaration, in 'Credences of Summer' VI (see p. 172) where the rock had embodied 'The brilliant mercy of a sure repose'. The first poem, 'Seventy Years Later', describes a desolation without words, without meaning, without 'the sounds of the guitar'. Out of this desolation, out of its poverty and need, there appears with the sudden radiance of the necessary angel himself something that can only be described as a revelation:

> As if nothingness contained a métier,
> A vital assumption, an impermanence
> In its permanent cold, an illusion so desired
>
> That the green leaves came and covered the high rock,
> That the lilacs came and bloomed, like a blindness cleaned,
> Exclaiming bright sight, as it was satisfied,
>
> In a birth of sight.

The second poem, 'The Poem as Icon', explores the nature of these miraculous leaves. They turn out to have much in common with the 'fictive covering' of Ozymandias's bride in 'Notes' II. VIII.

> The fiction of the leaves as the icon
>
> Of the poem, the figuration of blessedness,
> And the icon is the man...
>
> In this plenty, the poem makes meanings of the rock,
> Of such mixed motion and such imagery
> That its barrenness becomes a thousand things
>
> And so exists no more. This is the cure
> Of leaves and of the ground and of ourselves.
> His words are both the icon and the man.

'The Rock', particularly in these two parts – for the third, 'Forms of the Rock in a Night-Hymn', is less successful – creates a glowing atmosphere of conclusion and fulfilment. The leaves 'bloom as a man loves, as he lives in love', and the 'illusion so desired' seems to be the finally satisfying object of this love. But Stevens could not even now say 'This is the centre that I seek and this alone', and 'The Rock' was by no means his last poem.

12
The Last Phase

On 5 December 1950 Stevens wrote to the editor of the *Hudson Review* apologising for not being able to send him anything and adding:

I know what it is that I want to write about. The trouble is that I have not particularly felt like writing about it. Then, too, I have been overwhelmingly busy at the office – and in consequence too tired to do anything, except to read the evening paper, at home.

Three days later he wrote again:

I send you a poem after all. I had originally intended to write a long poem on the subject of the present poem but got no farther than the statement that God and the imagination are one. The implications of this statement were to follow, and may still...After writing to you I looked at the opening lines which I am now sending you and I thought that they might do.

The long poem was never written; the implications never followed. Stevens was now seventy-one and still working as a businessman in a full-time position of high responsibility. It is hardly surprising that another poem on his grandest scale was beyond him. Nevertheless the 'opening lines' which he sent to the *Hudson Review*,[1] calling them 'Final Soliloquy of the Interior Paramour', are by themselves remarkable enough, recording as they do a new conclusion and a new certainty:

> Light the first light of evening, as in a room
> In which we rest and, for small reason, think
> The world imagined is the ultimate good.

[1] A year later he chose to end the Faber Selection of his poems with these 'opening lines'.

This is, therefore, the intensest rendezvous.
It is in that thought that we collect ourselves,
Out of all the indifferences, into one thing:

Within a single thing, a single shawl
Wrapped tightly round us, since we are poor, a warmth,
A light, a power, the miraculous influence.

Here, now, we forget each other and ourselves.
We feel the obscurity of an order, a whole,
A knowledge, that which arranged the rendezvous.

Within its vital boundary, in the mind.
We say God and the imagination are one...
How high that highest candle lights the dark.

Out of this same light, out of the central mind,
We make a dwelling in the evening air,
In which being there together is enough.

These lines are a fine distillation, a quintessence, of thirty-five years of poetic thought and feeling on the most profound level. Much about them is by now familiar: poverty, and the revelation that redeems poverty; love, for there are, as so often in Stevens's most intense poems, two involved in a relationship of fulfilment and satisfaction: one and a mysterious other, the lover and the object of his love; self-reliance, for all that takes place in these lines takes place 'within its vital boundary, in the mind'; the image of the candle in the dark, which has been with Stevens ever since *Harmonium*'s 'Valley Candle' and has survived the 'Arctic effulgence' which assailed it in 'The Auroras of Autumn'. (He was to use it again in a speech[1] of the following year whose closing sentence tells of 'the interior paramour': the position of poetry 'is always an inner position, never certain, never fixed. It is to be found beneath the poet's word and deep within the reader's eye in those chambers in which the genius of poetry sits alone with her candle in a moving solitude.') But perhaps the single most striking characteristic of 'Final Soliloquy' is its humility. 'For small reason', 'a single shawl', 'since we are poor', 'a dwelling in the evening air', the candle itself against the vastness of the dark – all these words and phrases convey no flamboyant

---

[1] When accepting the medal of the Poetry Society of America 1951.

announcement of acquired belief but simply that the long search has ended, for the time being, in a quiet and secret sufficiency, in something that is 'enough'. Humility is not a new quality in Stevens's poetry. What is new, in these extraordinary lines, is a strengthening of that sense of 'otherness', of that separate thing in the face of which the poet can only be humble, which had begun to appear in some of the poems of *The Auroras of Autumn*.

> We feel the obscurity of an order, a whole,
> A knowledge, that which arranged the rendezvous.

These lines sketch the possibility that is immediately given its full force in the words:

> We say God and the imagination are one.

But even here we have only a suggestion – 'We say' – and it is not a 'truth' but this suggestion that is the 'highest candle'.

The line 'We say God and the imagination are one' may appear to suggest the very opposite of a sense of 'otherness'. It may appear, as it has to some critics,[1] to indicate the height or depth of romantic solipsism. But it should no more be taken in isolation as the statement of a creed than should Keats's 'Beauty is truth, truth beauty'. To jump to the kind of conclusion that Stevens himself throughout his life, including the period after 'Final Soliloquy', so steadfastly avoided would be deplorably inappropriate. The whole force of Stevens's long devotion to reality, the poet's 'inescapable and ever-present difficulty and inamorata', as he called it after[2] this poem was written, the resolute tentativeness which he never relaxed – 'I don't want to turn to stone', 'I have no wish to arrive at a conclusion' –, in particular the special quality of 'Final Soliloquy' itself, what one may call its extreme religious sensitiveness and reticence: all this should lead the reader away from any sensational summary of what is meant by the line 'We say God and the imagination are one.' Stevens himself no doubt would have been unwilling to commit himself beyond the almost experimental words of the poem. He occasionally tried con-

---

1 For instance Denis Donoghue in *Connoisseurs of Chaos*. He strengthens his case by quoting this line with the addition of the word 'human' before 'imagination'.
2 In a speech at Bard College in 1951, wrongly dated 1948 in *Opus Posthumous* (see letter to Mrs Church, 19 February 1951).

clusions in his notebook with this most crucial issue of his life in poetry. 'God is in me or else is not at all (does not exist).' 'The imagination is the liberty of the mind and hence the liberty of reality.' These two remarks taken together throw a little light on 'Final Soliloquy'. But the notebook entry that begins: 'Proposita: I, God and the imagination are one;' ends with a hint of rueful dubiousness at the logical consequence of such a proposition: 'Hence, I suppose, the imaginer is God.'

Meanwhile in his letters he went no further than the odd oblique reference to such things. For instance, late in 1951 he wrote to Sister Bernetta: 'Mr. Wagner indulges in over-simplifications.' [C. Roland Wagner was a sympathetic critic of Stevens's work] 'I am not an atheist although I do not believe to-day in the same God in whom I believed when I was a boy. But to talk to you about God is like explaining French to a Frenchman.' (21 December 1951.) And nearly a year later he said in the course of a rambling amiable letter to his friend Thomas McGreevy in Ireland: 'At my age it would be nice to be able to read more and think more and be myself more and to make up my mind about God, say, before it is too late, or at least before he makes up his mind about me.' (24 October 1952.)

In the autumn 1952 issue of the *Hudson Review* Stevens published a group of eight new poems. Apart from 'The Rock' itself, these poems were to form the most substantial part of the last section of the *Collected Poems*. They were headed by the great tribute to Santayana, 'To an Old Philosopher in Rome', which was perhaps the best poem of Stevens's last years, but two or three others were of almost equal weight and quality. 'To an Old Philosopher in Rome' was, among other things the most definitely religious poem Stevens had yet written. In it, as we have already seen (see above, p. 33), the contemplation of the imminent death of an old friend and hero merges imperceptibly into meditation on the poet's own approaching death. In it, also, there reaches a new intensity and a new explicitness that sense of 'otherness', of the saving existence of an ideal or a mysterious good outside himself, which had been gaining strength in Stevens's poetry since 'A Primitive Like an Orb'. At one moment in the poem, in his evocation of the convent room where Santayana lies dying, he writes of:

> A light on the candle tearing against the wick
> To join a hovering excellence, to escape
> From fire and be part only of that of which
>
> Fire is the symbol: the celestial possible.

Later the old man is said to be:

> alive
> Yet living in two worlds, impenitent
> As to one, and, as to one, most penitent,
> Impatient for the grandeur that you need
>
> In so much misery; and yet finding it
> Only in misery...

And towards the end of the poem in the words 'pillared porch' and 'threshold', Stevens uses an image familiar since some of the earliest poems in *Harmonium* to suggest the frontier and the momentous transition between one world and another.

In all this there is even now no more than suggestion. There is no declaration of anything that might be described as a truth, particularly as a truth as opposed to a fiction. Still less does anything in 'To an Old Philosopher in Rome' carry specifically Christian connotations. Nevertheless Stevens is here very near to a spiritual centre, a point of rest, that could as well be described in the traditional terms of Christian theology; and in 'Prologues to What is Possible', another poem of the 1952 group, this is even more the case.

This poem is, as it were, an exploration of the phrase 'the celestial possible', not by means of the archaic symbol, fire, beside which it is placed in 'To an Old Philosopher in Rome', but through a new image of strange dream-like vividness. Its first part consists only of this image. It begins:

> There was an ease of mind that was like being alone in a boat at sea,
> A boat carried forward by waves resembling the bright backs of rowers,
> Gripping their oars, as if they were sure of the way to their destination,
> Bending over and pulling themselves erect on the wooden handles,
> Wet with water and sparkling in the one-ness of their motion.

After more long, steady lines of gathering intensity, this part of the poem ends with one of those haunting intimations of the fulfilment of spiritual need that punctuate the whole extent of Stevens's poetry:

> ...he travelled alone, like a man lured on by a syllable without any
>   meaning,
> A syllable of which he felt, with an appointed sureness,
> That it contained the meaning into which he wanted to enter,
> A meaning which, as he entered it, would shatter the boat and leave
>   the oarsmen quiet
> As at a point of central arrival, an instant moment, much or little,
> Removed from any shore, from any man or woman, and needing none.

The magical tranquillity created by this image is broken by the opening words of the second part of the poem, which is in the form of an elaborate metaphysical commentary on the first part. 'The metaphor stirred his fear'. But in the course of this second part, fear gives way to a new vision of promise, as mysterious and as little-defined as the first but humbler and, in its surprising suddenness, more like the swift manifestations of sufficiency in various poems in the volume *The Auroras of Autumn*:

> What self, for example, did he contain that had not yet been loosed,
> Snarling in him for discovery as his attentions spread,
> As if all his hereditary lights were suddenly increased
> By an access of color, a new and unobserved, slight dithering,
> The smallest lamp, which added its puissant flick, to which he gave
> A name and privilege over the ordinary of his commonplace –
>
> A flick which added to what was real and its vocabulary,
> The way some first thing coming into Northern trees
> Adds to them the whole vocabulary of the South,
> The way the earliest single light in the evening sky, in spring,
> Creates a fresh universe out of nothingness by adding itself,
> The way a look or a touch reveals its unexpected magnitudes.

As usual, it would be rash to identify with any firmness the subject of this poem, the 'what is possible' to which its two parts are pro-logues. As usual, also, Stevens's preoccupation with the poet's particular relation to this subject, with the possibility of describing, somehow or other, that which cannot be named, lies close to the poem's centre. 'A syllable without any meaning' carries the full weight of what is evoked in the first part; 'A flick which added to what was real and its vocabulary' does the same in the second part. If one at last dares to suggest that the word 'God', with all its ancient complex of connotations, of meanings and meaninglessness, is the word that lies behind the moving evasions of this poem, as Stevens proposed it to lie behind 'the miraculous influence' in 'Final Soliloquy', it is by no means to suggest a simple answer to the problems Stevens faced in his poetry and thereby set his readers. It is rather, to hold all the elements of this one poem for a moment in one pattern and to see whether the poem gains in significance and coherence. If it does, we have proved nothing. We have merely suggested that a great creative mind may add to old words new life without so much as using them.

In the very subtle and very difficult Essay XI from *The Friend*, to which I have already referred, there is a passage in which Coleridge gives to the word 'God' exactly the kind of new life that Stevens, perhaps, does in 'Prologues to What is Possible'. It is a passage which certainly throws the light of a similar mind, a similar sense of the world, on the obscure unity that one feels to exist beneath the various different manifestations of 'The celestial possible' in Stevens's late poems, from 'the huge, high harmony that sounds a little and a little' and the figure of the necessary angel to the saving nuances of 'To an Old Philosopher in Rome' and 'Prologues to What is Possible'. Here is Coleridge:

Hast thou ever raised thy mind to the consideration of existence, in and by itself, as the mere act of existing? Hast thou ever said to thyself thoughtfully, It is! heedless in that moment, whether it were a man before thee, or a flower, or a grain of sand, – without reference, in short, to this or that particular mode or form of existence? If thou hast indeed attained to this, thou wilt have felt the presence of a mystery, which must have fixed thy spirit in awe and wonder.

He goes on to ask of 'the power, which evoked this idea of being' 'how shall we name it?' And, failing to define it further or to derive it from anything else, he continues:

And yet this power, nevertheless, is; – in supremacy of being it is; – and he for whom it manifests itself in its adequate idea, dare as little arrogate it to himself as his own, can as little appropriate it either totally or by partition, as he can claim ownership in the breathing air, or make an inclosure in the cope of heaven. He bears witness of it to his own mind, even as he describes life and light: and, with the silence of light, it describes itself and dwells in us only as far as we dwell in it. The truths which it manifests are such as it alone can manifest, and in all truth it manifests itself. By what name then canst thou call a truth so manifested? Is it not a revelation? Ask thyself whether thou canst attach to that latter word any consistent meaning not included in the idea of the former. And the manifesting power, the source and the correlative of the idea thus manifested – is it not God? Either thou knowest it to be God, or thou hast called an idol by that awful name.

Unless one believes, as Dr Leavis once[1] accused an opponent of believing, 'that poets put loosely what philosophers formulate with precision', one may well feel that Coleridge's attempt to argue a logical case for the connexion between the sense of reality which he begins by describing and the idea of God on which he ends is neither more nor less conclusive than Stevens's explorations of the same connexion by means of the images and illusions of poetry. Stevens himself would have been likely to say that this was a variety of thought, or simply a thought, by its nature poetic rather than rational. In 'A Collect of Philosophy', his last lecture, written in 1951 and therefore between 'Final Soliloquy' and 'Prologues to What is Possible', he said:

Essentially what I intend is that it shall be as if the philosophers had no knowledge of poetry and suddenly discovered it in their search for whatever it is that they are searching for and gave the name of poetry to that which they discovered.

And later in the same lecture he put into his peculiar prose a view of the relation between reality and the idea of God which is in spirit very close to Coleridge, however much Coleridge would have insisted that he, in distinction from Stevens, was dealing with truth rather than poetry:

The number of ways of passing between the traditional two fixed points of man's life, that is to say, of passing from the self to God, is fixed only by the limitations of space, which is limitless. The eternal philosopher is the eternal pilgrim on that road...In...the poem of the ascent into heaven, it is possible to say that there can be no faults, since it is precisely the faults of life that this

[1] In 'Criticism and Philosophy', his reply to Wellek's attack on *Revaluation*. (*The Common Pursuit*.)

197

poem enables us to leave behind. If the idea of God is the ultimate poetic idea, then the idea of the ascent into heaven is only a little below it. Conceding that not all philosophy is concerned with this particular poem, nevertheless a great deal of it is, and always has been.

One way of pinning down what the Coleridge passage has in common with poems like 'Final Soliloquy' and 'Prologues to What is Possible' is to say that in each of them there is a 'passing from the self to God', and that each of them, if one is willing to suspend in the case of Coleridge the normal assumptions about the word 'truth', is a part of 'the poem of the ascent into heaven'.

There is a sense in which 'the poem of the ascent into heaven' was the poem that Stevens had been writing all his life, ever since 'the strange unlike' of 'To The One of Fictive Music' and the 'starry *connaissance*' of 'Le Monocle de Mon Oncle' nearly forty years before. The 'flick which added to what was real and its vocabulary' was something that he had always known about, and his many years of devoted attention to its mysterious arrivals brought him in old age to a rare tranquillity. A third poem in the *Hudson Review* group of 1952 is an expression of this tranquillity, and also the description of a revelation, of a longed-for presence, in Coleridge's phrase, 'manifesting itself in its adequate idea'. The poem is called 'The World as Meditation'. It has as epigraph three sentences by Georges Enesco, the Romanian violinist, composer and teacher. 'J'ai passé trop de temps à travailler mon violon, à voyager. Mais l'exercice essentiel du compositeur – la méditation – rien ne l'a jamais suspendu en moi... Je vis un rêve permanent, qui ne s'arrête ni nuit ni jour.' Stevens had put the same self-analysis less directly in a letter to Feo dated 20 June 1945: 'Reality is the great *fond*, and it is because it is that the purely literary amounts to so little. Moreover, in the world of actuality, in spite of all I have just said, one is always living a little out of it.' 'The World as Meditation' is about the living of such a life, and about its object. It is a poem so perfectly achieved that it demands to be quoted in full:

> Is it Ulysses that approaches from the east,
> The interminable adventurer? The trees are mended.
> That winter is washed away. Someone is moving

On the horizon and lifting himself up above it.
A form of fire approaches the cretonnes of Penelope,
Whose mere savage presence awakens the world in which
    she dwells.

She has composed, so long, a self with which to welcome him,
Companion to his self for her, which she imagined,
Two in a deep-founded sheltering, friend and dear friend.

The trees had been mended, as an essential exercise
In an inhuman meditation, larger than her own.
No winds like dogs watched over her at night.

She wanted nothing he could not bring her by coming alone.
She wanted no fetchings. His arms would be her necklace
And her belt, the final fortune of their desire.

But was it Ulysses? Or was it only the warmth of the sun
On her pillow? The thought kept beating in her like her heart.
The two kept beating together. It was only day.

It was Ulysses and it was not. Yet they had met,
Friend and dear friend and a planet's encouragement.
The barbarous strength within her would never fail.

She would talk a little to herself as she combed her hair,
Repeating his name with its patient syllables,
Never forgetting him that kept coming constantly so near.

This was not Stevens's last good poem, but it was his last poem of the
very highest quality. In it he brings to a conclusion of exquisite
refinement, that is at the same time wonderfully fresh and new, a
theme that had been present in his poetry since the days of 'Sunday
Morning'. This theme is that love of which the human and sexual
passion of the poem is only an image. When the sexual reality dissolves – 'But was it Ulysses?' – the poem loses none of its intensity:
'The two kept beating together...The barbarous strength within
her would never fail.' The real subject of 'The World as Meditation'
(and its title should help us to realise this) is not love seen, as it were,
partially, from the point of view of the lover regarding the object of
his love. The poem's real subject is the complete relationship, the
full ambiguity of the genitive in such a phrase as 'the love of God',
which is in any case perhaps the most appropriate expression that

can be used to paraphrase the extraordinary sense of spiritual strength which the poem creates. This strength of course resides as much in the awe-inspiring, indefinite figure of Ulysses as in the long faithfulness of Penelope, and one of the poem's most powerful details is the touch of human pathos given to the hero, to the 'form of fire', by the two phrases, one at the beginning and one at the end, that make a frame for him: 'The interminable adventurer' and 'his name with its patient syllables'. The effect of manifold intensity, of a single figure seen simultaneously from different sides, is not unlike the effect of Blake's astonishing lines from *The Gates of Paradise*:

> Tho' thou art Worship'd by the Names Divine
> Of Jesus and Jehovah, thou art still
> The Son of Morn in weary Night's decline,
> The lost Traveller's Dream under the Hill.

In none of these late religious poems, which can be described in no other way, does Stevens use any of the ancient names and phrases of Christianity which Blake used and abused to his own revolutionary purposes. Nevertheless, at least in this last period, Stevens's thought and feeling on the central spiritual issues of ultimate meaning and value are related to the structure of orthodox Christianity in very much the same way as Blake's. In one poem of this period, printed in the *Collected Poems* immediately after 'The Rock', Stevens describes this relation in what is, for him, a surprisingly direct image. The poem is called 'St. Armorer's Church From the Outside'. It begins with a description of an abandoned church that 'was once an immense success'. Beside the ruin rises a chapel:

> His own: a chapel of breath, an appearance made
> For a sign of meaning in the meaningless,
>
> No radiance of dead blaze, but something seen
> In a mystic eye, no sign of life but life,
> Itself, the presence of the intelligible
> In that which is created as its symbol.

(One remembers again 'the scholar of one candle' against 'an Arctic effulgence' in 'The Auroras of Autumn'.) The rest of the poem contrasts the chapel more and more strongly with the desolation of

the church. The atmosphere of energy, freedom and change in which
the chapel stands recalls, in feeling if not in words, the fierce convictions of Blake, though Stevens is not feverishly preaching to a deaf
world but looking back at his own achievement with balance and
calm:

> The chapel rises, his own, his period,
> A civilization formed from the outward blank,
> A sacred syllable rising from sacked speech...
>
> St. Armorer's has nothing of this present,
> This *vif*, this dizzle-dazzle of being new
> And of becoming, for which the chapel spreads out
> Its arches in its vivid element,
>
> In the air of newness of that element,
> In an air of freshness, clearness, greenness, blueness,
> That which is always beginning because it is part
> Of that which is always beginning over and over.
>
> The chapel underneath St. Armorer's walls,
> Stands in a light, its natural light and day,
> The origin and keep of its health and his own.
> And there he walks and does as he lives and likes.

Although the most elaborate, 'St. Armorer's Church From the
Outside' is not the only poem of these last years in which Stevens
looked as if 'from the outside' at his own life and work. Nowhere
else did he, as here, compare the affirmations of his poetry to the
ruined certainties of the past. But in several shorter and simpler
poems he expressed the same final confidence, won for himself through
the groping efforts of a long search. In one of them, 'The Poem That
Took the Place of a Mountain' he uses to embody this confidence an
image that had been with him since 'the MacCullough' of 'Notes'
who 'lay lounging by the sea':

> As if the language suddenly, with ease,
> Said things it had laboriously spoken.

In 'An Ordinary Evening in New Haven' 'The Ruler of Reality'

> with the Queen
> Of Fact, lies at his ease beside the sea.

Now he has become more unequivocally the poet himself:

> There it was, word for word,
> The poem that took the place of a mountain...

> The exact rock where his inexactnesses
> Would discover, at last, the view toward which they had edged,

> Where he could lie and, gazing down at the sea,
> Recognize his unique and solitary home.

'The Planet on the Table', the most touching of these poems about himself, begins simply: 'Ariel was glad he had written his poems', and ends, more humbly than 'The Poem that Took the Place of a Mountain', with an acknowledgement of essential reality, of the other side of the old equation:

> It was not important that they survive.
> What mattered was that they should bear
> Some lineament or character,

> Some affluence, if only half perceived,
> In the poverty of their words,
> Of the planet of which they were part.

Even now, and even about himself and his work, he could not take a fixed view nor settle for one side of the equation to the neglect of the other. 'A Quiet Normal Life' says quite the opposite to what was so thankfully claimed in 'The Poem that Took the Place of a Mountain':

> His place, as he sat and as he thought, was not
> In anything that he constructed, so frail,
> So barely lit, so shadowed over and naught...

And in some of these poems that 'plain sense of things', or 'new knowledge of reality', which we have already seen to be one among several characteristics of this late phase of Stevens's work, impresses him with a fresh realisation of the world's separate existence from the meanings the poet may temporarily impose on it. Such are 'The Course of A Particular', a very fine poem which was left out of *The Rock* by mistake,[1] 'An Old Man Asleep', 'Vacancy in the Park', and

[1] It is printed in *Opus Posthumous* with a misprint 'air' for 'ear' in the penultimate line.

three beautiful poems about the sadness of leaving a world so much and so long beloved, 'The River of Rivers in Connecticut', 'Farewell Without a Guitar',[1] and 'Madame La Fleurie', where the 'Fat girl, terrestrial, my summer, my night' of 'Notes' takes on a new and terrifying aspect:

> He looked in a glass of earth and thought he lived in it.
> Now, he brings all that he saw into the earth, to the waiting parent.
> His crisp knowledge is devoured by her, beneath a dew.

It was not until 1954 that Stevens agreed to the publication of his collected poems, the idea being that the book's appearance should coincide with his seventy-fifth birthday which fell on 2 October of that year. Even then he was not particularly happy about the prospect. 'A collection is very much like sweeping under the rug', he wrote to one correspondent,[2] and to another:[3] 'I look forward to the appearance of this volume rather dismally. A book that contains everything that one has done in a lifetime does not reassure one. Then, the fact that I am 75 begins to seem like the most serious thing that has ever happened to me.' He knew, however, that there was now no alternative. The poems that made up *The Rock* section of the *Collected Poems* were not enough to constitute a whole new volume, and, in spite of what he must have recognised as the undimmed quality of these twenty-five poems, among which there is hardly a failure, he was aware that he was tiring. His work at the office was wearing him out more and more, leaving him exhausted at the end of each day, and, as we have seen, he refused to give it up even for the Charles Eliot Norton Chair at Harvard which he was offered for 1955–6.

One may guess, on the other hand, that this refusal to retire from a job for which he was already by the rules of the company five years too old was the result not so much of mere elderly stubborness as of a feeling that if he broke the routine of a lifetime he might write, instead of few poems, none at all. 'Here at home', he wrote in 1953,[4] 'it is just demnition grind day after day. This keeps me well, cheerful, prosperous, overweight and sober.' It is certainly possible that

---

1 Written in 1954, just too late for *Collected Poems* and also printed in *Opus Posthumous*.
2 Letter to N. H. Pearson, 27 April 1954.
3 To L. C. van Geyzel, 25 June 1954.
4 To Bernard Heringman, 7 January 1953.

without the 'demnition grind' that had for so long been the framework of his time, his creative work might simply have stopped from lack of support. In one of the few letters that reveal his own view of the two sides of his life, he shows how mixed his feelings were about the ordinary job which consumed so much of his energy and yet provided the secure base for his contemplative and imaginative freedom. He is writing to Thomas McGreevy in 1950:

If Beethoven could look back on what he had accomplished and say that it was a collection of crumbs compared to what he had hoped to accomplish, where should I ever find a figure of speech adequate to size up the little that I have done compared to that which I had once hoped to do. Of course, I have had a happy and well-kept life. But I have not even begun to touch the spheres within spheres that might have been possible if, instead of devoting the principal amount of my time to making a living, I had devoted it to thought and poetry. Certainly it is as true as it ever was that whatever means most to one should receive all of one's time and that has not been true in my case. But, then, if I had been more determined about it, I might now be looking back not with a mere sense of regret but at some actual devastation. To be cheerful about it, I am now in the happy position of being able to say that I don't know what would have happened if I had had more time. This is very much better than to have had all the time in the world and have found oneself inadequate. (17 February 1950.)

Such level and such truthful self-knowledge is not commonly to be found among poets nearing the end of their lives.

On 31 May 1954, four months before his seventy-fifth birthday, Stevens read at Columbia a Phi Beta Kappa poem that he had been asked to write and deliver as part of the University's two hundredth Commencement celebrations. A couple of days later when he was pressed for a copy of it he replied: 'Perhaps I shan't throw it away. But I shall certainly never use it in its present form nor allow anyone to see a copy of it...I am going to do a little more work on it and then, if I like it, I may at least keep it without any thought of doing anything with it.'[1] In the event he published a small, and not the best, part of it reworked under a new title in the *Times Literary Supplement* in the following September, and the poem itself, 'The Sail of Ulysses', remained among his papers until it was published in *Opus Posthumous*.

[1] To Babette Deutsch, 2 June 1954.

Perhaps he was right to be so reticent about this, his last piece of any considerable length and weight: it is an occasional poem on an unpromising subject – Columbia had wanted something on the theme of 'knowledge' – and much of it is certainly somewhat stiff and public in tone in comparison with his best work. Nevertheless it is 'The Sail of Ulysses' that is really his 'final soliloquy', his last summary of his long search and its goal:

> Under the shape of his sail, Ulysses,
> Symbol of the seeker, crossing by night
> The giant sea, read his own mind.

So the poem begins, the chosen figure of Ulysses having emerged perhaps from 'The World as Meditation' and from the distinctly Homeric atmosphere of the first part of 'Prologues to What is Possible' with its shining seascape, its rowers, and its long hexameter-like lines. The seeker's reading of his own mind, which forms the main body of the poem, is a religious meditation on knowledge as the precious connexion between the poor, lost, incomplete human being and that which can fulfil his need, find him, and make him whole. The poem's manner is, at least to begin with, quieter, less coloured, less demonstrative than Stevens's usual habit. Here, for instance, is part of section II (there are eight):

> There is a human loneliness,
> A part of space and solitude,
> In which knowledge cannot be denied,
> In which nothing of knowledge fails,
> The luminous companion, the hand,
> The fortifying arm, the profound
> Response, the completely answering voice,
> That which is more than anything else
> The right within us and about us...

The poem progresses not as a consecutive argument but as a proliferation of ideas set one against the other. The figure of the hero, 'the major abstraction...the idea of man', appears in section IV, which speaks of human self-sufficiency and 'A freedom at last from the mystical'. But in contrast section V, the poem's rhetorical summit, faces more directly than any other passage in Stevens's poetry the 'otherness' of whatever it is that may answer human need:

> Yet always there is another life,
> A life beyond this present knowing,
> A life lighter than this present splendor,
> Brighter, perfected and distant away,
> Not to be reached but to be known,
> Not an attainment of the will
> But something illogically received,
> A divination, a letting down
> From loftiness, misgivings dazzlingly
> Resolved in dazzling discovery.

A Christian would say that these lines are about grace, and that any other interpretation of them would be no more than a periphrasis for the theologian's single term. And indeed the closing lines of the section, describing an ultimate fulfilment 'in which the litter of truths becomes a whole', perhaps persuade us that at last Stevens's thought has moved past the 'fictive covering' that 'weaves always glistening from the heart and mind' to the nakedness of a timeless truth:

> The ancient symbols will be nothing then.
> We shall have gone beyond the symbols
> To that which they symbolized, away
> From the rumors of the speech-full domes,
> To the chatter that is then the true legend,
> Like glitter ascended into fire.

But even now the poet must speak in fictive images, and the creation or recognition – which it is perhaps, as I have earlier suggested, does not matter as much as we are used to thinking – of such a truth is a manifestation and a triumph of the human 'heart and mind'. Knowledge, this poem's theme, is that which lies between the mind and truth, linking the one with the other; and sections VI and VII celebrate on the one hand the power of the mind of man, who 'has nothing but the truth to leave':

> The mind renews the world in a verse,
> A passage of music, a paragraph
> By a right philosopher...

and, on the other hand, the pull of the truth, of the 'stellar large-
nesses' which exist behind 'the particular thought', 'the difficult
inch':

> This is not poet's ease of mind.
> It is the fate that dwells in truth.
> We obey the coaxings of our end.

The last and most completely successful section of the poem
begins with a question: 'What is the shape of the sibyl?' The answer
turns away from lofty and mysterious intimations of fulfilment to
that without which there can be no fulfilment, to human awareness
of human necessity. This is Stevens's final expression of a vision of
humanity which had informed some of his best poetry. It is a vision
without which his hopes, his affirmations, his discoveries would have
lacked an essential realism, an essential compassion, 'His poverty
becomes his heart's strong core'.

> It is the sibyl of the self,
> The self as sibyl, whose diamond,
> Whose chiefest embracing of all wealth
> Is poverty, whose jewel found
> At the exactest central of the earth
> Is need. For this, the sibyl's shape
> Is a blind thing fumbling for its form,
> A form that is lame, a hand, a back,
> A dream too poor, too destitute
> To be remembered, the old shape
> Worn and leaning to nothingness,
> A woman looking down the road,
> A child asleep in its own life.

Though it contains several passages almost the equal of this one,
'The Sail of Ulysses' is too diffuse, in places too obscurely abstract
(which was his own objection to it), to be reckoned among Stevens's
masterpieces. There is one quality, however, which this poem has
more strongly than any of those masterpieces, though most of them
have it to some degree. This quality is, as it were, a double strength,
the double strength that comes from the expression of a recognition
of the possible power of human love and human intelligence and the
simultaneous demonstration of that power. Like other of Stevens's

poems but more so, and particularly when we know how late in his life it was written, 'The Sail of Ulysses' leaves us feeling that here was a man who not only knew what humanity at its best is capable of achieving but himself went a long way towards achieving it.

In a speech Stevens made in January 1955, accepting in New York the National Book Award for his *Collected Poems*, he referred to this double strength, this simultaneity of perception and demonstration, in terms that show most movingly by how far he felt himself to have fallen short of the possibilities he had glimpsed, by how much he felt, in his own case, perception to have outdistanced demonstration. But the passage also shows how high he rated the importance of that perception, that glimpse:

We can never have great poetry unless we believe that poetry serves great ends. We must recognize this from the beginning so that it will affect every-thing that we do. Our belief in the greatness of poetry is a vital part of its greatness, an implicit part of the belief of others in its greatness. Now, at seventy-five, as I look back on the little that I have done as I turn the pages of my own poems gathered together in a single volume, I have no choice except to paraphrase the old verse that says that it is not what I am, but what I aspired to be that comforts me. It is not what I have written but what I should like to have written that constitutes my true poems, the uncollected poems which I have not had the strength to realize.

Humble as my actual contribution to poetry may be and however modest my experience of poetry has been, I have learned through that contribution and by the aid of that experience of the greatness that lay beyond, the power over the mind that lies in the mind itself, the incalculable expanse of the imagination as it reflects itself in us and about us. This is the precious scope which every poet seeks to achieve as best he can.

During this last winter of his life Stevens spent part of the time left over from the office working on Valéry. He had been asked to write an introduction to a volume of the Bollingen Collected Works in English, and chose to write two pieces on the dialogues *Eupalinos* and *L'Âme et la Danse* for Volume IV. Several times over many years he had spoken in his letters of Valéry as a writer whose works he must one day read thoroughly, and he told Mrs Church that he was accepting this assignment because 'I want to know Valéry better and this is an opportunity to do so, even though, living at the center of the world, he is far beyond me in so many things.' (2 December 1954.) That there were some things in common between himself and Valéry Stevens obviously knew. 'Je vaux par ce qui me manque'. 'Mon exigence est ma ressource': these epigrams could have been placed to good effect over several of Stevens's key passages. And, on a deeper level, they shared an intense interest in the poetic process examined against a metaphysical background. But the similarities between them were entirely a matter of coincidence rather than influence, and the differences were far more profound than the similarities. Like all the 'influences' on Stevens except that of Santayana this one is overrated almost as soon as it is mentioned, as is Stevens's debt to French literature in general. He was throughout his life devoted to the French language and to the idea of France – 'the center of the world' as he says with rather absurd self-deprecation in the letter quoted above – but neither the theory nor the practice of French poetry left any considerable mark on his work. As he once wrote,[1] denying the influence of Mallarmé, 'Verlaine meant a good deal more to me...But I was never a student of any of these poets; they were simply poets and I was the youthful general reader.' The great difference between his own poetry and that of the best French poets with whom he has been associated, Mallarmé and Valéry, is the firm hold on ordinary ways of thought, on what one might call common sense, that Stevens never abandoned and that Mallarmé and Valéry each in his way thought quite irrelevant to the concerns of poetry. Neither of them would ever have written: 'For myself, the inaccessible jewel is the normal and all of life, in poetry, is the difficult pursuit of just that.'

Similarly, Valéry's prose moves in an atmosphere of rarefied intellectual purity quite alien to Stevens's much less detached and more accidental, more gritty, observations about poetry and life. The single word 'Whitman', his loyalty to whom Stevens never abandoned and about whom he wrote[2] during this very winter: 'The good things, the superbly beautiful and moving things, are those that he wrote naturally, with an extemporaneous and irrepressible vehemence of emotion', should be enough to explain the irritation that occasionally shows through the respectful admiration of his Valéry introductions.

---

[1] To Heringman, 3 May 1949.   [2] Letter to Joseph Bennett, 8 February 1955.

These last pieces of Stevens's prose are in any case interesting not so much for what they say about Valéry, which is little, as for the note of personal conclusion that Stevens failed to keep out of them. He ends the *Eupalinos* piece by pointing out that Rilke's translation of the dialogue was 'the last work he did before he died', and he adds, inconsequentially but in the circumstances touchingly,

It seems sometimes, in the fluidity of the dialogue, as if the discussion was casual and fortuitous or, say, Socratic. But a discussion over which the mind of Socrates presides derives much of its vitality from this characteristic, so that when the talk is over, we have a sense of extended and noble unity, a sense of large and long-considered form.

And the introduction to *L'Âme et la Danse* ends:

What *Dance and the Soul* requires is not so much explanation as...attentive and fervent critics or, say, readers, willing to experience the transformation which knowing a little about themselves brings about as by miracle or, say, by art. Man has many ways to attain the divine, and the way of Eupalinos and the way of Athikte and the various ways of Paul Valéry are only a few of them.

These remarks, however unconsciously, have a great deal more to do with Stevens, coming 'somewhat sadly'[1] to the end of his life, than they have to do with Valéry.

On 24 March the manuscript of these introductions was sent off to the editor of the Bollingen Edition. Less than a month later Stevens went into hospital for an exploratory operation. It revealed the incurable cancer from which he died on 2 August, having emerged from hospital for a few weeks to spend an obstinate two or three hours a day at the office, too ill and exhausted to think about poetry. His last few poems, written in the autumn and winter of 1954-5 and printed in *Opus Posthumous* after 'The Sail of Ulysses', have the same wistful humility as the National Book Award speech. In one of them, 'As You Leave the Room', a reworking of a little poem he had inscribed in a copy of *Transport to Summer* in 1947, he adds to his original lines slightly altered ('left' is put in for 'lived', for instance) a final couplet which looks back at all that he has tried to do with a wry melancholy rather than with any pride:

[1] Stevens loved Santayana's remark in a letter to Feo 'I have always, somewhat sadly, bowed to expediency or fate.' (Stevens to Feo, 22 April 1949.)

Now, here, the snow I had forgotten becomes

Part of a major reality, part of
An appreciation of a reality

And thus an elevation, as if I left
With something I could touch, touch every way.

And yet nothing has been changed except what is
Unreal, as if nothing had been changed at all.

This melancholy is no sudden shadow. It is the sharp, hard fruit of an old and deeply rooted honesty. Even now, at the very end, there are no easy certainties in Stevens's mind. In various poems he has reached various moments of peace, each seeming, perhaps, to bring him nearer to the goal of his search. But he builds upon them no structure to be recommended to others as the truth or as any firm conclusion. He knows that the day for structures and conclusions is over: 'The truth about the poet in a time of disbelief is not that he must turn evangelist. After all he shares the disbelief of his time. He does not turn to Paris or Rome...He turns to himself.' The last poem to be published[1] in Stevens's lifetime, 'July Mountain', is on this theme, its ten lines capturing for a final suspended instant the poet himself, one imagination in its own reality, 'he in the substance of his region' as he said in a fragment[2] left at his death.

> We live in a constellation
> Of patches and of pitches,
> Not in a single world,
> In things said well in music,
> On the piano, and in speech,
> As in a page of poetry –
> Thinkers without final thoughts
> In an always incipient cosmos,
> The way, when we climb a mountain,
> Vermont throws itself together.

As he had required of the supreme fiction, 'It Must Change'. But now and then 'in a constellation of patches and of pitches' 'things said well' suffice our need. The satisfaction and the order of 'July Mountain'

---

[1] 'July Mountain' appeared in *Atlantic Monthly*, April 1955.
[2] Called in *Opus Posthumous* 'A Mythology Reflects its Region'.

are very close to the satisfaction and order that Stevens had long ago found a related image for in 'Anecdote of the Jar':

> I placed a jar in Tennessee
> And round it was, upon a hill.
> It made the slovenly wilderness
> Surround that hill.
>
> The wilderness rose up to it,
> And sprawled around, no longer wild.

These lines, written in 1919, define lightly but as well as any he ever wrote Stevens's hope for poetry, his belief that through it the slovenly wilderness of the modern world can be made, for however transient a time, to yield modern man something that will satisfy his need. And whatever moves and stirs us about the jar in Tennessee is, in the end, that which moves and stirs us about Stevens himself and the poetry he wrote which seems to go so much of the distance towards fulfilling his hope. He called it 'nobility', 'that nobility which is our spiritual height and depth', and the sentences at the end of 'The Noble Rider and the Sound of Words' where he explained what he meant explain also, as far as a few words can, the meaning and value of his life's work.

Someone had prefaced the catalogue of an exhibition of Epstein flower paintings with the line 'How with this rage can beauty hold a plea...' Stevens said:

What ferocious beauty the line from Shakespeare puts on when used under such circumstances While it has its modulation of despair, it holds its plea and its plea is noble. There is no element more conspicuously absent from contemporary poetry than nobility. There is no element that poets have sought after, more curiously and more piously, certain of its obscure existence ...It is hard to think of a thing more out of time than nobility. Looked at plainly it seems false and dead and ugly...But as a wave is a force and not the water of which it is composed, which is never the same, so nobility is a force and not the manifestations of which it is composed, which are never the same...It is not an artifice that the mind has added to human nature. The mind has added nothing to human nature. It is a violence from within that protects us from a violence without. It is the imagination pressing back against the pressure of reality. It seems, in the last analysis, to to have something to do with our self-preservation; and that, no doubt, is why the expression of it, the sound of its words, helps us to live our lives.

.   .   .   .   .

The ultimate question about Stevens has to be answered from outside his own terms. Does his work really substantiate the claims he was in the habit of making for poetry? Does it actually 'help us to live our lives', as distinct from merely helping him to live his, and, if it does, why and how does it do it?

The world in which religion has collapsed has been described as a world without an absolute sanction for morality. According to this description, the most important result of the decay of Christianity is the fact that all moral codes, including those that happen to be closest in content to the Christian code, are relative and merely coexist in a metaphysical void. This relativism might not have been very noticeable, since concepts such as the social good can masquerade as absolutes, were it not that simultaneously with the decay of Christianity there took place the triumphant rise of a scientific cast of mind, formed in particular by evolutionary biology, which appeared to abolish the significance of specifically human qualities and aspirations by reducing them to accidents of genetic progress. The situation of modern European man was described in this way by Nietzsche in the 1880s and his description has seemed accurate enough to many thinkers, writers and scientists, whether or not they have been familiar with his works or with his ideas for a way out of the nihilistic impasse, for nearly a hundred years. Many philosophers, for example, assuming that such fields of enquiry are no longer of provable value, have given up ethics and metaphysics for the first time since Plato; while psychologists have tended to see in all human activity, including artistic creation and religious aspiration, behaviour theoretically as susceptible to programming as the behaviour of a rat or a computer – though the studies of the psycholinguists are now pointing in a new and contrary direction.

Dissenters from the nihilist description, whether they are conscious of it or not, and most are not, identify themselves by a belief in the soul – or something which essentially distinguishes the human from the merely animal – and a belief in the absolute – or something which enables them to judge that one set of ethical rules is better than another and not just different, as social goods may be different. Liberal humanists, if really liberal (judging one set of ethical rules to be better than another) and really humanist (believing man essentially distinct from animals), are such dissenters, whatever their feelings about the soul and the absolute as words. Arnold, who talked about reason and the will of God, and Santayana, who talked about reason and the ideal, were consciously such dissenters. Dr Leavis, whose words are *humanitas*, creativity, responsibility, is passionately such a dissenter, and the 'Two Cultures' debate was a locus classicus of the conflict between Nietzsche's description of the world and dissent from it.

One may guess that in the Christian period the great majority of people simply accepted belief, the given meaning, the given truth, as the object of their faith, and that religion impinged upon their lives primarily as ritual and as a set of moral imperatives backed by the truth. It was for a minority that religion was above all faith and progress in faith, its ultimate disclosures the goal for the contemplative life, its ritual and its moral imperatives necessary but subsidiary to more significant demands. For the heirs of this minority a world without religion is primarily a world without a goal for the contemplative life. Since the nihilist description of our situation sees religion only as an erroneous account of the world that used to serve as a sanction for morality, these people have no place in it except as psychological invalids infected with illusory needs. But such people are, as they have always been, a very small minority, and they are unlikely to be offered a place in the scheme of things even by the dissenters. For most of the dissenters, like most of the nihilists, are the heirs of the old majority; and therefore on the most fundamental level, the level of belief, of ultimate meaning, they simply accept what is given. And what is given nowadays is the absence of the possibility of belief, the absence of ultimate meaning, the absence of an object of faith. That there is here a gap, a major inconsistency, in the conscious position of most dissenters is a fact they cannot overlook indefinitely. They suppose that what they stand for can be sanctioned in the metaphysical void, but they are wrong. They need, if only to make them aware of the gap, the contemplative minority for whom belief or its absence is not given but is an issue of extreme personal urgency.

Stevens was an heir of the contemplative minority and his work is the record of his progress in a faith whose existence and whose object could be defined, the old defining words being dead, only in the new words of his poetry. For the supporters of the description of the world that does not countenance the soul and the absolute Stevens's work can presumably have only the marginal interest of a decorative linguistic pattern informed here and there with nostalgia for the past. Their case against him is in their terms unanswerable. For the majority of the dissenters, whose preoccupations are primarily moral, Stevens's work will seem at first sight almost equally marginal since his overt concern with ordinary questions of emotional, social and political life is almost non-existent. Their case, on the other hand, is answerable, at least with a suggestion.

Just as in the Christian past the morality of the many was sanctioned by beliefs which the many took as read but a few devoted their lives to understanding and serving, so now, perhaps, the humanist ethics of social justice and balanced freedoms which many see as the best hope of our civilisation should be sanctioned by a belief in the ideal, a belief that has to do with the soul and the absolute, which the many can take as read but a few must devote their lives to understanding and serving. That the ideal which sanctions the ethics of the west cannot be a materialist ideal is becoming more obvious every day, and those – they are by definition dissenters – who acknowledge that what is needed is the restoration of value to the individual soul, to its course through life and to its death, are those who have something to learn from Stevens. He presents them not with an answer but with an example. What 'helps us to live our lives' in Stevens's poetry is not its conclusions, where any can be found; it is not a belief in 'the supreme fiction', a phrase that in isolation can only be inspected as interesting or rejected as absurd, which is 'what will suffice' us, his readers. What in Stevens's case 'helps us to live our lives' is the affirmation that is there in his poetry, that he earned over a lifetime through faith, patience, honesty and the refusal to give up, and that is in the end an affirmation of the value of the individual soul and of the meaning of its relation to the absolute. If, in fact, we are prepared really to understand Stevens's poetry, what we will learn is what in the past the ordinary person learnt from the writings of those whose talent was for the contemplative life – that there is such a thing as the progress of the soul, that what is valuable has to be earned, that the virtues of the soul, faith, patience, honesty, humility, persistence, have their meaning in time and in time earn rewards which are worth having. Lives being lived that could teach us all this are probably not uncommon, but we do not often know about them. 'The expression of it, the sound of its words '– new words, of and for our world – are very rare.

SELECT BIBLIOGRAPHY

I WALLACE STEVENS

The Collected Poems of Wallace Stevens, New York (Knopf), 1954; London (Faber), 1955.

The Necessary Angel; Essays on Reality and the Imagination, New York (Knopf), 1951; London (Faber), 1960.

Opus Posthumous, Edited, with an Introduction, by Samuel French Morse, New York (Knopf), 1957; London (Faber), 1959.

Letters of Wallace Stevens, Edited by Holly Stevens, New York (Knopf), 1966; London (Faber), 1967.

NOTE

Opus Posthumous contains poems and prose pieces uncollected or unpublished at Stevens's death. It also contains aphorisms from his notebooks, two of the three short plays he wrote in 1916–17, and one prose fragment, 'On Poetic Truth', 'mistakenly attributed to Stevens, but actually excerpts from an essay of the same title by R. D. Lewis' (S. F. Morse, 1970).

The only important piece not to be found in any of these books is the revised version of 'Owl's Clover' which was published in *The Man with the Blue Guitar and Other Poems*, New York (Knopf), 1937. 'Owl's Clover' in the much longer original version is in *Opus Posthumous*.

The third play, 'Bowl, Cat and Broomstick', can be found in the *Quarterly Review of Literature*, Volume XVI, no. 1–2 (1969).

Thirteen youthful poems appear in *The Harvard Advocate Anthology* edited by Donald Hall, New York (Twayne), 1951.

SELECTIONS

Selected Poems, London (Faber), 1953. (Selected by Stevens.)

Poems by Wallace Stevens, Selected, with an Introduction, by Samuel French Morse. New York (Vintage Books), 1959.

II BOOKS AND ARTICLES ON WALLACE STEVENS

BEWLEY, Marius: *The Complex Fate*, London (Chatto), 1952, pp. 171–92.
– *Masks and Mirrors*, London (Chatto), 1970, pp. 271–80.
BORROFF, Marie, ed.: *Wallace Stevens; A Collection of Critical Essays*, Englewood Cliffs (Prentice-Hall), 1963. (Includes essays by Sister M. Bernetta Quinn and Northrop Frye.)
BROWN, Ashley and Robert S. Haller, eds.: *The Ahievement of Wallace Stevens*, Philadelphia (Lippincott), 1962. (Includes essays by Marianne Moore, R. P. Blackmur, Hi Simons and Randall Jarrell.)
BUTTEL, Robert: *Wallace Stevens, The Making of Harmonium*, Princeton (University Press), 1967.
DOGGETT, Frank: *Stevens' Poetry of Thought*, Baltimore (Johns Hopkins), 1966.
DONOGHUE, Denis: *Connoisseurs of Chaos*, London (Faber), 1966, pp. 190–215.
– *The Ordinary Universe*, London (Faber), 1968, pp. 221–40, 267–90.
FUCHS, Daniel: *The Comic Spirit of Wallace Stevens*, University of North Carolina Press, 1963.
KERMODE, Frank: *Wallace Stevens*, Edinburgh and London (Oliver and Boyd), 1960; New York (Grove Press), 1961.
– *Continuities*, London (Routledge), 1968, pp. 77–91.
MARTZ, Louis L.: *The Poem of the Mind*, New York (Oxford), 1966, pp. 183–223.
MORSE, Samuel French: *Wallace Stevens; Poetry as Life*, New York (Pegasus), 1970. (Includes interesting biographical material.)
PEARCE, Roy Harvey and J. Hillis Miller, eds.: *The Act of the Mind; Essays on the Poetry of Wallace Stevens*, Baltimore (John Hopkins), 1965. (Includes essays by the editors and by Bernard Heringman.)
VENDLER, Helen Hennessy: *On Extended Wings: Wallace Stevens' Longer Poems*, Cambridge, Mass. (Harvard University Press), 1969.
WINTERS, Yvor: *In Defense of Reason*, London (Routledge), 1960, pp. 431–59.

SELECTION

EHRENPREIS, Irvin, ed.: *Wallace Stevens: A Critical Anthology*, London (Penguin), 1973.

INDEX

INDEX